VeBS!

GOOD NEWS CLUES ™

CLUES

SEARCHING FOR
NEW LIFE IN JESUS

MW01230793

DIRECTOR'S GUIDE

KJV Version

Very **e**xciting **B**ible **S**chool® Curriculum

© 2004 Cook Communications Ministries. All rights reserved.

Editorial Managers: Janet Lee, Doug Schmidt
Product Developer: Karen Pickering
Art Director: Randy Maid
Cover Design: idesignetc, Keith Sherrer
Interior Design: idesignetc, Keith Sherrer
Illustrations: Heiser Graphics, Inc. and Brent Hale Artography
Photography: Brad Armstrong Photography
Writers: Cheryl Crews, Gail Rohlfing, Karen Schmidt
Music: Music Precedent, Ltd.

4050 Lee Vance View · Colorado Springs, CO 80918-7100 · Colorado Springs, CO/Paris, Ontario
www.CookMinistries.com/NexGen
Printed in South Korea

ISBN: 0-7814-4071-8

103423

Table of Contents

GOOD NEWS CLUES™

SEARCHING FOR NEW LIFE IN JESUS

Your kids are geared up for excitement— ready for a week of discovery and action. But this VBS is much more than just fun!

Kids will learn to be Jesus' disciples and to look forward to their home in heaven as they solve the mystery adventures in five different sites.

Good News Clues™ is a Very exciting Bible School® curriculum based on Revelation 3:20.

> *"Behold, I stand at the door, and knock: if any man hear my voice, and open the door, I will come in to him, and will sup with him, and he with me."*

Each of the *Good News Clues*™ opening skits features a skit involving one or two leaders and the puppet dog detective or interaction between two leaders.

Five separate Discovery Sites have been developed, based on the theme verse. At each Discovery Site the children will learn how to be Jesus' disciples in their everyday lives—

■ The Garden

WE NEED TO BE FORGIVEN.

From the Bible story of the Garden of Eden, children will learn that all people are sinners but that God wants us to turn to Him.

■ The Dining Room

WE CAN BE SAVED FROM OUR SIN THROUGH JESUS.

Children will study the last week of Jesus' life, which will help them understand that salvation comes through the death and resurrection of Jesus Christ.

■ The Family Room

WE CAN BE WELCOMED INTO GOD'S FAMILY.

As they study the story of the Prodigal Son *(and in Preschool the Parable of the Lost Sheep)*, the children will learn about the love and forgiveness of God.

■ The Kitchen

WE CAN GROW IN JESUS.

The children will begin to discover how to grow in the Christian life as they study the Parables of the Mustard Seed and the Yeast *(and in Preschool the Parable of Salt and Light)*.

■ The Living Room

WE CAN LIVE WITH JESUS FOREVER.

The children will learn more about the place God is preparing for us to live someday, as they study the Parables of the Hidden Treasure and the Pearl.

Each site includes a take-home paper called "The Quest Continues." Reproduce these pages to give to your children before they go home from each VBS Discovery Site. The take-home papers will inform parents about what their child experienced at the day's Discovery Site and encourage parents to get involved with their child's spiritual growth.

Introduction to VeBS®

Kids love activity! This adventure will bring a wonderful meaning to the familiar rooms of home as the children learn Bible stories about new life in Jesus that relate to each room. Exploring the Scriptures through fun-filled activities, while solving daily mysteries throughout the "house and yard," your children will gain new insights about what it means to become part of God's family.

Visiting five Discovery Sites, the children will open the Scriptures to learn that they need to be forgiven, that salvation comes through Jesus, that God desires to have them in His family, how to grow in their faith, and that they can look forward to their future home in heaven.

Learning Models

For Small Groups:

If your total VBS attendance is expected to be small, or if you have trouble recruiting enough leaders to assist you, you may choose to present each Discovery Site separately—one each day of the week.

For Large Groups:

If your total VBS attendance is large enough, and if you have plenty of assistants, you may opt to hold each session simultaneously at five locations in your church building or auditorium. A unique feature of this VBS learning model is that each leader (or pair of leaders) prepares ONLY one lesson. That lesson is presented by the same leader(s) every day to a different group of children. All the activities for the day, including the interactive Bible story, crafts, activities, games, and snacks can all be done at this one location. There is no particular order for the visits, but by the end of the week, each of the five groups will have visited all five sites. This method allows the children to be immersed in single environments where all aspects of the lesson tie together and reinforce one core concept. It also gives the leaders the freedom to focus on the needs of the kids, not the clock.

These five sites remain intact for the entire week. If you wish, divide children into five groups by age or grade. Key Verses and materials for each site have been age-graded as follows:

PRESCHOOL—children who have completed preschool or have not yet attended school.

EARLY ELEMENTARY—children who have completed kindergarten or first grade.

ELEMENTARY—those who have completed second or third grade.

UPPER ELEMENTARY—those who have completed fourth or fifth grade. Alter these divisions if needed.

Discovery Sites

Regardless of the learning model you choose, each Discovery Site will present an exciting experience for your kids to learn about Jesus. Each Discovery Site will be decorated according to the day's sub-theme to help the children learn about growing as Jesus' disciples.

Goals

- Introduce children to Jesus as Savior.
- Change children from the inside out as their hearts are transformed by God's love for them and the hope He offers through Jesus.
- Develop in children an understanding of the relationship God wants to have with them through stories from the Bible.
- Match leaders' abilities with tasks so they are free to enjoy the children.
- Develop meaningful relationships between leaders and children in an interactive environment.
- Build a bridge between church and home as families are encouraged and challenged by the VBS ministry.

We hope these are your goals too as you seek to provide your kids with the best VBS program possible. Have fun as you join with your kids on an adventure to search for new life in Jesus.

Custom VeBS® Options

Are you looking for a new way to maximize your Bible school investment? Do you see needs in your church and community that would be better met with a different format than the standard five-day Bible school? Look no further! Here are some helpful tips for customizing our VBS to meet those needs. Be creative and make it your own!

BACKYARD BIBLE CLUB

Backyard Bible clubs are an excellent way to do outreach and you can easily customize this VBS program to meet the unique needs of this setting. Backyard Bible clubs take place in the neighborhoods of people in your church. *Good News Clues™* is designed so that you can set up all the Discovery Sites at once, one Discovery

Site each day, or create a general setup with small changes each day. If your schedule does not allow for five meetings, you can cut it down to meet your schedule—each lesson stands alone so children will have a complete experience in one day or five!

The Purpose:

Outreach: Backyard Bible clubs provide a unique opportunity for outreach into your community. Instead of asking people to come to the church, the church is going to them. Children are invited into a neighbor's home, a safe and fun place where they can learn about the love of Jesus. Backyard Bible clubs also provide a unique opportunity for outreach to parents who can be casually involved in what their child is doing without the commitment of being a church volunteer.

Evangelism: Backyard Bible clubs are a great way to reach kids who do not usually attend church with

the good news of salvation in Jesus. Because the invitations are sent out into the neighborhoods, many families are introduced to the love of Jesus Christ for the first time through backyard Bible clubs.

Church Growth: Backyard Bible clubs often bring new people to your church. When new families in the area are introduced to the church and develop relationships with people in the church, they are likely to get involved in other ways as well. Instead of taking away from another church's membership, backyard Bible clubs are a way to grow the church with new Christians who might not otherwise attend any church at all.

The benefits of backyard Bible clubs are great. Kids have a fun, safe setting in which to learn about Jesus, parents get involved and are introduced to the church and the Christian community, and most importantly, children and adults alike are introduced to Jesus and to a church family in which meaningful relationships can continue to grow after VBS is over.

How It Works:

A backyard Bible club is just what it says it is—a Bible club that is held in someone's backyard. So the only real differences in implementing a backyard Bible club instead of a traditional VBS are the location and the use of facilities and materials.

One option is to have five backyard Bible clubs going on in neighborhoods during one week, set up and run just like VBS, except there will only be one Discovery Site set up per session. Each backyard Bible club teacher develops only one Discovery Site. This includes collecting all of the materials, creating the site scene, and so on. On the first day of VBS, each backyard Bible club teacher runs the Discovery Site he or she developed. Later in the day, all five teachers meet to exchange materials so each Bible club teacher does another Discovery Site on the second day. The teachers continue exchanging materials until all have done each Discovery Site. This way, the work of developing the Discovery Site is divided between five leaders.

Another option is to run separate clubs throughout the summer. This way, each club will get all the materials at once and then pass them on to the next club when they have finished all five sessions.

Who You Need:

Backyard Bible clubs are a wonderful way to match people with jobs that fit their spiritual gifts! Each person involved has specific responsibilities that allow him or her to use their gifts to honor God and serve others.

The first thing you need is a host(ess). This person is a member of the church who has the gift of hospitality and desires to open his or her home and life to others. The size of the home is not important as long as there is space to tell the story, a place to do crafts and have snacks, and an open area in the yard or even in a nearby park for kids to play games. It is good if this person is already a respected and trusted member of the neighborhood or community, but it is also a great way for someone who is new to an area to develop relationships with neighbors.

You will also need a leader (called Investigator) for the backyard Bible club. This person should have the gifts of teaching and shepherding as his or her attention will be focused on helping the kids learn about Jesus and apply the lessons to their own lives. It is also helpful for this person to be gifted in administration, as he or she will coordinate and facilitate the overall program. If your church is running multiple clubs at one time, you may also need a director to oversee the coordination and staffing of all the club programs.

Finally, you will need some assistants (called Assistant Investigators), based on the number of children attending the backyard Bible club. This is a wonderful chance to get parents and others from the neighborhood involved! They are there to do just what their name says—assist. Generally two assistants are sufficient as long as there are not more than 20 kids attending. However, extra hands are always helpful, and it is a great opportunity to build relationships with neighborhood adults as well as children.

Individual Responsibilities:

Host(ess):

- Pray for the children and families of the neighborhood and for the staff involved.

- Hand out invitations to parents in the neighborhood, inviting kids to take part.

- Host a meeting for the leader and assistants in his or her home a couple of weeks before the backyard Bible club begins.

- Provide a safe, clean place for the kids to come each day of the backyard Bible club.

- Provide snacks each day of the club.

- Follow up with families and continue to build relationships after the club is over.

Leader (Investigator): (If your clubs have a director, he/she would share some of these responsibilities.)

- Understand and facilitate each step of the schedule.

- Provide all needed supplies and props.

- Lead a planning meeting with all staff before the backyard Bible club begins.

- Present the Discovery Site materials and Bible story to the children.

- Lead or make sure that someone is prepared to lead the other sections of the lessons.

- Make sure the host's/hostess's home is clean and in good shape after the backyard Bible club.

- Follow up with the kids and families after the club has ended.

Helpers (called Assistant Investigators):

- Follow the direction of the Investigator in whatever capacity has been decided on.

- Assist children who need extra attention.

- Build relationships with and love the children.

Helpful Hints:

Send invitations and then have a registration day in a nearby park or common area. Make it fun with

GOOD NEWS CLUES™

games, balloons, and so on. Even those in the area who did not receive invitations will be drawn to this and it gives parents a safe, non-threatening place to ask questions and find out about your backyard Bible club.

Always make sure that the parents register their kids—it is important that the parents know where the child is and have given their permission.

Follow up with the children and the parents! Hand out invitations to your church with the location and service times on the card. Provide a way for the families to go along with someone they have met during the backyard Bible club. You may also want to follow up with the parents by having dinner or coffee and dessert in the host's/hostess's home sometime after the club ends. You might even consider starting a neighborhood Bible study!

INTERGENERATIONAL OPTION

To involve more of your church in the excitement of VBS, shape your activities to include the diverse and valuable people within your church body. While "intergenerational" may mean different things to different people, the basic idea of several generations learning God's Word together is a great way to get involved and learn from each other.

What Is Intergenerational?

The most direct use of "intergenerational learning" in the Bible is found in Deuteronomy 6:6-7: "And these words, which I command thee this day, shall be in thine heart: And thou shalt teach them diligently unto thy children, and shalt talk of them when thou sittest in thine house, and when thou walkest by the way, and when thou liest down, and when thou risest up."

Parents have been given an immense responsibility to teach and instruct their children. This responsibility extends even beyond the parents to other members of the family of God. In the church, we often divide the family into different "age levels." The goal of intergenerational learning is to bring many people back together to share in a common learning experience centered around God's Word. Intergenerational learning activities enable you to include adults, senior citizens, youth, and children

in one dynamic learning environment. In that one learning environment, they can learn from the teacher and also from the wealth of experience and new perspectives that old and young alike can bring.

How Does It Work?

Intergenerational activities are fun and challenging. Often the real challenge is not convincing people that it is a good idea, but showing them how it can work. To have a successful intergenerational component to your VBS activities, remember that the teaching will be primarily focused on the children. Keep in mind that the passage from Deuteronomy is written for the instruction of the child. The youth and adults, however, will also benefit from the teaching. It is often the simple messages that we learn as children that we go back to time and again because they are foundational to our faith. It may be a re-learning for some of the older participants, but it can still be a meaningful and life-changing experience.

There are a number of ways that you can incorporate intergenerational learning into your VBS program. If the intergenerational learning model is new for your church, you may choose to do VBS just for the kids but use the intergenerational options presented in the Closing Program included in this *Good News Clues*™ book. Or you may want to design VBS so that families are together during the opening and closing assembly times but break into age groups for the Bible story and main activity times.

Another option is to teach just one of the Discovery Sites to an intergenerational group. Invite the members of children's families to come to VBS on the day that their child or children will be in that particular Discovery Sites. This option could easily be combined with the opening and closing assembly option. You may also choose to do a one-day event where all the Discovery Sites are set up as learning centers and families are free to travel to each one in one-hour intervals, participating in the activities, games, and Bible stories at each.

Finally, the youth, adults, and kids of your church will get excited about an entire intergenerational VBS. Read on for ideas and tips to make your intergenerational event run smoothly.

What Does a Five-Session, Intergenerational Program Look Like?

Preparation for this intergenerational VBS will follow the same basic steps outlined for the traditional VBS, including planning, recruiting, training, promoting, and so on. Set up your registration and attendance just as you would for the traditional VBS, assigning families to different groups that will rotate to a different Discovery Site each day. You will need three leaders *(typically a Investigator and two "site coordinators")* in each Discovery Site as well as one Assistant Investigator to travel with each group. Only one Assistant Investigator will be needed since parents will be in the Discovery Site with the kids. However, you will want to communicate to parents from the beginning that you want their participation to keep things running smoothly and to take care of any discipline issues.

Before VBS begins, talk to five families who will be involved and ask them for their help in the opening assemblies. Give each of the five families one of the songs on the *Good News Clues*™ CD and ask that they learn it, come up with some hand motions, and be ready to teach it to the others at VBS during the opening assembly time. If you have a number of families willing to participate, you may also want to write a short *(five-minute)* skit for each day and have families act it out.

In the Discovery Site each day, the activities and Bible story will be presented just as they are for the traditional VBS. Encourage the Investigators to choose the games and crafts that will appeal to the widest variety of ages. Parents and youth should participate in making the crafts but may need to be reminded that it is the process of the whole family doing it together, not the best finished product, that is most important. For some of the crafts, you may want to assign different steps to different age levels so that each person contributes a specific thing to the final product.

The Bible Memorization activity will be a great time for all age levels to participate together, as many of the youth and adults may not already know the Key Verse for the day. Use the Bible Memorization activities suggested in the Discovery Sites. You may want to divide your group into families or age levels.

If the groups are made up of families, they should learn the verse that corresponds to the age of the youngest child.

Since VBS is designed so all of the activities of one session happen in the individual Discovery Sites, there is a great deal of flexibility in adapting the program to meet your schedule. An intergenerational learning time can last between one hour and three hours simply by picking and choosing the games and crafts that you would like to do in each Discovery Site. Feel free to adapt the materials to meet your needs and enjoy the process of learning together.

Above all, keep in mind that the church is about bringing people together. As the writer of Hebrews put it, "Not forsaking the assembling of ourselves together, as the manner of some is; but exhorting one another: and so much the more, as ye see the day approaching" *(Heb. 10:25)*.

As you prepare for your VBS, look for ways to teach the entire church about God's love for His children—even the adults!

Outdoor Option

Kids love to be outdoors! If the weather in your area permits and you have a park or open area nearby, consider doing an outdoor VBS. Being outside will help kids feel part of the outdoor settings and give them even more opportunities for experiential learning. If you choose this custom option, the program can be used exactly as it is described in the Director's Guide section—but outside!

Be sure to think through the following issues:

- If you are using a public park, does the area need to be reserved or do you need a permit?

- Does your schedule need to change at all to allow more time for transitions?

- How will you transport the items needed?

- Is there a covered, secure area where you can set things up and leave them during VBS?

- Is there a place at the church where you can store items before and during VBS?

- Do you have plenty of water for the kids to drink throughout the days of VBS?

- Do you have plenty of sunscreen for the kids and leaders?
- What is the backup plan in case the weather turns bad?

If this custom option sounds good to you but you can't work out all the details, you might try one of these ideas: Simplify the outdoor option by having only a couple of Discovery Sites outside; hold a one-day VBS where all the Discovery Sites are set up outside for a day; or have an area where kids from any of the Discovery Sites can go outside for some of the crafts, activities, and games. Even a few minutes of fresh air during a game can make the day more fun and exciting. Be creative and enjoy the beautiful world around you that God created!

CAMP

Good News Clues™ is a great curriculum to use for camp! It is easy to expand and fits well into a camp setting. The VBS part of the camp can run just as a basic VBS would run in a church. The Discovery Sites can remain set up all week and groups of kids can rotate between them during the VBS time. You will want to add some camp activities as well. Below is a sample of what a VBS camp schedule might look like.

Use the people and resources in your church and at your camp to come up with the sports activities and electives for the afternoon time.

Alternative Schedules:

Besides the more extensive custom options mentioned here, there are many ways to adapt the VBS schedule to meet your needs. Here are some sample adaptations of the basic VBS schedule. Feel free to mix and match until your VBS is the way you like it.

FIVE CONSECUTIVE SATURDAYS

If time, space, or staffing are issues for you, consider doing VBS on five consecutive Saturdays! This will spread out the time for preparation and allow working adults to participate. You may set up all five Discovery Sites and leave them set up for the five weeks, or set up one Discovery Site for each Saturday. If you choose to set up only one Discovery

Site per week, you will need to consider that all of your kids will be in one place and how to move them all smoothly through the Discovery Site.

EVENING VBS

Evening VBS is also an excellent way to get volunteers involved who may work during the day. You can use the basic three-hour schedule *(given on page D·28)* and adapt it to fit into the evenings. This is also a great way to provide VBS for the entire family. By using the free, downloadable Youth and Adult Guides that correlate with *Good News Clues™ (see www.cookvbs.com)*, family members will all be studying the same lessons. You may want to hold VBS from 6:00–9:00 p.m. to make sure that people have time to make it after work.

ONE-DAY VBS

A one-day VBS can be a big hit! Because each of the Discovery Sites stands alone, children can participate in any of the Discovery Sites during the day and still have a great time. If space is limited, you may want to choose three Discovery Sites and have children rotate throughout the day. Here is a suggested one-day schedule using three of the Discovery Sites.

Daily schedule for camp:

7:45	Rise and Shine!
8:15	Breakfast
9:00	Cleanup time
9:15	Leaders meet for prayer
9:30	Opening assembly with singing
10:00	VBS sites
12:00	Lunch
1:00	VBS wrap-up and closing assembly
1:30	Rest and reflection time
2:00	Sports activities and electives
4:00	Singing and preparation for closing program
5:30	Cleanup
6:00	Dinner
7:30	Evening entertainment/campfire
8:30	Small group prayer time in cabins
9:00	Lights out

10-DAY VBS

Expanding VBS is simple! There are plenty of crafts and games to choose from, and children often like playing a favorite game or doing a favorite activity more than once! To expand this VBS, you can present the opening activity and the Bible story, plus choose a craft and a game from those provided in the Discovery Site. On the second day, do a review of the Bible story and then start with the Bible Memorization activity and finish out the lesson using the crafts and games that you did not use during day one. Children will spend two days in each Discovery Site, reinforcing the lesson and the Key Verse for that site. To make up time that would have been spent on the whole lesson in the Discovery Site, consider spending part of each day preparing for the closing program or extending the missions and/or singing time each day.

One-day VeBS schedule:

8:30	Staff meets for prayer and devotion
9:00	Opening ceremony and group formation
9:45	Rotation to one of three sites (*Intro and Bible Story, Game, Craft, or Snack*)
11:00	Rotation to another of three sites (*Intro and Bible Story, Game, or Craft*)
12:15	Gather for box lunch
1:00	Rotation to last of three sites (*Intro and Bible Story, Game, or Craft*)
2:45	Gather for cafeteria style snacks
3:00	Wrap-up and closing assembly
3:30	Dismissal

Alternative Uses

CHILDREN'S CHURCH

Good News Clues™ is a great curriculum to use in your children's church ministry. It's easy to expand and fits well into a children's church setting. Each VBS site can be set up to use for two weeks. There are plenty of crafts and games to choose from, and children often like playing a favorite game or doing a favorite activity more than once! On the first Sunday for each Discovery Site, you can present the opening activity and the Bible story, plus choose a craft and a game from those provided. On the second Sunday, do a review of the Bible story and then start with the Bible Memorization activity and finish out the lesson using the crafts and games that you did not use the previous week. Children will spend two days in each Discovery Site, reinforcing the lesson and the Key Bible Verse for that site. On the eleventh and twelfth Sundays of the quarter, consider spending time preparing for a program to present to parents. The children can work on the songs and Key Bible Verses. Older children or helpers can work on the puppet skits as shown for the closing program. Then on the last Sunday of the quarter, invite the parents to join the children for a time of worship as the children present their program.

CHRISTIAN SCHOOL BIBLE STUDY

Good News Clues™ would also be an excellent way to involve your students in a Christian school setting to make discoveries about new life in Jesus. Involve your class in creating the murals for each of the Discovery Sites. A team-teaching approach to this would work well if several classes joined together. Each classroom could be responsible for creating a mural and decorating for one of the Discovery Sites. Each teacher could prepare to teach the Bible story for that Discovery Site. Then each class could rotate on a following day (*or week*) to one of the other classrooms to learn about the Bible truths taught in that lesson. At the end of five days (*or weeks*) the children will have covered all the material. The curriculum could also be expanded to fit a 10-day schedule.

VeBS® as Outreach

Good News Clues™ is designed as a fun-filled experience that clearly presents the good news of Jesus Christ. The fun aspect of this mystery theme will appeal to unchurched children in your community. Children come for the fun, but discover the love and grace of the Lord while being challenged to follow Him. VBS is about outreach and discipleship.

This VBS book provides two resources to help your Investigators and Assistant Investigators talk with children who are seeking salvation. One resource is the Leader Hint "How to lead children to Jesus and into God's family" (*page R·12*). The second is the "Discovering Jesus as Your Savior" brochure on

pages R·84-85. Copy the "Discovering Jesus" path for Investigators to use and then give to children to take home. The parent letter on the back will help parents understand and support decisions their child has made. The blank area on the back side can be customized to provide information about the worship and Bible study opportunities at your church. You might include an invitation too! Use the space to inform new Christians and their families on how your church can support them in their growing faith.

Online Resources

Valuable resources for you, your VBS leaders, plus your kids and their families are online now at www.cookvbs.com. Leaders will find spiritual encouragement, practical teaching tips, and helpful printable resources. When your VBS gets underway, tell your kids and their families about the web site. They'll find additional resources to help parents lead their families to discover Jesus. Get connected and explore the many ways God can work through VBS.

VBS FOR YOUTH

Most young people want to win in life but many aren't sure how. *Good News Clues™ Youth Guide* is the VBS youth guide that correlates to the *Good News Clues™* VBS. This resource helps church leaders teach teens about God's promises for these times. *Good News Clues™ Youth Guide* will lead your teens, and the friends they invite to VBS, to explore Bible stories that teach us about God's goodness in times of trouble. Teens will encounter the truth that God is seeking them. "Behold, I stand at the door, and knock: if any man hear my voice,

and open the door, I will come in to him, and will sup with him, and he with me"— Revelation 3:20. *Good News Clues™ Youth Guide* is available free, online, through the Cook Communications Ministries' VBS web site, www.cookvbs.com. When you log on, the home page will show an icon for the *Good News Clues™ Youth Guide* for use with *Good News Clues™* VBS. Click on the *Good News Clues™ Youth Guide* icon and follow the instructions for downloading and printing.

Each *Good News Clues™ Youth Guide* session is based on high-energy games and real small-group discussion. Your students will be challenged to Reach In and deepen their own commitments to Jesus through personal Bible study and reflection. *Good News Clues™ Youth Guide* also challenges kids to Reach Out and get involved in leading their friends to Christ. Your students will belong and take ownership of their youth ministry as well as take the lead in inviting their friends into a relationship with Christ. *Good News Clues™ Youth Guide* leads your youth to take

Bible truths and put them into faithful action by asking Jesus into their hearts and trusting Him with the challenges and trials of their lives.

VBS FOR ADULTS

There might be some parents who would like to stick around while their kids are in VBS. Some of them might like to be in a study of their own. If this happens, we have FREE Bible studies just for adults that correspond with the five Training Camps in *Good News Clues*™ VBS, so parents and kids will have something to talk about on the way home from VBS. As with all Cook materials, these studies are age-appropriate, and tackle relevant issues that many "grown-ups" face today. You can find a link to download the studies on Cook's VBS site, www.cookvbs.com. When you log on, you'll see an icon for the adult guides. Click on the icon and follow the instructions for downloading and printing your own copy of the *Good News Clues*™ VBS Adult Guide.

www.cookvbs.com

Using This Guide

There are many tasks and responsibilities on the shoulders of a director, so we have given you a guide to take you through VBS from beginning to end without a hitch. The resources and information in this step-by-step guide will help you with all your key responsibilities as a director. From Introduction to Closing Program you will be guided step-by-step through the events of *Good News Clues*™ and what needs to be done in each area. The Planning Calendar (*on pages D·14-15*) will help you to plan out your time and manage the different aspects of directing VBS.

Referring to the Table of Contents you will notice that each section starts with a unique prefix:

D• — (Director's Guide)
E1• — (Site 1 Guide)
E2• — (Site 2 Guide)
E3• — (Site 3 Guide)
E4• — (Site 4 Guide)
E5• — (Site 5 Guide)
P1• — (Preschool Site 1 Guide)
P2• — (Preschool Site 2 Guide)
P3• — (Preschool Site 3 Guide)
P4• — (Preschool Site 4 Guide)
P5• — (Preschool Site 5 Guide)
R• — (Reproducible Resources)

There are four sections featuring a durable, colorful, tabbed section divider for the Director's Guide, Elementary Sites, Preschool Guide, and Reproducible Resources. Page numbers for each section run sequentially starting with the first page of each section. However, notice that the Elementary and Preschool Site Guides are numbered individually to assist the Investigators as they work with each of them.

Comprehensive Supply Lists

You will find a comprehensive general supply list on pages D·18-26 for the five Elementary Sites, and a list of Preschool supplies on pages P·4-10. These lists are broken down by Sites and by activity (*e.g., crafts, snacks, etc.*), allowing you to coordinate your supply needs before requesting donations or making purchases. For your Investigators' convenience, each Site section lists the supplies needed for that particular Site.

Everything in this guide is fully reproducible for use in the purchaser's VBS program. Pages have been perforated for your convenience and ease of use. Feel free to make this book your own! Add your own flair and ideas to it as you develop the program best suited to the kids who regularly attend your church and live in the community around your church.

Finally, trust God, and have fun! And before you go any further in this guide, stop and ask God to help you throughout this process. Then prepare to see Him touch the hearts of children with the knowledge that they can learn and grow in their walk with Jesus.

QUICK VIEW ICONS

The icons shown below will help Investigators and Assistant Investigators quickly get to specific points in their lesson. The Preschool Guide will use some different/additional icons as noted below.

 **Preparing to Search**

 **Putting the Pieces Together**

 **Focus on the Bible**

 **Elementary Deduction**

 **Bible Memorization**

 **Detectives' Departure**

 **Music Time**

Preschool Icons

 **Hands-on Exploration**

 **Gumshoe Grub**

 **Bible Memorization**

 **Case Cracking Games**

Electronic Clip Art

In addition to the lively music on the *Good News Clues*™ CD, we've added a collection of electronic images for use in creating your promotional materials. Images are accessible by Macintosh or PC users. Thumbnail representations of the images are printed on the inside front cover of this guide.

Please consult your software manual for the proper way to import images.

In addition to the clip art images, we've also included editable PDF documents so that you can "fill-in-the-blanks" with specific event information. These include a full-color poster, bulletin insert, doorknob hangers, name badges, postcards, and certificate of completion.

Planning Calendar

4 MONTHS PRIOR

☐ Begin praying for the leaders and children who will be part of VBS.

☐ Establish a VBS planning committee and/or select the director *(page D·15)*.

☐ Establish the VBS dates on your church's calendar.

☐ Establish a working budget for VBS *(page D·17)*.

3 MONTHS PRIOR

☐ Begin holding regular planning meetings. Assign responsibilities to the members of the VBS committee. Smaller churches can ask one person to fill multiple positions. *(Refer to Recruit section on pages D·59-61 for recruitment resources and descriptions of all positions.)*

☐ Recruit someone to oversee setup of all Discovery Sites. *(See **Creating Discovery Sites** on page D·31.)*

☐ Choose Investigators and Assistant Investigators *(one Assistant Investigator per 6 to 8 kids)* for each site.

☐ Recruit someone to be in charge of daily opening assembly time when all children meet together *(page D·31)*.

☐ Recruit someone to be in charge of the Closing Program *(page D·52)*.

☐ Recruit someone to be responsible for nursery and preschoolers.

☐ Recruit craft coordinators *(one per Discovery Site would be ideal, but since all crafts are done within the Discovery Sites, Assistant Investigators can also fill this role)*.

☐ Recruit someone to be in charge of snacks. *(Again, use your Assistant Investigators in this area.)*

☐ Recruit outreach and publicity staff.

☐ Recruit someone to coordinate registration.

☐ Recruit people to pray, to provide transportation, and to do follow-up.

2 MONTHS PRIOR

☐ Have the Investigators who are responsible for each Discovery Site select committees to plan how each environment will be created. *(See **Creating Discovery Sites** on page D·31.)*

☐ Make assignments for each Discovery Site, such as one person to organize and order craft materials, someone to be in charge of props, refreshments, etc.

☐ Begin publicity within your church. *(See **Promote** beginning on page D·74.)*

☐ Begin holding regular staff training sessions. *(See **Training** beginning on page D·62 for information, training resources, and meeting agendas.)*

6 WEEKS PRIOR

☐ Begin community publicity through posters, newspapers, and "community events" radio spots *(page D·74-76)*.

☐ Make sure committees continue to meet regularly.

☐ Make sure leaders *(Investigators)* are beginning to prepare.

☐ Continue training for all VBS staff.

4 WEEKS PRIOR

☐ Make announcements in your church to create interest and enthusiasm *(page D·75)*.

☐ Begin a registration drive. As kids are registered, decide how you will group them *(by age, grade, mixed ages, etc.)* and assign them to a team of children. *(Registration on page D·27)*

☐ Begin preparing for the closing program and decide which option to use. *(See page D·52.)*

☐ Double-check all props, costumes, music, snacks, and so on.

☐ Continue training for all VBS staff.

Key Players

- [ ] Review details with Investigators and committees.

- [ ] Make signs to help the first day go smoothly ("Check-in," "Registration," and so on).

- [ ] Prepare a checklist for each Discovery Site, detailing all items that will be needed the first day of VBS.

- [ ] Make copies of the take-home pages and Detective's Diaries for each Discovery Site (based on the number of registered children) and distribute to leaders.

- [ ] Prepare for a devotion time with staff before VBS each day (pages D·67-72).

DAY BEFORE

- [ ] Set up the sites and make sure everything is ready for the first day!

- [ ] See that final plans have been made for the closing program at the end of VBS.

- [ ] Meet with the VBS staff for prayer.

1 WEEK AFTER

- [ ] Families, staff, and director complete evaluations (pages R·44-46).

- [ ] Activate the follow-up committee (pages D·77-78).

- [ ] Review your budget and keep information along with other general comments on file for next year's VBS director.

- [ ] Update the name and address list of leaders and children for follow-up as well as next year's registration and promotion.

Use the following information as you look for people to be key players in VBS. This information will help you as you plan and will give people a good idea of what you are asking them to do as they consider their involvement in VBS. *(See pages D·59-61 for more information on recruiting staff.)*

VBS Director

This person oversees the entire VBS, coordinating and helping the staff as needed with promotion, preparation, and follow-up.

Investigators *(2 per Discovery Site)*

Investigators, or teachers, should be people who enjoy interacting with or leading groups. They will remain at their designated Discovery Sites and should portray only one role during VBS. The two Investigators per Discovery Site work as a team to present the activities and Bible story. The Investigators prepare only one lesson and give that lesson to each of the five groups of kids.

Investigators and Assistant Investigators should dress in character for the site they are working in. Suggestions for appropriate attire are listed at the beginning of each site *(See Site Coordinators.)* Keep your attire comfortable while enhancing the theme.

Assistant Investigators

Recruit one Assistant Investigator for every six to eight children. As children go to a different Discovery Site every day, they are accompanied by the same Assistant Investigator. As the children arrive, Assistant Investigators should gather their groups, go with them to opening assembly, accompany them daily to each site, and assist as needed. Mature junior high and senior high young people make excellent Assistant Investigators. The Assistant Investigators have the unique and exciting opportunity to build meaningful relationships with the children and guide them toward God's love through their actions and informal teaching times.

Other Staff

Depending on how many volunteers you use, you could have people coordinate snacks or crafts. You may also want people to create the Discovery Sites and to promote and follow up within the church and your community. You can also rely on volunteers to gather props before VBS. Refer to page D-59 for more information on recruiting people based on their spiritual gifts.

Overview Chart

SITE	Garden *Site Color: Dark*	Dining Room *Site Color: Red*	Family Room *Site Color: White*	Kitchen *Site Color: Green*	Living Room *Site Color: Gold*
BIBLE STORY	Adam and Eve sin. *(Genesis 1:26-31; 2:4—3:23)*	Jesus dies and comes back to life. *(Matthew 21:1-11; 26:17-29; 26:47—28:10)*	The Prodigal Son is welcomed home by his father. *(Luke 15:11-32)*	The Parables of the Mustard Seed and the Yeast give clues about growing in our faith. *(Matthew 13:31-33)*	The Parables of the Hidden Treasure and the Pearl give clues about our future home. *(Matthew 13:44-46)*
KEY VERSE	*"For all have sinned, and come short of the glory of God."* — Romans 3:23	*"But God commendeth his love toward us, in that, while we were yet sinners, Christ died for us."* — Romans 5:8	*"For God so loved the world that he gave his only begotten Son, that whosoever believeth in him should not perish, but have everlasting life."* — John 3:16	*"But grow in grace, and in the knowledge of our Lord and Saviour Jesus Christ."* — 2 Peter 3:18	*"But lay up for yourselves treasures in heaven, where neither moth nor rust doth corrupt, and where thieves do not break through nor steal. For where your treasure is, there will your heart be also."* — Matthew 6:20-21
CONCEPT	We need to be forgiven.	We can be saved from our sin through Jesus.	We can be welcomed into God's family.	We can grow in Jesus.	We can live with Jesus forever.
RESPONSE	Children will understand that they've sinned and turn to God.	Children will ask Jesus to be their Savior.	Children will believe God loves them and ask to be part of His family.	Children will take steps to grow in their spiritual life.	Children will believe that those who trust Jesus as Savior can look forward to a heavenly home.

Budget

Developing a budget is one of the most important things you will do to plan your VBS.

Most churches will already have an amount budgeted for VBS. Once you know the total amount, it is a good idea to break down how much of that budget will be spent in each of the areas of VBS. Whether your budget is large or small, good planning means that money is available right up to the end of VBS. If VBS has been done in your church in previous years, the budgets from those VBS programs will be your best tools.

To develop your budget, it is a good idea first to make a list of all the categories in which money could be spent and break those down into specifics. Next, determine how many children you will have and how much income (*if any*) there will be from registration or other sources. Use the budget chart (*see page R·2*) to help you plan your budget. Some of the main expenses are listed. List any other main categories you can think of that apply to your situation and then break them down into specifics and keep track of money spent as you go.

Keeping track of a budget is as important as creating one, but sometimes more difficult—especially if there are a number of people involved. If other people from your VBS team are purchasing props or supplies, be sure they know how much to spend and how to report to you the amount spent. The reimbursement form (*see page R·3*) is one way to handle reimbursement records. This form can be copied and handed out to VBS staff at the beginning of the program or as needs arise.

The records that you keep will be very valuable to next year's director, so do your best to keep them accurate. Make notes on the budget at the end of VBS for next year!

- Take a VBS offering in your church.
- Hold a fund-raising event.
- Get supply donations.
- Get snack donations.
- Allow church members to sponsor a child by giving a certain amount to VBS.
- *(This is also a great way to get people without kids involved in VBS—you may want to choose the intergenerational option for the closing program so they can see what the child they sponsored has been doing all week!)*
- Choose ways of showing appreciation and doing follow-up using the services of people in the church rather than purchasing and giving gifts.
- Network with other churches in your area that are doing *Good News Clues*™ to see if there are ways to share props and supplies.

Supplies

All of the supplies for *Good News Clues*™ are common items and easy to obtain. This may seem to be a daunting task; however, with the aid of some organized volunteers and the comprehensive supply list below, you'll have it done in no time!

Your church may already have some supplies available for your use during VBS. For the remaining supplies, you may want to get donations from church members by sending out a list of needed supplies. After donations have been gathered, purchase the remaining items on the list.

Each activity, craft, game, and snack in this *Good News Clues*™ Step-by-Step Guide has a corresponding list of supplies that are referenced in the PG *(page number)* column in the compiled list below. You may want to cross off the items you already have on hand, and pencil in the quantities you need for each item based on the estimated number of children attending your VBS.

Supplies for Activities, Games, Snacks and Crafts have been placed in categories denoted by the prefix A, G, S, or C in front of each item. Numerals are listed after the prefix to keep all the supplies needed for a specific game, craft, or snack together *(C1)*. If you choose not to use a particular craft, game, or snack option, you can simply ignore the list of supplies needed for that particular option.

Supplies for Discovery Site decorations will vary, depending on your VBS plan. Please refer to suggested Discovery Site decorations in the **Setting the Scene** section of each site for recommended items and tips.

NOTE: The number of supplies listed in the TOT *(Total)* column will vary depending on the number of children attending each site, and/or the total number of teams that children are divided into. These quantities will need to be calculated when VBS registration is complete. You may want to have some extra supplies on hand for walk-in attendees.

CATEGORY & ITEM	PG	QTY	/UNIT	TOT	HAVE	NEED	✔
Common Supplies needed at each site							
Bibles		1	/site	6			
Good News Clues™ CD (Duplicate CDs or cassettes)		1	/site	6			
CD Player or cassette player		1	/site	6			
Song lyrics on overhead transparencies		1	/site				
Overhead projector		1	/site				
Scissors, pens, pencils and markers		1	ea./child				
Glue, tape, stapler							
Paper plates, cups, and napkins for snacks		1	ea./child/site				
Paper towels for cleanups							
SITE 1: THE GARDEN							
Garden Mural	R·72	1	/site				
Copy of "The Quest Continues" student take-home paper (page E1·14)	E1·14	1	/child				

CATEGORY & ITEM	PG	QTY	/UNIT	TOT	HAVE	NEED	✔

CATEGORY & ITEM	PG	QTY	/UNIT	TOT	HAVE	NEED	✔
Copy of the "Detective's Diaries" (pages R·61-68)	E1·8	1	each/child				
(A1) Actual dead plant in a pot of dry dirt	E1·5	1	each/site				
(A1) Broken garden tool	E1·5	1	each/site				
(A1) Clue 1 on dark paper	E1·5	1	each/site				
(A2) Fragrant flower	E1·6	1	each/site				
(A3) Small pieces of paper with 1 or 2 words of the verse printed on them.	E1·8	1	set/site				
(A3) Inflated balloons, each with 1-2 words of the verse inside, taped into flower shape	E1·8	1	ea./4-5 children				
(A3) Clue 2 on dark paper	E1·8	1	each/site				
(A3) Key Verse Poster	E1·8	1	each/site				
(A3) Key Verse Cards (page R·60)	E1·8	1	each/child				
(A4) Puppet (optional)	E1·9	1	each/site				
(A5) Dark beads	E1·12	1	each/child				
(A5) Lacing or cord	E1·12	1	piece/child				
(A5) Emily's Bracelet (optional)	E1·12	1	each/site				
(A5) Treasure Basket	E1·12	1	each/site				
(A5) Clue 3 on dark paper	E1·12	1	each/site				
(S1) Healthy veggies to dip, such as carrot sticks, celery sticks, cucumber slices, and other vegetables	E1·10	2-4	pieces/child				
(S1) One or two soft dips, such as ranch dip (already prepared or use your own recipe)	E1·10	2	containers/site				
(S1) Small paper plates	E1·10	1	each/child				
(S1) Spoons for dip	E1·10	1	each/container				
(S2) Red crepe paper cut into 10-inch circles	E1·10	1	each/child				
(S2) Pretzels, small crackers, or candy	E1·10	1	handful/child				
(S2) Green floral tape or green twist ties	E1·10	1	each/child				
(S2) Bushel Baskets	E1·10	1-2	each/site				
(G1) Ball	E1·10	1-2	each/site				
(G2) Dirt or potting soil	E1·10	1	bag/2 buckets				
(G2) Buckets	E1·10	2	ea./5-6 children				
(G2) Plastic spoons	E1·10	1	each/bucket				
(G2) Plastic cups	E1·10	1	each/bucket				
(C1) Scratch paper (art paper that has multicolors underneath a layer of black (cut into 1-3/4" x 8" strips)	E1·11	1	each/child				
(C1) Satin ribbon cut into 12" lengths	E1·11	1	piece/child				
(C1) Wooden scratching tools or paperclips	E1·11	1	each/child				
(C1) Hole punch	E1·11	1-2	each/site				
(C2) Gel pens or markers made to draw on dark paper	E1·11		variety/site				
(C2) Dark-colored paper cups (or use paper cups covered with dark construction paper)	E1·11	1	each/child				
(C2) Potting soil	E1·11	3/4	cup/child				

CATEGORY & ITEM	PG	QTY	/UNIT	TOT	HAVE	NEED	✔

SITE 1: THE GARDEN (Continued)

CATEGORY & ITEM	PG	QTY	/UNIT	TOT	HAVE	NEED	✔
(C2) Scoop for potting soil	E1·11	1-2	each/site				
(C2) Small annual flowers or nontoxic houseplants	E1·11	1	each/child				
(C2) Clear self-adhesive paper *(cut to cover outside of cups)*	E1·11	1	piece/child				

SITE 2: THE DINING ROOM

CATEGORY & ITEM	PG	QTY	/UNIT	TOT	HAVE	NEED	✔
Dining Room Mural	R·73	1	each/site				
Copy of "The Quest Continues" student take-home paper *(page E2·14)*	E2·14	1	each/child				
Copy of the "Detective's Diary" *(pages R·61-68)*	E2·8	1	each/child				
(A7) Two large bread rolls	E2·5	1	each/site				
(A7) Plate of bite-size crackers or bread pieces spread with grape jelly	E2·5	1	piece/child				
(A7) Napkins	E2·5	1	each/child				
(A7) Clue 1 written on red paper	E2·5	1	set/site				
(A9) Dining table shapes *(spoon, knife, fork, plate, and napkin)*	E2·8	1	set/site				
(A9) Key Verse poster	E2·8	1	each/site				
(A9) Key Verse Cards *(page R·60)*	E2·8	1	each/child				
(A9) Clue 2 written on red paper	E2·8	1	each/site				
(A10) Copy of song lyrics for each child or have the words on an overhead transparency *(page R·21-26)*	E2·9	1	each/site				
(A10) Puppet *(optional)*	E2·9	1	each/site				
(S3) A variety of pieces of red fruit such as cherries, watermelon balls, or strawberries	E2·9	4-5	pieces/child				
(S3) A variety of red candies such as red licorice, red sour balls, red hots, etc.	E2·9	4-5	pieces/child				
(S3) Small paper cups	E2·9	1	each/child				
(S3) Napkins	E2·9	1	each/child				
(S4) Matzo crackers or other crackers	E2·10	4-5	each/child				
(S4) Cheese Slices *(American Swiss, cheddar, etc.)*	E2·10	4-5	slices/child				
(S4) Napkins	E2·10	1	each/child				
(S4) Sharp knife for slicing cheese	E2·10	1	each/site				
(G3) Clue 3 written on red paper	E2·10	1	each/site				
(G3) White towel or cloth	E2·10	1	each/team				
(G3) Tray	E2·10	1	each/team				
(G3) Plastic cup	E2·10	1	each/team				
(G3) Plastic plate	E2·10	1	each/team				
(G3) Plastic knife, fork, spoon	E2·10	1	set/team				
(G3) Napkin	E2·10	1	each/team				
(G4) Assortment of crackers, cheese cubes, apple wedges, juice or milk, and carrot sticks	E2·11	1	assortment/team				
(G4) Table, placemats, candlesticks, place settings for six players	E2·11	1	set up/team				
(G4) Index cards numbered 1 through 6	E2·11	1	set/team				
(C3) Clear photo key chains	E2·11	1	each/child				
(C3) White drawing paper, 2-1/4" x 3-1/4" or to fit key chains	E2·11	1	each/child				

CATEGORY & ITEM	PG	QTY	/UNIT	TOT	HAVE	NEED	✔
SITE 2: THE DINING ROOM (Continued)							
(C3) Red drawing paper, 2-1/4" x 3-1/4" or to fit key chains	E2·11	1	each/child				
(C3) Thin-line markers	E2·11	1	set/3-4 children				
(C4) Inexpensive white fabric placemats or white fabric cut to the size of placemats and hemmed	E2·11	1	each/child				
(C4) Fabric markers	E2·11	1	set/3-4 children				
(C4) Fabric scissors and sewing machine if making placemats	E2·11	1	each/site				
(A11) Bleach	E2·12	1	bottle/site				
(A11) Red food coloring	E2·12	1	bottle/site				
(A11) Measuring spoons	E2·12	1	set/site				
(A11) Clear glass cups with water	E2·12	1	each/site				
(A11) Red beads	E2·12	1	each/child				
(A11) Lacing	E2·12	1	piece/child				
(A11) Detective's Diary	E2·12	1	each/child				
(A11) Crayons, colored pencils, markers	E2·12	1	assortment/table				
(A11) *Emily's Bracelet* (optional)	E2·12	1	each/site				
(A11) Clusters of grapes on a plate	E2·12	1-2	grapes/child				
(A11) Clue 4 written on red paper	E2·12	1	each/site				
SITE 3: THE FAMILY ROOM							
Family Room Mural	R·74	1	each/site				
Copy of "The Quest Continues" student take-home paper (page E3·15)	E3·15	1	each/child				
Copy of the "Detective's Diary" (pages R·61-68)	E3·9	1	each/child				
(A13) Jigsaw puzzle altered to read 4 GIVE N	E3·5	1	each/site				
(A13) Large mirror	E3·5	1	each/site				
(A13) Clue 1 on white paper	E3·5	1	each/site				
(A14) Bible	E3·7	1	each/site				
(A14) Regal-looking robe	E3·7	1	each/site				
(A14) Large costume jewelry ring	E3·7	1	each/site				
(A14) Sandals	E3·7	1	pair/site				
(A14) Fabric bag of coins	E3·7	1	each/site				
(A14) Ragged clothing	E3·7	1	set/site				
(A15) Key Verse poster	E3·9	1	each/site				
(A15) Card stock puzzle pieces with verse phrases on them (See pattern on page R·49 in Resources.)	E3·9	1	set/site				
(A15) Detective's Diaries	E3·9	1	each/child				
(A15) Clue 2 written on white paper	E3·9	1	each/site				
(A16) Copy of song lyrics for each child or have the words on an overhead transparency (page R·21-26)	E3·10	1	each/site				
(S5) Regular or microwave popcorn in a variety of flavors, such as kettle corn, cheese, popcorn, buttered popcorn	E3·10	1	handful/child				
(S5) Large serving bowls	E3·10	1-3	each/site				

CATEGORY & ITEM	PG	QTY	/UNIT	TOT	HAVE	NEED	✔
(S5) Scoops	E3·10	1-3	each/site				
(S5) Small paper bowls	E3·10	1	each/child				
(S5) Napkins	E3·10	1	each/child				
(S6) White cake mix	E3·10	1	ea/24 cupcakes				
(S6) Eggs	E3·10		/cake mix				
(S6) Oil	E3·10		/cake mix				
(S6) Cupcake tin	E3·10		/cake mix				
(S6) Cupcake liners	E3·10	1	each/cupcake				
(S6) Canned or homemade white frosting	E3·10	1	each/cake mix				
(S6) White decorating sprinkles	E3·10	1	each/cake mix				
(S6) Napkins	E3·10	1	each/child				
(G6) Taped or chalked shapes *(circles, squares, rectangles)* on floor	E3·11	1	each/site				
(G6) Music *(CD or video)*	E3·11	1	each/site				
(C5) Magnet strips with adhesive on one side	E3·11	2	each/child				
(C5) Puzzle pieces	E3·11	35-40	each/child				
(C5) White spray paint	E3·11	1	can/site				
(C5) Cardboard frames	E3·11	1	each/child				
(C5) Craft glue	E3·11	1	bottle/table				
(C5) Newspapers	E3·11	1	batch/site				
(C5) Tempera paint in different colors	E3·11	1-3	bottles/site				
(C5) Photo insert paper *(copy on page R·53 in Resources)*	E3·11	2	each/child				
(C6) Yarn cut to 15" lengths	E3·12	1	each/child				
(C6) Cotton fabric cut into 12" x 6" rectangles	E3·12	1	each/child				
(C6) Sewing machine, thread	E3·12	1	each/site				
(C6) Safety pins	E3·12	2	each/child				
(C6) Shiny pennies for each word of Bible Memory Verse	E3·12		each/child				
(C6) Fabric paint	E3·12	1-3	bottles/site				
(C6) Newspapers	E3·12	1	batch/site				
(C6) Paint Shirts	E3·12	1	each/child				
(A17) Detective's Diaries	E3·13	1	each/child				
(A17) Scissors	E3·13	1	each/child				
(A17) Glue Sticks	E3·13	1	each/two children				
(A17) Pens/pencils	E3·13	1	each/child				
(A17) Key Verse poster from Bible Memorization activity	E3·13	1	each/site				
(A17) White beads	E3·13	1	each/child				
(A17) Lacing	E3·13	1	piece/child				
(A17) Clue 3 on white paper	E3·13	1	each/site				
(A17) *Emily's Bracelet (optional)*	E3·13	1	each/site				

CATEGORY & ITEM	PG	QTY	/UNIT	TOT	HAVE	NEED	✔
SITE 4: THE KITCHEN							
Kitchen Mural	R·75	1	each/site				
Copy of "The Quest Continues" student take-home paper (page E4·14)	E4·14	1	each/child				
Copy of the "Detective's Diaries" (pages R·61-68)	E4·8	1	each/child				
(A19) Yeast dough that is prepared and ready to be kneaded	E4·5	1	handful/child				
(A19) Wet wipes, basins with water, soap and paper towels or a place for kids to wash and dry their hands	E4·5	1	each/site				
(A19) Tables	E4·5	1	ea/6-8 children				
(A19) Flour	E4·5	1	pkg/site				
(A19) Baking sheets	E4·5	1	each/16-20 rolls				
(A19) One loaf of homemade bread baked without yeast	E4·5	1	each/site				
(A19) Clue 1 written on green paper	E4·5	1	each/site				
(A20) Bible	E4·7	1	each/site				
(A20) Container of yeast	E4·7	1	each/site				
(A20) Box or bag of mustard seed	E4·7	1	each/site				
(A21) Key Verse Poster	E4·8	1	each/site				
(A21) Key Verse Cards	E4·8	1	each/child				
(A21) Detective's Diary	E4·8	1	each/child				
(A21) Tape	E4·8	1	roll/site				
(A21) Clue 2 written on green paper	E4·8	1	each/site				
(A22) Copy of song lyrics for each child or have the words on an overhead transparency (page R·21-26)	E4·9	1	each/site				
(A22) Overhead projector	E4·9	1	each/site				
(A22) Puppet (optional)	E4·9	1	each/site				
(S7) Small hot dogs or sausages	E4·9	1-2	each/child				
(S7) Refrigerated crescent rolls	E4·9	1	tube/8 hot dogs				
(S7) Baking sheet	E4·9		site				
(S7) Ketchup	E4·9	1	bottle/site				
(S7) Mustard	E4·9	1	bottle/site				
(S7) Multi-colored fish crackers	E4·9	1	scoop/child				
(S7) Serving plates or trays	E4·9		site				
(S7) Small bowls for ketchup and mustard	E4·9		site				
(S7) Spoons for ketchup and mustard	E4·9		site				
(S7) Small plates	E4·9	1	each/child				
(S7) Napkins, cups	E4·9	1	each/child				
(S8) Lime green gelatin	E4·10	1	pkg/4-6 children				
(S8) Clear 8-oz. cups	E4·10	1	each/child				
(S8) Whipped topping	E4·10	2	scoops/child				
(S8) Spoons	E4·10	1	each/child				
(S8) Napkins, cups	E4·10	1	each/child				

SITE 4: THE KITCHEN (Continued)

CATEGORY & ITEM	PG	QTY	/UNIT	TOT	HAVE	NEED	✔
(G8) Inflated balloons	E4·10	1-2	each/child				
(G9) Hardboiled eggs	E4·10	1	each/team				
(G9) Kitchen items: skillets, serving spoons, tongs, plates, bowls, mugs, cookie sheets	E4·10	1	set/team				
(C7) Copy of bird pattern *(see page R·48 in Resources)*	E4·11	1	each/child				
(C7) Utility knife	E4·11	1	each/site				
(C7) Drawing paper cut into 6" x 4" pieces	E4·11	1	each/child				
(C7) Hole punch	E4·11	1	each/site				
(C7) String cut into 24" pieces	E4·11	1	each/child				
(C7) Markers	E4·11	1	set/table				
(C7) Scissors	E4·11	1	each/site				
(C7) Pictures of various types of birds *(available at your local library, etc.)*	E4·11	1	set/site				
(C8) Yellow foam board, 6" wide x height of child plus 1 foot	E4·12	1	each/child				
(C8) Inexpensive measuring tape *(or use the pattern on page R·47 in Resources)*	E4·12	1	each/child				
(C8) Stickers of flowers	E4·12	10-12	each/child				
(C8) Red craft foam	E4·12	1	each/child				
(C8) Black markers	E4·12	2-3	each/table				
(C8) Tacky material to attach pieces	E4·12	1	piece/child				
(C8) Utility knife	E4·12	1	each/site				
(A23) Index cards	E4·12	1-2	each/child				
(A23) Markers or colored pencils	E4·12	1	assortment/site				
(A23) Sample recipe cards (any kind)	E4·12	1	set/site				
(A23) Detective's Diaries	E4·12	1	each/child				
(A23) Pencils	E4·12	1	each/child				
(A23) Green beads	E4·12	1	each/child				
(A23) Lacing	E4·12	1	piece/child				
(A23) *Emily's Bracelet (optional)*	E4·12	1	each/site				
(A23) Treasure of the day: yeast rolls	E4·12	1	each/child				
(A23) Clue 3 on green paper	E4·12	1	each/site				

CATEGORY & ITEM	PG	QTY	/UNIT	TOT	HAVE	NEED	✔
SITE 5: THE LIVING ROOM							
Living Room Mural	R·76	1	each/site				
Copy of "The Quest Continues" student take-home paper (page E5·14)	E5·14	1	each/child				
Copy of the "Detective's Diaries" (pages R·61-68)	E5·9	1	each/child				
(A25) Small tabletop-size treasure chest with working lock and key	E5·5	1	each/site				
(A25) Clue #1 on yellow paper	E5·5	1	each/site				
(A26) King-size white bedsheet hanging to be used as a screen	E5·6	1	each/site				
(A26) Bright lights (photographic lights or strong work lights)	E5·6	2-4	each/site				
(A26) Shovel	E5·6	1	each/site				
(A26) Small ball (smaller than golf ball)	E5·7	1	each/site				
(A26) Treasure box	E5·7	1	each/site				
(A26) Armload of "stuff" such as boxes, bags, and clothing	E5·7	1	assortment/site				
(A26) Cloth bag of jingling coins	E5·7	1	each/site				
(A26) Poster boards (phrases to write found on E5·7)	E5·7	7	each/site				
(A27) Key Verse Posters	E5·9	2	each/site				
(A27) Poster board	E5·9	1	sheet/4 kids				
(A27) Markers	E5·9	1	set/4 kids				
(A27) Detective's Diaries	E5·9	1	each/child				
(A27) Key Verse Cards	E5·9	1	each/child				
(A28) Copy of song lyrics for each child or have the words on an overhead transparency (page R·21-26)	E5·9	1	each/site				
(A28) Overhead projector	E5·9	1	each/site				
(A28) Puppet (optional)	E5·9	1	each/site				
(S9) Pudding (store bought or homemade)	E5·10	2	spoonfuls/child				
(S9) Clear cups—8 oz. size	E5·10	1	each/child				
(S9) Spoons	E5·10	1	each/child				
(S9) Chocolate chips, butterscotch chips, or mini marshmallows	E5·10	1	tablespoon/child				
(S10) Small decorated cookies (store bought or homemade)	E5·10	1-2	each/child				
(S10) Juice, such as apple juice	E5·10	1	cupful/child				
(S10) Doilies on trays	E5·10	1-3	each/site				
(S10) Fancy napkins	E5·10	1	each/child				
(S10) Cups	E5·10	1	each/child				
(G10) Clue #2 on yellow paper	E5·10	1	each/child				
(G10) Couch	E5·10	1	each/site				
(G10) Ottoman	E5·10	2-3	each/site				
(G10) Carpet squares	E5·10	2-3	each/site				
(G10) End tables	E5·10	2-3	each/site				
(G10) Small lamp shades	E5·10	2-3	each/site				
(G11) Garbage bags full of paper wads	E5·11	2	each/site				

CATEGORY & ITEM	PG	QTY	/UNIT	TOT	HAVE	NEED	✔
SITE 5: THE LIVING ROOM (Continued)							
(G11) Bags of cotton balls or foam packing peanuts	E5·11	2-3	each/site				
(G11) Grocery bags	E5·11	1	each/2-3 kids				
(C9) Treasure Boxes (use pattern on page R·50 or purchase them)	E5·11	1	each/child				
(C9) Glue	E5·11	1	bottle/3-4 kids				
(C9) Gold spray paint	E5·11	1	can/site				
(C9) Newspapers	E5·11	1	bunch/site				
(C9) Pasta—different shapes like elbow, bow-tie, etc.	E5·11	1	assortment/site				
(C10) Needles	E5·12	1	each/child				
(C10) Thread—36" lengths (white or gold)	E5·12	1	each/child				
(C10) Pearl-like beads of various sizes	E5·12	5-8	each child				
(C10) Gold ribbon, 1-1/2" wide, cut into 10" lengths	E5·12	1	each/child				
(C10) Spring clothespins	E5·12	1	each/child				
(A29) Detective's Diaries	E5·13	1	each/child				
(A29) Yellow or gold beads	E5·13	1	each/child				
(A29) Lacing or cording	E5·13	1	piece/child				
(A29) Clue #3 on yellow paper	E5·13	1	each/child				

Registration

Registering kids for your VBS is another very important step in planning. Once registration starts, it is important to have a system to track each student and his or her information. Use the registration card, or design a similar card with the specific information that your church needs. *(See page R·4.)* Be sure to have one file that contains a card for each child attending VBS. Along with a registration card, you need to have a medical release form for each child, signed by a parent or guardian. This allows the VBS staff to obtain medical help for a sick or injured child. Check with your church and/or local government for the information and format they recommend.

Attendance

Once VBS begins, you will need a system for tracking attendance and knowing which kids are in the different Discovery Sites each day. Following the instructions below will help make the first day, including last minute registrations, run smoothly. This will also give you an ongoing record of the location of each child.

Once the majority of children have been registered, the director should divide the children into five groups and assign a color to each group. Reproduce the Group Color attendance sheet on page R·5, making a separate chart for each group in your VBS. On the first few lines of the chart write in the names of the Investigators for that group of kids, then list the children's names. *(Use as many pages as necessary if you have more children in a group than spaces on the chart.)* At the top of each chart are five boxes, noting the order in which that group will go to the Discovery Site. Fill in the days that your VBS sessions will be held and the order that the group will go through the Discovery Sites. *(Example: The red group might go through Discovery Sites 1-5; group yellow would then start with Discovery Site 2 and go through Discovery Site 5 and then to Discovery Site 1.)*

When your charts are complete, make name tags for the children. You may want to choose electronic clip art on the *Good News Clues*™ CD to create custom name tags that tie into the *Good News Clues*™

theme, or use the name tag layout provided on the CD. Write each child's name using the color of marker that matches the color of the group he or she is assigned to. Put the name tags all together in one box, alphabetized, regardless of color. Then make a photocopy of the chart pages and hand them off to the person in charge of registration and attendance during VBS. Also give this person extra name tags and the markers used to write the names.

For the first session, each child will come to the attendance desk and tell the VBS staff his or her name. The VBS staff will find the child's name tag in the box and give it to the child. Then the VBS staff will look at the list that corresponds to the name tag color and mark the child present for that session. The VBS staff can then direct the child to the area where he or she is to meet the rest of his or her group. If any new children come, they should fill out a registration card. The VBS staff will then assign them to a group, write each child's name on the appropriate attendance page, and make a name tag using the corresponding color. Once all the children have arrived, the VBS staff in charge of attendance should give any new names to the Director to add to his or her lists.

Schedule

Good News Clues™ is flexible enough to fit the most diverse schedules and needs. Adjust the program as you wish. A typical morning schedule might look like this:

8:15	Staff meets for prayer and devotions
8:30	Investigators and Assistant Investigators organize kids into their groups
8:45	Opening Assembly
9:15	Children dismissed to go to their Discovery Sites
11:15	Closing Assembly
11:30	Dismissal

The schedule for each Discovery Site is loaded with activities that are designed to last two hours. Investigators may find that they don't have enough time for everything. They should decide in advance which activities are optional. It's better to have too much planned than too little. But do avoid rushing children through activities. If you find that your location requires extra time for transitions, be sure to build this into your schedule by extending it by a few minutes at the beginning or end.

If you decide not to include the missions project in your opening assembly, you may want to adopt the following schedule since you may not need as much time in the Opening Assembly:

8:30	Staff meets for prayer and devotions
8:50	Investigators and Assistant Investigators organize kids into their groups
9:00	Brief Opening Assembly
9:15	Children dismissed to travel to their Discovery Sites
11:15	Closing Assembly
11:30	Dismissal

Good News Clues™ is also designed to give you flexibility within the lessons as well. If your schedule only allows for a shorter VBS, you can easily take time from each of the five Discovery Sites by cutting back on the number of activities or games. The Investigators have the flexibility to decide which activities to keep and which to cut in order to meet the time requirements and the skill level of the children. If, however, the needs of your church require a completely different format and schedule, see Custom VeBS® Options on pages D·3-8 for more ideas for creative VBS formats.

Puppet Option

Many children's ministries have found puppets to be effective ministry tools, capturing attention, and adding fun and variety to lessons and programs. That's why this year's VBS program offers you a creative Puppet Option.

The Puppet Option is a lively enhancement to existing program material. The puppet can be used to enhance all opening and closing skits. And puppets can be used to interact with the Investigator during the time in each Discovery Site, leading the children to activities, leading the children during the music time, etc.

The VBS Puppet Option includes an easy, enlargeable puppet pattern, featuring *Good News Clues*™ puppet named BOSWORTH. See the resources section *(pages R·55-59)* for the pattern to make your own puppet to use during *Good News Clues*™.

The puppet may be operated from behind a simple detective's desk, a sheet draped over chairs, or even behind a church piano. Use your imagination, and you'll come up with a great idea for each Discovery Site that's tailored to your own facilities and resources.

PUPPETEERS
(Consider youth participation)

While some tireless VBS leaders can switch between puppeteering and handling other aspects of the programs, there may be options available for those who cannot. Consider that some of the best church and ministry puppeteers come from preteen and youth groups. If you have a group of motivated teenagers, they may add a wonderful, energetic dimension to your VBS program. Let them participate in the VBS effort by rehearsing and performing with the puppet. In addition, they can assist in other practical ways, such as serving snacks and monitoring games. By working together in this way, they will experience the reward of being a part of a vital community effort! Plus, they'll have a great time doing it.

Motivating Ideas for Young Puppeteers:

- Provide uniforms such as identical T-shirts or polo shirts and jeans.
  - Plan the schedule of who operates the puppet for each session. Be sure to give everyone a chance to participate during the week!
- Schedule rehearsals with pizza.
- Give your troupe an official name.

Puppets can both entertain and teach. On the hand of a skillful puppeteer, the puppet becomes alive, and its message will most likely be remembered for a long time.

PUPPETRY BASICS

Get to know the puppet well. What is its personality? What are its likes and dislikes, its characteristics, and the sound of its voice? Remind the puppeteers repeatedly that they need to speak very loudly in order for the audience to hear. Even if using a microphone backstage, the reader should speak more slowly and clearly than in normal conversation.

When the audience laughs, have the puppet pause in speaking so parts of the dialogue are not missed. To make the puppet look like it's talking *(realistically)*, open the puppet's mouth on each syllable spoken. This takes much practice, and at first it will feel unnatural. If the puppet's mouth doesn't move, work the head and arms appropriately to simulate movement while speaking. Puppets who are "listening" should turn to face the speaker. They should hold their heads up—no drooping hands inside of the puppets—to show they are attentive. Puppets onstage that are not speaking should hold completely still, unless otherwise indicated in the script. Otherwise, the audience gets confused about which puppet is speaking. Remember that the puppet is a role model. Avoid having the puppet display negative behavior (such as fighting), use bad grammar, or rude language.

In addition, do these helpful things for the puppeteers:

Make a copy of the skit for each puppet handler. To help readers keep their place on the page, use highlighter markers to designate a character's name each time it appears. You could use a different color for each character.

Give copies of the scripts to the puppeteers at least a week before they are to do the presentation.

Encourage the puppeteers to practice at home in addition to set rehearsal times together. Send the skit home so they can practice with their parents or other family member. Be sure to send along a parent note explaining what to do.

Have the puppeteers use one of the skits included on pages D·32-51 to practice with. Then have them actually perform the skit for each other to learn how to do these things.

For inexperienced puppeteers, you could have one child work the puppet while another reads the script.

MAKING A PUPPET STAGE

A puppet stage can be as simple or elaborate as you wish to make it. Use or adapt one of the ideas below to create a stage that works well with your group and the class space.

Cardboard Box Theater

Obtain a large cardboard box from an appliance store. Cut a hole four inches from the top in the front of the box at least 18 inches wide by 8 inches high. Then cut off the flap of the box that hangs down in the back. Cut the stationary part of the rear of the box straight down the middle to create "swing doors" for the puppeteer to enter and exit.

Decorate the exterior of the box as you desire to make it into the room represented in each Discovery Site. Use paint, wallpaper, colorful adhesive paper, or fabric. Pleat and staple fabric to the front of the stage for curtains. A glue gun also works well to attach the curtain fabric across the top.

Garment Rack Theater

Buy a metal garment rack. Many of these have rollers or wheels on the bottom to make moving the theater simple. Slipstitch a length of curtain to the top of the rack to make a valance (or use a shower curtain cut to fit along with shower curtain rings). Place curtains behind the valance so they can be opened and closed for the stage. Include strips of fabric or ribbon for each side so they can be tied back when the puppets are performing. Attach a piece of fabric to the bottom half of the garment rack to cover the area where the puppeteer sits. This can be hung by slipping a dowel or tension rod through a hem at the top of the fabric.

Doorway Theater

You will need a tension rod a little wider than the door opening and some fabric for this theater. Stitch a casing along the back of the fabric and insert the tension rod. Or use a shower curtain and rings. Place the curtain in the doorway at a height that will hide the puppeteer. Puppeteers can crouch down or sit on a chair behind the curtain.

Creating Discovery Sites

In each Discovery Site, there are specific suggestions for creating the learning environment for that Discovery Site. Transparencies found in the Reproducible Resources section contain art, directions, and suggestions to enhance your sites.

You may want to involve your whole church! Invite youth, Bible study groups, senior citizens, and others to help create the Discovery Sites. Be sure to have materials ready for your "paint party" and serve light refreshments if you like. Many props for the Discovery Sites can also be borrowed or rented. Be as creative as you'd like in order to give a "feel" for the various settings. The most important thing is that it is safe, colorful, fun, and kid-friendly.

Opening and Closing Assemblies

The Opening and Closing Assemblies are the times in the VBS when all the kids are together, doing the same things, and learning the same things. This is a great time to make announcements, celebrate birthdays, etc. This is also a time to get excited about VBS by singing the songs on *Good News Clues*™ CD. Be sure to sing the Theme Song, *Good News Clues*, each day. Kids will enjoy learning the songs together and singing them throughout all of VBS. You may also want to add some songs that are well known to the kids.

There are two versions of each Opening Assembly skit—one with only people and one using the puppet. Along with the opening assembly skits provided on the following pages, the Opening Assembly time is a great chance to practice the songs and skits in preparation for the Closing Program. The Opening Assembly is also designed as an opportunity to include a missions emphasis in your VBS. This year's missions project is called **Project Share God's Treasure** and is a partnership with Cook Communications Ministries International. Through this program, your VBS can send New Testament Picture Bibles to kids throughout South America, Africa, the Middle East, Asia, and India who would not otherwise be able to have a Bible. Pages D-80-81 further explain the mission project.

Because the children rotate through the Discovery Sites simultaneously, the skit for each day may not match their Discovery Site. That is okay because they'll be learning more about the overall program and the truth about salvation with each presentation.

The Closing Assembly is designed as a wrap-up of the day and a chance to communicate any information that needs to be given to all the children and leaders. Since the children have all been to a different Discovery Site each day, this is a good time to reinforce the overall theme for VBS and review the song(s) learned in the Opening Assembly.

Assembly Decorations

Decorate the assembly area with a welcome banner. Organize groups of kids by assigning a different color or group name to each. *(See Attendance on page D-27.)* Make matching group banners and attach them to seat sections in the assembly area so kids can easily find places to sit with their group. Encourage Assistant Investigators to dress in their group colors, or provide colored VBS T-shirts. Have music from *Good News Clues*™ CD playing as children arrive.

Opening Skit – Day 1

CAST: *Host, Detective*

PROPS: *Magnifying glass, cap, mirror*

SCENE: *Host is onstage.*

HOST: **Morning, kids.** *(Wait for children to respond.)* **My name is __(Host's Name)__ .** *(Detective enters with a magnifying glass and a cap on his head. Detective looks at the ground, the edge of the stage, and the host, saying "Aha!" after each.)* **__(Detective's Name)__ , what are you doing?**

DETECTIVE: **I'm solving a mystery.**

HOST: **A mystery? What happened?**

DETECTIVE: **Someone stole my pet rock!**

HOST: **What have you done to find the culprit?**

DETECTIVE: **I've run around saying, "Aha!"**

HOST: **Maybe you should try a different tactic.**

DETECTIVE: **Good idea.** *(To kids.)* **Kids, did you steal my pet rock?** *(Wait for kids to say, "No.")* **Some of you didn't answer. Did you kids steal my pet rock?** *(Wait for kids to say, "No!")*

HOST: **I didn't mean for you to accuse the kids.**

DETECTIVE: **But what if they stole it?**

HOST: **The kids didn't steal it. Instead of accusing people, you should look for clues, things that have changed since you found your pet rock missing.**

DETECTIVE: **Good idea. I'll look for clues in this mirror.** *(Detective picks up a mirror and looks into it.)* **Aha!**

HOST: **What did you find?**

DETECTIVE: **This morning, I didn't have anything in my hand. Now there's a magnifying glass there.**

HOST: **__(Detective's Name)__ , you're using the magnifying glass to look for clues.**

DETECTIVE: **Oh yeah. I forgot.** *(Turns back to mirror.)* **Aha! This morning, there was nothing on my head. Now there's a hat!**

HOST: **__(Detective's Name)__ , you put that hat on your head..**

DETECTIVE: **Oh yeah. I thought it would make me look more like a detective.**

HOST: **And it does. Wait. Turn this way. You have a smudge of dirt on your arm.** *(Host wipes off the smudge.)*

DETECTIVE: **I must have gotten it while I was in the yard.**

HOST: **What were you doing there? Playing soccer?**

DETECTIVE: **No, digging in the garden.**

HOST: **Why were you digging in the garden?**

DETECTIVE: **Because I love hiding things in the rock garden.**

HOST: **Aha!**

DETECTIVE: **What?**

HOST: *You hid your pet rock in the garden with the other rocks.*

DETECTIVE: *You're right! How did you know? You're an amazing detective. Now I feel bad that I blamed the theft on all these great kids. I'm sorry, kids.*

HOST: *Don't feel too bad. We all mess up. None of us are perfect. But next time, don't hide your pet rock from yourself.*

DETECTIVE: *Well, all I can promise is that I won't blame anyone. I love playing hide-and-seek with my pet rock. It's our favorite game. Come on. I'll show you how to play.*

(Everyone exits.)

Opening Puppet Skit – Day 1

CAST: *Leader, BOSWORTH (the puppet)*

PROPS: *Magnifying glass, puppet hat*

SCENE: *Leader is onstage.*

LEADER: **Morning, kids.** *(Wait for children to respond.)* **My name is __(Leader's name)__ .** *(BOSWORTH enters with a magnifying glass and a hat on his head. BOSWORTH looks at the ground, the edge of the stage, and the leader, saying "Aha!" after each.)* **BOSWORTH, what are you doing?**

BOSWORTH: *I'm solving a mystery.*

LEADER: **A mystery? What happened?**

BOSWORTH: *Someone stole my bone!*

LEADER: **Are you sure?**

BOSWORTH: *Of course I am.*

LEADER: **What have you done to find the culprit?**

BOSWORTH: *I've run around saying, "Aha!"*

LEADER: **Maybe you should try a different tactic.**

BOSWORTH: *Right. (To kids.) Kids, did you steal my bone? (Wait for kids to say, "No.") Some of you didn't answer. Did you kids steal my bone? (Wait for kids to say, "No!")*

LEADER: **I didn't mean for you to accuse the kids.**

BOSWORTH: *I think they stole my bone.*

LEADER: **The kids didn't steal your bone. Instead of accusing people, you should look for clues, things that have changed since you found your bone missing.**

BOSWORTH: *Good idea. I'll look for clues in this mirror. (BOSWORTH looks offstage, as if a mirror is just out of the audience's view.) Aha!*

LEADER: **What did you find?**

BOSWORTH: *This morning, I didn't have anything in my hand. Now there's a magnifying glass in it.*

LEADER: **BOSWORTH, you're using the magnifying glass to look for clues.**

BOSWORTH: *Oh yeah. I forgot. (Turns back to mirror.) Aha!*

LEADER: **What now?**

BOSWORTH: *This morning, there was nothing on my head. Now there's a hat!*

LEADER: **BOSWORTH, you put that hat on your head.**

BOSWORTH: *Oh yeah. I thought it would make me look more like a detective.*

LEADER: **And it does. Wait. Turn this way. You have a smudge of dirt on your arm.** *(Leader wipes off the smudge.)*

BOSWORTH: *I must have gotten it while I was in the yard.*

LEADER: **What were you doing there? Playing soccer?**

BOSWORTH: *No, digging up tulips.*

LEADER: *Why were you digging up tulips?*

BOSWORTH: *Because I always hide my bones under tulips.*

LEADER: *Aha! You dug up the tulips in your yard and hid your bone beneath them.*

BOSWORTH: *You're right! You are an amazing detective. I can't believe I blamed all these great kids for stealing my bone. I'm sorry, kids.*

LEADER: *Don't feel too bad. We all mess up. None of us are perfect. But next time, don't hide your bone from yourself.*

BOSWORTH: *Well, next time, I won't blame anyone, but I can't say that I'll never hide it again.*

LEADER: *Why not?*

BOSWORTH: *Because I love playing hide-and-seek with my bones, even when I hide them from me.*

LEADER: *Come on. I'll help you dig it up.*

(Everyone exits.)

Opening Skit – Day 2

CAST: Host, Friend, Culprit

PROPS: Napkins

SCENE: Host and Friend are onstage. Friend has a stack of napkins.

FRIEND: <u>(Host's Name)</u> , would you put these away for me? (Holds up a stack of napkins.)

HOST: No problem, <u>(Friend's Name)</u> .

(Friend hands Host the napkins and then exits. Host walks toward the door. Culprit hurries onstage.)

CULPRIT: Don't go in there!

HOST: I have to put these napkins away.

CULPRIT: No. Run! Get out of here!

HOST: Why?

CULPRIT: Danger! Danger!

HOST: What's the matter?

CULPRIT: Someone is in big trouble!

HOST: Who?

CULPRIT: That's not important. Flee! Flee!

HOST: This sounds like a mystery. (Turns to kids.) Should we solve it? (Wait for kids' responses.)

CULPRIT: No! There's no mystery. There's danger.

HOST: Let's open the door and find out what's going on.

CULPRIT: No! Don't! You don't understand. There's blood everywhere!

HOST: (Stops.) Is someone hurt?

CULPRIT: No, but someone's in really big trouble.

HOST: Well, let's go and help him.

CULPRIT: You can't. The person in trouble isn't in the room anymore.

HOST: Is there blood all over the table?

CULPRIT: Well, no.

HOST: All over the chairs?

CULPRIT: Not exactly, but there's a big spot on one of the chairs.

HOST: It's not all over <u>(Friend's Name)'s</u> brand new white carpet, is it?

CULPRIT: Not all over, but there are two big red spots.

HOST: Of blood?

CULPRIT: Well, not blood, exactly.

HOST: Exactly what made these spots?

CULPRIT: Something that looks like blood.

HOST: Kids, what is something that is found in the dining room that could look like blood? (Have kids guess things. As soon as someone says, "Ketchup," Culprit should say his next line. If no child mentions ketchup, the Host could say, "Was it ketchup?")

CULPRIT: I confess! I confess! I did it! I was eating a hamburger in the dining room, and I spilled the ketchup. Now I am in really, really big trouble.

HOST: Yes, you are. You spilled ketchup on __(Friend's Name)'s__ new carpet. But I will help you out of this fix.

CULPRIT: You can do that?

HOST: If Jesus could figure out a way for all of us to get into heaven, I think I can figure out a way to clean up ketchup in the dining room.

CULPRIT: What're you going to use?

HOST: Let's start by using these, (Holds up napkins.) and then we'll get a rag, soap, and water to finish the job. Come on. It's time to open the door to the dining room.

(They exit.)

Opening Puppet Play – Day 2

CAST: Leader, Friend, BOSWORTH (the puppet)

PROPS: Napkins

SCENE: Leader and Friend are onstage. Friend has a stack of napkins.

FRIEND: _(Leader's Name)_ , would you put these away for me? (Holds up a stack of napkins.)

LEADER: No problem, _(Friend's Name)_ .

(Friend hands Leader the napkins and then exits. Leader walks toward the door. BOSWORTH pops onto stage gasping.)

BOSWORTH: Don't go in there!

LEADER: I have to put these napkins away.

BOSWORTH: No. Run! Get out of here!

LEADER: Why?

BOSWORTH: Danger! Danger!

LEADER: What's the matter?

BOSWORTH: Someone is in big trouble!

LEADER: Who?

BOSWORTH: That's not important. Flee! Flee!

LEADER: This sounds like a mystery. (Turns to kids.) **Should we solve it?** (Wait for kids' responses.)

BOSWORTH: No! There's no mystery. There's danger.

LEADER: Let's open the door and find out what's going on.

BOSWORTH: No! Don't! You don't understand. There's blood everywhere!

LEADER: (Stops.) Is someone hurt?

BOSWORTH: No, but someone's in really big trouble.

LEADER: Well, let's go and help him.

BOSWORTH: You can't. The person in trouble isn't in the room anymore.

LEADER: Is there blood all over the table?

BOSWORTH: Well, no.

LEADER: All over the chairs?

BOSWORTH: Not exactly, but there's a big spot on one of the chairs.

LEADER: It's not all over _(Friend's Name)'s_ brand new white carpet, is it?

BOSWORTH: Not all over, but there are two big red spots.

LEADER: Of blood?

BOSWORTH: Well, not blood, exactly.

LEADER: Exactly what made these spots?

BOSWORTH: Something that looks like blood.

LEADER: Kids, what is something that is found in the dining room that could look like blood? (Have kids guess things. As soon as someone says, "Ketchup," BOSWORTH should say his next line. If no child mentions ketchup, the leader could say, "Was it ketchup?")

BOSWORTH: I confess! I confess! I did it! I was eating a hamburger in the dining room, and I spilled the ketchup. Now I am in really, really big trouble.

LEADER: Yes, you are. You spilled ketchup on __(Friend's Name)'s__ new carpet. But I will help you out of this fix.

BOSWORTH: You can do that?

LEADER: If Jesus could figure out a way for all of us to get into heaven, I think I can figure out a way to clean up ketchup in the dining room.

BOSWORTH: What're you going to use?

LEADER: Let's start by using these, (Holds up napkins.) and then we'll get a rag, soap, and water to finish the job. Come on. It's time to open the door to the dining room.

(They exit.)

Opening Skit – Day 3

CAST: *Host, Friend, Prodigal*

PROPS: *Four chairs, bag of candy, wrapping paper*

SCENE: *Host folds a candy in wrapping paper. Friend sits in a chair. Prodigal sits and eyes the candy.*

FRIEND: *__(Host's Name)__, this room is a great place to relax. I don't have a family room at my home.*

HOST: *Well, __(Friend's Name)__, you're always welcome to relax in my family room.*

PRODIGAL: *Relax. Ha! Family rooms have too many rules.*

FRIEND: *Like what?*

PRODIGAL: *Like don't put your feet on the coffee table.*

HOST: *Some people don't allow feet on the furniture, but my stuff is so old, you can put your feet up.*

FRIEND: *Cool. (Puts his feet on a chair.)*

PRODIGAL: *How about the other rules?*

FRIEND: *What other rules?*

PRODIGAL: *Like don't eat food in the family room.*

HOST: *Food crumbs on the floor do attract bugs, but I vacuum every night. I often eat in here.*

PRODIGAL: *Great! Let me have that piece of candy. I'm starving.*

HOST: *__(Prodigal's Name)__, this candy isn't for you . . .*

PRODIGAL: *Come on. You're not eating it. Let me have it. My stomach's growling.*

HOST: *No, __(Prodigal's Name)__.*

PRODIGAL: *You don't mean that.*

HOST: *Yes, I do.*

PRODIGAL: *You have a piece of candy, and you're not going to give it to me?*

HOST: *I can't. You see . . .*

PRODIGAL: *Oh, I see. It's okay for you to eat in the family room, but not for me.*

HOST: *It's not that . . .*

PRODIGAL: *Fine. Just fine. I'm out of here.*

HOST: *__(Prodigal's Name)__, wait!*
(Prodigal exits.)

FRIEND: *What got into him?*

HOST: *It's a mystery to me.*

FRIEND: *Want to listen to some music? (Host nods.) How about the Holy Roly Bagatolies?*

HOST: *No, they're too loud.*

FRIEND: *Totally Terrible Tunes from the Twenties?*

Host: *No, they're really awful.*

PRODIGAL: *(From offstage.) Can I come back in?*

HOST: *Sure, __(Prodigal's Name)__.*
(Prodigal re-enters.)

GOOD NEWS CLUES™

PRODIGAL: *(Sighs.)* **I'm sorry, __(Host's Name)__ . I shouldn't have demanded the candy. It's yours. I had no right to get upset with you. Will you forgive me?**

HOST: **Of course, I forgive you, __(Prodigal's Name)__ . God showed us how to forgive so that everything is forgotten, but let me explain. I can't give you this piece of candy because I'm wrapping it up for your friend's, Aaron's, birthday party tomorrow. You can't have this one, but you can have all these candies.** *(Holds up bag of candy.)*

FRIEND: **You're being unfair. I was here the whole time, and you didn't offer me any candy.**

HOST: **I didn't know you had a sweet tooth. Let's go to the other room, and I'll give you each a bag.**

(Everyone exits.)

Opening Puppet Play – Day 3

CAST: Leader, Friend, BOSWORTH (the puppet)

PROPS: Three chairs, bag of doggy treats, wrapping paper

SCENE: Leader folds a doggy treat in wrapping paper. Friend sits in a chair. Bosworth eyes the doggy treat.

FRIEND: _(Leader's Name)_ , this room is a great place to relax. I don't have a family room at my home.

LEADER: Well, _(Friend's Name)_ , you're always welcome to relax in my family room.

BOSWORTH: Relax. Ha! Family rooms have too many rules.

FRIEND: Like what?

BOSWORTH: Like don't put your feet on the coffee table.

LEADER: Some people don't allow feet on the furniture, but my stuff is so old, you can put your feet up.

FRIEND: Cool. (Puts his feet on a chair.)

BOSWORTH: How about the other rules?

FRIEND: What other rules?

BOSWORTH: Like don't eat food in the family room.

LEADER: Food on the floor does attract bugs, but I vacuum every night. I often eat in here.

BOSWORTH: Great! Let me have that doggy treat. I'm starving.

LEADER: BOSWORTH, this doggy treat isn't for you . . .

BOSWORTH: Come on. It's not like you're going to eat it. Let me have it. My stomach's growling.

LEADER: No, BOSWORTH.

BOSWORTH: You don't mean that.

LEADER: Yes, I do.

BOSWORTH: You have a doggy treat, and you're not going to give it to me?

LEADER: I can't. You see . . .

BOSWORTH: Oh, I see. It's okay for you to eat in the family room, but not for me.

LEADER: It's not that . . .

BOSWORTH: Fine. Just fine. I'm out of here.

LEADER: BOSWORTH, wait! (BOSWORTH exits.)

FRIEND: What got into him?

LEADER: It's a mystery to me.

FRIEND: Want to listen to some music? (Leader nods.) How about the Holy Roly Bagatolies?

LEADER: No, they're too loud.

FRIEND: Totally Terrible Tunes from the Twenties?

LEADER: No, they're really awful.

BOSWORTH: *(From offstage.)* **Can I come back in?**

LEADER: **Sure, BOSWORTH.** *(BOSWORTH re-enters.)*

BOSWORTH: *(Sighs.)* **I'm sorry, __(Leader's Name)__ . I shouldn't have demanded the doggy treat. It's yours. I had no right to get upset with you. Will you forgive me?**

LEADER: **Of course, I forgive you, BOSWORTH. God showed us how to forgive so that everything is forgotten, but let me explain. I can't give you this doggy treat because I'm wrapping it up for your friend's, Biscuit's, birthday party tomorrow. You can't have this one, but you can have all these doggy treats.** *(Holds up bag of remaining doggy treats.)*

FRIEND: **You're being unfair. I was here the whole time, and you didn't offer me food.**

LEADER: **I didn't know you were hungry. Come on. Let's go and get snacks. Then we can come back to the family room and relax together.**

FRIEND: **Great idea.**

BOSWORTH: **We're right behind you.**

(Everyone exits.)

Opening Skit – Day 4

CAST: Leader, Friend, Neighbor, Detective

PROPS: Large plant, three paper plates, flashlight

SCENE: Detective is measuring himself against the plant. Leader, Friend, and Neighbor enter and pass out the plates.

LEADER: Hi, _(Detective's Name)_. Can _(Friend's Name)_, _(Neighbor's Name)_, or I get you something to eat?

DETECTIVE: No thanks, _(Leader's Name)_. I'm in the middle of solving a mystery.

NEIGHBOR: Really? What's the mystery?

DETECTIVE: *(Points to plant)* _(Name of Leader)_, do you remember when you planted the seed for this plant?

LEADER: It was probably last March sometime.

DETECTIVE: Exactly!

FRIEND: Exactly what? Are you okay? *(Friend pats Detective's arm.)* **Hey, you're wet.**

DETECTIVE: Of course, I'm wet. This plant started to grow last March, and it's already bigger than my hand. I've been growing for a lot longer than it has. If it keeps growing at this rate, it will pass me up next year.

LEADER: True, but what does that have to do with a mystery and being wet?

DETECTIVE: Everything. I've soaked myself in water, just like you soak this plant. Here, shine this on me. *(Detective hands Friend a flashlight. Friend shines the flashlight on Detective.)* **And now, I'm standing in the light, just like the plant sits in the sunlight.**

NEIGHBOR: But the plant is in dirt, and you're not.

DETECTIVE: You're right. I'd better go roll around in mud. I'll be right back.

LEADER: Wait a minute. How we grow is a mystery, but it's not one you can solve by pretending to be a plant.

DETECTIVE: How do you know?

FRIEND: Look at us. *(Leader, Friend, and Neighbor stand in a line from tallest to shortest.)*

DETECTIVE: You're different sizes.

NEIGHBOR: We've grown differently inside and out.

DETECTIVE: How can you grow inside?

LEADER: Unlike our bodies, we do have some control over how much we grow on the inside. Depending on how much time we spend with God, we grow spiritually. Depending on how much we study our schoolwork, our minds grow.

NEIGHBOR: If you keep dousing yourself with water, rolling in the mud, and standing in sunlight, you won't become taller, you'll get weaker, which will hurt how your body grows.

GOOD NEWS CLUES™

FRIEND: *The best thing you can do to grow is eat healthy food, get a lot of rest, and exercise by running around every day.*

LEADER: *Are you disappointed that you can't solve this mystery?*

DETECTIVE: *Not really, because if I'm finished solving this case, I can eat food again. I'm really, really hungry.*

FRIEND: *Well, you've come to the right room to eat.*

NEIGHBOR: *Here in the kitchen, we have whatever you like.*

DETECTIVE: *Great! I'll take a peanut butter, jelly, and tuna fish sandwich, please.*

LEADER, FRIEND, AND NEIGHBOR:
Eww!

Opening Puppet Play — Day 4

CAST: *Leader, Friend, Neighbor, BOSWORTH (the puppet)*

PROPS: *Large plant, three paper plates, flashlight*

SCENE: *BOSWORTH is measuring himself against the plant. Leader, Friend, and Neighbor enter and pass out the plates.*

LEADER: *Hi, BOSWORTH. Can __(Friend's Name)__, __(Neighbor's Name)__, or I get you something to eat?*

BOSWORTH: *No thanks, __(Leader's Name)__. I'm in the middle of solving a mystery.*

NEIGHBOR: *Really? What's the mystery?*

BOSWORTH: *(Points to plant) __(Name of Leader)__, do you remember when you planted the seed for this plant?*

LEADER: *It was probably last March sometime.*

BOSWORTH: *Exactly!*

FRIEND: *Exactly what? Are you okay? (Friend scratches BOSWORTH's head.)* **Hey, you're wet.**

BOSWORTH: *Of course, I'm wet. This plant started to grow last March, and it's already taller than I am. I've been growing for a lot longer than it has.*

LEADER: *True, but what does that have to do with a mystery and being wet?*

BOSWORTH: *Everything. I have soaked myself in water, just like you soak this plant. Here, shine this on me. (BOSWORTH hands Friend a flashlight. Friend shines the flashlight on BOSWORTH.)* **And now, I'm standing in the light, just like the plant sits in the sunlight.**

NEIGHBOR: *But the plant is in dirt, and you're not.*

BOSWORTH: *You're right. I'd better go roll around in mud. I'll be right back.*

LEADER: *Wait a minute. How we grow is a mystery, but it's not one you can solve by pretending to be a plant.*

BOSWORTH: *How do you know?*

FRIEND: *Look at us. (Leader, Friend, and Neighbor stand in a line from tallest to shortest.)*

BOSWORTH: *You're different sizes.*

NEIGHBOR: *We've grown differently inside and out.*

BOSWORTH: *How can you grow inside?*

LEADER: *Unlike our bodies, we do have some control over how much we grow on the inside. Depending on how much time we spend with God, we grow spiritually. Depending on how much we study our schoolwork, our minds grow.*

NEIGHBOR: *If you keep dousing yourself with water, rolling in the mud, and standing in sunlight, you won't become taller, you'll get weaker, which will hurt how your body grows.*

FRIEND: The best thing you can do to grow is eat healthy food, get a lot of rest, and exercise by running around every day.

LEADER: Are you disappointed that you can't solve this mystery?

BOSWORTH: Not really, because if I'm not solving this case, then I can eat food again. I'm really, really hungry.

FRIEND: Well, you've come to the right room to eat.

NEIGHBOR: Here in the kitchen, we have whatever you like.

BOSWORTH: Great! I'll take a peanut butter and jelly sandwich with dog food, please.

LEADER, FRIEND, AND NEIGHBOR:
Eww!

Opening Skit – Day 5

CAST: Leader, Friend, Neighbor, Puzzler

PROPS: None

SCENE: Leader, Friend, Neighbor, and Puzzler are onstage

LEADER: Good word puzzle _(Friend's Name)_ and _(Neighbor's Name)_ .

FRIEND: Thanks, _(Leader's Name)_ .

PUZZLER: Okay. Okay. It's my turn. I have a puzzle for you to solve.

NEIGHBOR: Oh good. Another puzzle.

PUZZLER: I do not breathe, but I'm alive,
I do not eat, but I'll survive,
I'm quarters that you do not spend,
Inside, in sight, my space won't bend.
What am I?

NEIGHBOR: That's a hard one. *(Throughout the following conversation, Puzzler should be dancing and carrying on in the background.)*

FRIEND: But we can figure it out. We just have to search through the words.

LEADER: Kids, what do you think the second line means?

PUZZLER: I do not eat, but I'll survive.

(If children suggest an inanimate object, "a thing" that doesn't need food, have Leader say, "Good answer! Maybe it's a thing, not a person.")

FRIEND: That's right. It can't be a person, animal, or plant, because living things eat.

NEIGHBOR: But it is alive. Remember the first line?

PUZZLER: I do not breathe but I'm alive.

LEADER: If it doesn't breathe, it has to be a thing. Maybe the word "alive" is a play on words. Kids, what are some other words that mean being "alive"?

(Let kids answer. If anyone mentions the word "living" have Leader say, "That's a good answer.")

NEIGHBOR: Look at the first word in the last line.

PUZZLER: Inside.

NEIGHBOR: Wouldn't that mean it's not outside of a building?

FRIEND: Good. And the second and third word of the last line . . .

PUZZLER: In sight.

FRIEND: That would mean that we could see it. It's not imaginary.

LEADER: And the rest of the line . . .

PUZZLER: My space won't bend.

LEADER. Do you think it's the space in a room?

NEIGHBOR: That's it!

FRIEND: We've got it! We know the answer. We know which quarters can't be spent. These quarters are not money. They are a person's residence, where they live.

LEADER: *Let's listen to   (Puzzler's Name)   as he says the riddle one more time:*

PUZZLER: *I do not breathe, but I'm alive,*
I do not eat, but I'll survive,
I'm quarters that you do not spend,
Inside, in sight, my space won't bend. What am I?

LEADER: *Kids, do you know which room the puzzle is about? (Let kids guess. If they don't get the answer, have Neighbor blurt out, "It's the Living Room.")*

LEADER: *You're right. It's the living room.*

FRIEND: *Riddles are so fun. They let you search for hidden messages.*

LEADER: *That was a great riddle. Kids, what was the answer again? (Let kids repeat, "Living Room.") I couldn't hear you. (Let kids shout, "Living Room.") That's right. And now it's time for us to go to the living room together.*

(Everyone exits.)

Opening Puppet Play – Day 5

CAST:	Leader, Friend, Neighbor, BOSWORTH (the puppet)
PROPS:	None
SCENE:	Leader, Friend, Neighbor, and BOSWORTH are onstage

LEADER: Good word puzzle _(Friend's Name)_ and _(Neighbor's Name)_ .

FRIEND: Thanks, _(Leader's Name)_ .

BOSWORTH: Okay. Okay. It's my turn. I have a puzzle for you to solve.

NEIGHBOR: Oh good. Another puzzle.

BOSWORTH: I do not breathe, but I'm alive,
I do not eat, but I'll survive,
I'm quarters that you do not spend,
Inside, in sight, my space won't bend.
What am I?

NEIGHBOR: That's a hard one. (Throughout the following conversation, BOSWORTH should be dancing and carrying on in the background.)

FRIEND: But we can figure it out. We just have to search through the words.

LEADER: Kids, what do you think the second line means?

BOSWORTH: I do not eat, but I'll survive.

(If children suggest an inanimate object, "a thing" that doesn't need food, have Leader say, "Good answer! Maybe it's a thing, not a person.")

FRIEND: That's right. It can't be a person, animal, or plant, because living things eat.

NEIGHBOR: But it is alive. Remember the first line?

BOSWORTH: I do not breathe but I'm alive.

LEADER: If it doesn't breathe, it has to be a thing. Maybe the word "alive" is a play on words. Kids, what are some other words that mean being "alive"?

(Let kids answer. If anyone mentions the word "living" have Leader say, "That's a good answer.")

NEIGHBOR: Look at the first word in the last line.

BOSWORTH: Inside.

NEIGHBOR: Wouldn't that mean it's not outside of a building?

FRIEND: Good. And the second and third word of the last line . . .

BOSWORTH: In sight.

FRIEND: That would mean that we could see it. It's not imaginary.

LEADER: And the rest of the line . . .

BOSWORTH: My space won't bend.

LEADER. Do you think it's the space in a room?

NEIGHBOR: That's it!

FRIEND: We've got it! We know the answer. We know which quarters can't be spent. These quarters are not money. They are a person's residence, where they live.

LEADER: Let's listen to BOSWORTH as he says the riddle one more time:

GOOD NEWS CLUES™

BOSWORTH: *I do not breathe, but I'm alive,*
I do not eat, but I'll survive,
I'm quarters that you do not spend,
Inside, in sight, my space won't bend. What am I?

LEADER: *Kids, do you know which room the puzzle is about?* (Let kids guess. If they don't get the answer, have Neighbor blurt out, "It's the Living Room.")

LEADER: *You're right. It's the living room.*

FRIEND: *Riddles are so fun. They let you search for hidden messages.*

LEADER: *That was a great riddle. Kids, what was the answer again?* (Let kids repeat, "Living Room.") *I couldn't hear you.* (Let kids shout, "Living Room.") *That's right. And now it's time for us to go to the living room together.*

(Everyone exits.)

Closing Program

As the finale for the *Good News Clues*™ experience, this program is designed to celebrate the goodness of God. It encourages program participants and the audience to respond to the gifts of God's grace, and presents a great opportunity for your church to reach out to neighborhood families who have sent their children to your VBS but do not attend church regularly. The skits offer relevant principles that children and their parents can easily recognize and apply to their lives. And the participation by the children is just plain fun! Make sure the children invite their parents, friends, and neighbors to share in this celebration! The traditional program is designed to follow this basic schedule:

10 minutes:	Welcome by Director
5 minutes:	Prayer by Pastor
60 minutes:	Closing Program
30 minutes:	Awards, missions, refreshments

Fifteen minutes before the closing program begins, play music from the *Good News Clues*™ CD or some other Christian children's music softly through the sound system.

When it is time to begin, play the VBS theme song, *Good News Clues* while the children enter from the back of the sanctuary or auditorium. Children can step in time with the music and line up in front of the church, facing the audience. *(If a particularly ambitious group of young performers happens to be among your attendees, they might choose to choreograph the processional to this song during the week and perform it while the other children are entering, lining up, and singing.)*

At this point, the Director welcomes the audience, followed by prayer by the pastor. The pastor should introduce *Good News Clues*™ program, which starts on the next page. You will need to select the version of the program you desire to use—the version with only people or the version which includes BOSWORTH the puppet.

CLOSING

The Director might give each child who attended VBS a Certificate of Completion *(on the CD, or see page R·9)*. The Director should thank the children and their families for participating. Close with a prayer followed by a reprise of the children singing this year's VBS theme song, *Good News Clues.*

During a time for greeting people and enjoying refreshments, you might provide Family Evaluation forms *(see page R·44)* and invite families to give you their feedback by completing a form.

INTERGENERATIONAL OPTION

This option allows for a fun two-hour family experience! *(Note: There are 10 extra minutes in this two-hour schedule to allow for transitions.)*

Follow this schedule:

15 minutes: As families arrive, greet them and place them into five groups. If any children do not have family present, team them up with a friend's family. Assign two Investigators to each group. Investigators should remain in costume.

75 minutes: Have each group start at one Discovery Site. Groups then rotate through each of the five Discovery Sites *(15 minutes each)* until each group has visited all five.

At each Discovery Site, the families will watch the Opening Assembly Skit for that Discovery Site *(see skits on pages D·32-51)*, hear children recite the Bible verse, and sing the song that was learned at that site. The Director should keep time and give a signal for the groups to move on to the next Discovery Site.

20 minutes: Gather the groups together for a closing awards assembly and refreshments. See the Closing suggestions given above.

Closing Skit

CAST: Leader, Friend, Neighbor, Detective

PROPS: Binoculars

SCENE: Detective is looking through binoculars. Leader, Friend, and Neighbor are onstage.

NEIGHBOR: _(Friend's Name)_ and _(Leader's Name)_, thank you for helping me move into my new home.

FRIEND: Our pleasure, _(Neighbor's Name)_.

LEADER: It's going to be great having you live so close. To welcome you to the neighborhood, we have a surprise for you.

NEIGHBOR: You do? What is it?

LEADER: First, we have kids who want to recite their memory verses from this week. *(Have individual children or the children as a group recite the memory verses from the week.)*

NEIGHBOR: That was wonderful kids!

FRIEND: But that's not all. We have some children who want to sing a song for you. *(Have individual children or the children as a group sing one of the songs they have learned during the week.)*

DETECTIVE: I love that song! How did they know that that was my favorite song this week?

LEADER: _(Detective's Name)_, you like all the songs.

DETECTIVE: You're right. If only I could remember them all. But I do remember a lot. In the garden we studied creation and sin.

LEADER: Who can tell me one thing you learned about creation and sin? *(Have one child share what they learned about in Site 1: The Garden.)*

FRIEND: When we visited the dining room, we learned about Jesus' life, death, burial, and resurrection.

LEADER: Who can tell me one thing you learned about salvation? *(Have one child share what they learned about in Site 2: The Dining Room.)*

NEIGHBOR: In the family room, we studied the prodigal son and how Jesus is a personal Savior.

LEADER: Who can tell me one thing you learned about asking for forgiveness? *(Have one child share what they learned about forgiveness in Site 3: The Family Room.)*

DETECTIVE: When we were in the kitchen, we learned about how we can grow spiritually, which is what VBS is all about, and in the living room we learned about hidden treasures.

FRIEND: _(Detective's Name)_, what are you searching for?

DETECTIVE: Neighborhood safety.

NEIGHBOR: Why are you using binoculars?

DETECTIVE: I'm keeping an eye on the neighborhood to make sure it'll be safe for you.

LEADER: Wait a minute. I know it's safe. I live here.

DETECTIVE: You can never be too careful.

FRIEND: Have you seen anything odd?

DETECTIVE: No. Someone's washing a car. Someone else is mowing the yard. Someone else is breaking into a home.

NEIGHBOR: What?

DETECTIVE: Oh no! Someone just opened a window and got into a home. I just saw a robbery. Help! Help! Kids, yell help! Help! *(Detective and kids yell help.)*

LEADER: Quiet. Quiet. *(Waves hands.)* __(Detective's Name)__ , are you sure you saw a break-in?

DETECTIVE: Yes, yes. I'm sure. With these binoculars, I can see things far away as clear as if they were happening in this room.

LEADER: Let's not panic.

FRIEND: We should call the police. *(Friend runs around the room saying, "Where's the phone?")*

NEIGHBOR: I don't have a phone yet. I just moved in.

LEADER: Does anyone have a cell phone?

FRIEND: I do . . . but it's at home.

NEIGHBOR: I don't have one.

LEADER: I have one, but it's not charged. Let's go to my house. We can call from there.

DETECTIVE: I wouldn't do that if I were you.

LEADER: I live across the street. It won't take long.

DETECTIVE: Hit the deck! *(Everyone falls to the floor.)* The thief is coming out the front door.

FRIEND: Too late to call the police.

NEIGHBOR: We need to stop him. *(All but Detective begin to crawl toward the door. Detective has climbed back up to the window and is using his binoculars.)*

LEADER: When we get outside, we'll run toward the house and scare him away. Which house is he robbing?

DETECTIVE: The one across the street.

LEADER: The one across the street? My house is across the street.

DETECTIVE: I know. He's robbing your house. You're too late. He just drove away. *(Everyone stands up.)*

LEADER: What did he look like?

DETECTIVE: He was big and mean and angry and not someone you would want to meet in a dark alley. Actually, __(Leader's Name)__ , he looked a lot like you.

LEADER: I'd better go home and see if anything's missing.

DETECTIVE: I wouldn't do that if I were you.

FRIEND: He has to see what was taken.

DETECTIVE: But . . . hit the deck! *(Everyone drops to the floor again, and Detective ducks.)*

NEIGHBOR: What is it __(Detective's Name)__ ?

DETECTIVE: He's back.

FRIEND: *Why would a criminal return to the scene of the crime?*

LEADER: *(Stands.)* **This is ridiculous. I'm going over there. It's my house.** *(Leader exits while everyone else yells, "No!")*

NEIGHBOR: *What's happening?*

DETECTIVE: *(Looking through binoculars.)* **He's walking down the sidewalk. He's crossing the street. He's walking up the sidewalk. Oh no. Oh no. The thief just walked out of the house.**

FRIEND: *What are they doing now?*

DETECTIVE: *They're . . . they're hugging.*

FRIEND AND NEIGHBOR:
Hugging?! *(They both look out the window.)*

DETECTIVE: **Now they're both waving at us.** *(Friend, Neighbor, and Detective wave back.)* **(Leader's Name) is coming back.**

(Leader enters.)

DETECTIVE: **What happened? What were you doing? Who was that?**

LEADER: *Relax.*

NEIGHBOR: *Did he break into your house?*

LEADER: **Yes, he did. My son forgot his keys and broke into the house through his bedroom window.**

FRIEND: *Your son?*

NEIGHBOR: *I didn't know you had a son.*

LEADER: *He's been away for a long time, but I'm thrilled that he's back. Why don't you all come over for dinner at my house tonight? We'll have a big party to welcome him home.*

FRIEND: *Sounds good.*

NEIGHBOR: *I'm always up for dinner.*

DETECTIVE: *But isn't he the one who left years ago without saying goodbye?*

LEADER: *Yes, that's him. I think he's grown up a lot. I can't wait to get to know him again. I'll see you guys later. I've got to go now.* *(Leader exits.)*

ALL: *Bye.*

NEIGHBOR: *Well, this has been an exciting day. I guess there are a lot of wonderful stories hidden in every neighborhood.*

FRIEND: *Kids, it's been a lot of fun this week having you visit. I hope you remember to invite Jesus into your home so that you can continue to grow and learn about Him all year long. And then someday, we'll all be in the same neighborhood in heaven.*

DETECTIVE: *We've got to go now. We're going to visit (Leader's Name)'s home. Bye.*

(Everybody exits.)

Closing Puppet Play

CAST: Leader, Friend, Neighbor, BOSWORTH

PROPS: Binoculars

SCENE: BOSWORTH is looking through binoculars. Leader, Friend, and Neighbor are onstage.

NEIGHBOR: _(Friend's Name)_ and _(Leader's Name)_, thank you for helping me move into my new home.

FRIEND: Our pleasure, _(Neighbor's Name)_.

LEADER: It's going to be great having you live so close. To welcome you to the neighborhood, we have a surprise for you.

NEIGHBOR: You do? What is it?

LEADER: First, we have kids who want to recite their memory verses from this week. *(Have individual children or the children as a group recite the memory verses from the week.)*

NEIGHBOR: That was wonderful kids!

FRIEND: But that's not all. We have some children who want to sing a song for you. *(Have individual children or the children as a group sing one of the songs they have learned during the week.)*

BOSWORTH: I love that song! How did they know that that was my favorite song this week?

LEADER: BOSWORTH, you like all the songs.

BOSWORTH: You're right. If only I could remember them all. But I do remember a lot. In the garden we studied creation and sin.

LEADER: Who can tell me one thing you learned about creation and sin? *(Have one child share what they learned about in Site 1: The Garden.)*

FRIEND: When we visited the dining room, we learned about Jesus' life, death, burial, and resurrection.

LEADER: Who can tell me one thing you learned about salvation? *(Have one child share what they learned about in Site 2: The Dining Room.)*

NEIGHBOR: In the family room, we studied the prodigal son and how Jesus is a personal Savior.

LEADER: Who can tell me one thing you learned about asking for forgiveness? *(Have one child share what they learned about forgiveness in Site 3: The Family Room.)*

BOSWORTH: When we were in the kitchen, we learned about how we can grow spiritually, which is what VBS is all about, and in the living room we learned about hidden treasures.

FRIEND: BOSWORTH, what are you searching for?

BOSWORTH: Neighborhood safety.

NEIGHBOR: Why are you using binoculars?

BOSWORTH: I'm keeping an eye on the neighborhood to make sure it'll be safe for you.

LEADER: *Wait a minute. I know it's safe. I live here.*

BOSWORTH: *You can never be too careful.*

FRIEND: *Have you seen anything odd?*

BOSWORTH: *No. Someone's washing a car. Someone else is mowing the yard. Someone else is breaking into a home.*

NEIGHBOR: *What?*

BOSWORTH: *Oh no! Someone just opened a window and got into a home. I just saw a robbery. Help! Help! Kids, yell help! Help! (BOSWORTH and kids yell help.)*

LEADER: *Quiet. Quiet. (Waves hands.) BOSWORTH, are you sure you saw a break-in?*

BOSWORTH: *Yes, yes. I'm sure. With these binoculars, I can see things far away as clear as if they were happening in this room.*

LEADER: *Let's not panic.*

FRIEND: *We should call the police. (Friend runs around the room saying, "Where's the phone?")*

NEIGHBOR: *I don't have a phone yet. I just moved in.*

LEADER: *Does anyone have a cell phone?*

FRIEND: *I do . . . but it's at home.*

NEIGHBOR: *I don't have one.*

LEADER: *I have one, but it's not charged. Let's go to my house. We can call from there.*

BOSWORTH: *I wouldn't do that if I were you.*

LEADER: *I live across the street. It won't take long.*

BOSWORTH: *Hit the deck! (Everyone falls to the floor. BOSWORTH ducks.) **The thief is coming out the front door.***

FRIEND: *Too late to call the police.*

NEIGHBOR: *We need to stop him. (They begin to crawl toward the door.)*

LEADER: *When we get outside, we'll run toward the house and scare him away. Which house is he robbing?*

BOSWORTH: *The one across the street.*

LEADER: *The one across the street? My house is across the street.*

BOSWORTH: *I know. He's robbing your house. You're too late. He just drove away. (Everyone stands up.)*

LEADER: *What did he look like?*

BOSWORTH: *He was big and mean and angry and not someone you would want to meet in a dark alley. Actually, (Leader's Name) , he looked a lot like you.*

LEADER: *I'd better go home and see if anything's missing.*

BOSWORTH: *I wouldn't do that if I were you.*

FRIEND: *He has to see what was taken.*

BOSWORTH: *But . . . hit the deck! (Everyone drops to the floor again, and BOSWORTH ducks.)*

NEIGHBOR: *What is it BOSWORTH?*

BOSWORTH: *He's back.*

FRIEND:	*Why would a criminal return to the scene of the crime?*
LEADER:	*(Stands.)* **This is ridiculous. I'm going over there. It's my house.** *(Leader exits while everyone else yells, "No!")*
NEIGHBOR:	*What's happening?*
BOSWORTH:	*(Looking through the binoculars.)* **He's walking down the sidewalk. He's crossing the street. He's walking up the sidewalk. Oh no. Oh no. The thief just walked out of the house.**
FRIEND:	*What are they doing now?*
BOSWORTH:	*They're . . . they're hugging.*
FRIEND AND NEIGHBOR:	
	Hugging?! *(They both look out the window.)*
BOSWORTH:	**Now they're both waving at us.** *(Friend, Neighbor, and BOSWORTH wave back.)* **_(Leader's Name)_ is coming back.**

(Leader enters.)

BOSWORTH:	**What happened? What were you doing? Who was that?**
LEADER:	*Relax.*
NEIGHBOR:	*Did he break into your house?*
LEADER:	*Yes, he did. My son forgot his keys and broke into the house through his bedroom window.*
FRIEND:	*Your son?*

NEIGHBOR:	*I didn't know you had a son.*
LEADER:	*He's been away for a long time, but I'm thrilled that he's back. Why don't you all come over for dinner at my house tonight? We'll have a big party to welcome him home.*
FRIEND:	*Sounds good.*
NEIGHBOR:	*I'm always up for dinner.*
BOSWORTH:	*But isn't he the one who left years ago without saying goodbye?*
LEADER:	*Yes, that's him. I think he's grown up a lot. I can't wait to get to know him again. I'll see you guys later. I've got to go now. (Leader exits.)*
ALL:	*Bye.*
NEIGHBOR:	*Well, this has been an exciting day. I guess there are a lot of wonderful stories hidden in every neighborhood.*
FRIEND:	*Kids, it's been a lot of fun this week having you visit. I hope you remember to invite Jesus into your home so that you can continue to grow and learn about Him all year long. And then someday, we'll all be in the same neighborhood in heaven.*
BOSWORTH:	*We've got to go now. We're going to visit (Leader's Name)'s home. Bye.*

(Everybody exits.)

Spiritual Gifts

One of your most important jobs as VBS Director is recruiting your volunteers. God has already given your church the very best people to help you this summer, and now it's your task to find them and put them in the right jobs!

Pray—While you most certainly have already started to do this, add this next line to your prayer requests: "Lord, help me see how You have gifted people." Too often, recruiting is seen as the necessary filling of slots with warm bodies. But God's Word treats serving in the Body of Christ much differently. First Corinthians 12:4-7 says, "Now there are diversities of gifts, but the same Spirit. And there are differences of administrations, but the same Lord. And there are diversities of operations, but it is the same God which worketh all in all. But the manifestation of the Spirit is given to every man to profit withal." Paul was writing about the fact that God has created us all in special ways to build up and support God's works in the church. And VBS is work that you cannot do alone. That's why you must start seeing people as vital members of a dynamic ministry community.

Seek—Ironically, the first step in recruiting is watching. Think of the people in your church. Who offers to come early to set up for your church's functions? Who loves to teach others about God's Word? Who offers to help with food? Who is gifted in arts or crafts? If you were to ask these people why they do what they do, most if not all of them will tell you that they help in certain areas because they enjoy it. That's one of the amazing things about spiritual gifts—people enjoy working in the areas in which God has gifted them. Your job as VBS director is to help people identify the jobs they can do that match their gifts. There may also be people in your church that you do not know but who would enjoy being part of VBS. To locate these people and get them involved, you can make announcements during worship services as well as distributing a volunteer flyer where people can express interest in helping with VBS. *(See page R·11.)*

The chart on the next page gives a brief overview of key questions to ask yourself, how they match spiritual gifts, and how that might translate into a role for VBS. You may want to copy it and give it to others who may be helping with recruiting or considering volunteering.

Ask—Once you have prayed about your staff of volunteers and looked for their spiritual gifts and talents, you are in a position to ask them to help. When you approach potential volunteers, make sure you tell them the specific job duties and responsibilities that you have in mind for them, and why you think they would be a good fit for a specific task. Be sure to listen as they respond—they certainly know themselves better than you do!

Spiritual Gifts Chart

GIFT	QUESTIONS	POSSIBLE ROLE
Based on: Romans 12; 1 Corinthians 12:28		
Helper	Who is always willing to lend a hand? Who thinks of ways to support and give, even when it is not asked of him or her?	Craft helper Snack coordinator Supply gatherer
Exhorter	Who is encouraging to be around? Who greets others with a smile and has a kind word, no matter who the person is?	Greeter Team leader Follow-up Leader
Administration	Who is looking for ways to organize programs? Who seems to be organized and able to help others because of it?	Craft/Snack coordinator Registration Assistant director
Giver	Who is always willing to give to your ministries? Who looks to fill the needs of those around him or her?	Craft/Snack donation Closing Program sponsor
Mercy	Who is willing to reach out to others who are hurting or in crisis? Who is motivated to show God's love to others?	Greeter Team leader
Server	Who is willing to stay in the background, content to help in other ways?	Snack preparer Craft coordinator
Leader	Who likes to tell others about God's Word? Who is primarily interested in how God changes others' hearts by revealing His Word?	Leader Team leader

Note: *While this list is not exhaustive, it can provide a good starting point to ask key questions about the gifts and abilities of those in your church. For other listings of gifts, see also Ephesians 4:11 and 1 Corinthians 12:8-10.*

Volunteers

In addition, make sure that your church is protected from liability by screening your volunteers. Hopefully you will personally know all the people who volunteer. However, some churches do not always have this luxury. Use your children's ministry's existing volunteer application or create one that asks for a volunteer's history of work with children, an official form of identification, Social Security number, and other information such as address and phone number(s), a brief testimony, and references. Unfortunately, these sorts of precautions are now standard in churches today, and VBS is no exception. Be sure that you talk with your pastor or Children's Minister to make sure you have met your church's screening standards so you can have the safest, most enjoyable VBS possible!

Personnel Chart

As you recruit and select team members for your VBS, the chart below will help you keep track of who is doing what and which positions still need to be filled.

DISCOVERY SITE 1
THE GARDEN—We need to be forgiven.

Leader 1	
Leader 2	
Location	
Other staff	

DISCOVERY SITE 2
THE DINING ROOM—We can be saved from our sin through Jesus.

Leader 1	
Leader 2	
Location	
Other staff	

DISCOVERY SITE 3
THE FAMILY ROOM—We can be welcomed into God's family.

Leader 1	
Leader 2	
Location	
Other staff	

DISCOVERY SITE 4
THE KITCHEN—We can grow in Jesus.

Leader 1	
Leader 2	
Location	
Other staff	

DISCOVERY SITE 5
THE LIVING ROOM—We can live with Jesus forever.

Leader 1	
Leader 2	
Location	
Other staff	

Training Your Staff

One of the many things your volunteers need to take with them as they set out to affect the lives of God's children is a trained mind. Training is one of the most important and stabilizing components to a successful VBS. Not only do your volunteers need to know what the VBS is all about, they need to know the specifics of their jobs and the best way to do their jobs. Make sure you schedule at least two training opportunities before the VBS begins so your volunteers can get to know each other and become a team, as well as become familiar with the roles they will perform.

As you recruit VBS staff, you will probably know who your Investigators will be before you have recruited all the people to be Assistant Investigators *(those who travel with each group of kids.)* These two groups of workers have different roles and will need some slightly different training for the jobs they will be doing. Included below are two meeting agendas:

one for the Director and Investigators and one for all of the VBS staff. Each meeting is designed to last two hours. *(Note: You may want to ask your Investigators to come only to the second half of the second meeting or to help lead parts of the first half.)* Adjust these agendas to match the number of meetings you are able to have and the length of your VBS meetings. You may want to combine this time with other planning meetings, but be sure to set aside the specific time to spend on training.

Agenda 1:

Director and Investigators

10 min.	Welcome, prayer, introductions
15 min.	Team Building activity *(Page D·66.)*
10 min.	Review all VBS materials and resources that are available to the teachers.
10 min.	Discuss the role of the Investigators. *(See **Key Players**, page D·15.)*
15 min.	Overview of age-level characteristics *(see **Age Characteristics Charts**, pages R·17-20)* and how to adapt teaching to different age levels.
10 min.	BREAK
40 min.	Break into teaching teams *(two Investigators per Discovery Site)* to work on lesson preparation.
10 min.	Wrap-up discussion, questions, prayer

Agenda 2:

Director and all VBS Staff

10 min.	Welcome, prayer, introductions
15 min.	Team Building activity *(Page D·66.)*
10 min.	Review all materials and resources.
10 min.	Discuss the roles of the different staff who are present. *(See **Key Players**, page D·15.)*
10 min.	Discuss the logistics of how VBS will run in your particular setting.
15 min.	Overview of relationship building and the age-level characteristics *(See **Age Characteristics Charts**, pages R·17-20.)*
10 min.	BREAK
20 min.	Overview of Leader Hints *(See **Leader Hints**, pages R·12-16.)*
10 min.	Overview of important information *(include emergency procedures, safety tips, special education issues, and legal responsibilities)*
10 min.	Wrap-up discussion, questions, prayer

Good News Clues™
Assistant Investigators

Inviting the middle school and high school youth to assist in your VBS program gives them a unique way to learn about God and minister to younger children. As they prepare and help lead, they will be listening and thinking more carefully about the Bible truths being taught. As they help and serve, they will be developing their Christian character. As they interact with you and other teachers, along with the younger children, they will be developing bonds in the Body of Christ and friendships within your congregation.

In addition, lessons are much easier to teach with helpers along. With extra hands, feet, and voices, you will be much better able to befriend, teach, and meet the needs of the preschool and early elementary children. And when a lesson calls for extra helpers, the VBS Assistant Investigators will conveniently be available to lend a hand.

FINDING AND RECRUITING ASSISTANT INVESTIGATORS

First, establish with your church's childrens ministries' team what age group you will be recruiting as your assistants. Be sure to follow your church's screening procedures and rules for those who work with young children.

- Have the middle school and high school Sunday school announce the opportunity for youth to participate as VBS Assistant Investigators.

- Send flyers home with the youth explaining the opportunity so it can be discussed with parents.

- Host a short reception or "VBS Assistant Investigators' Party" and invite the youth of your church to come and find out what it's all about. Keep it fun and brief. Clearly define the jobs of a VBS Assistant Investigator.

- Present the opportunity to work as a VBS Assistant Investigator as a positive experience rather than a chore for kids with "nothing else to do" during your VBS program. Make participation as a VBS Assistant Investigator a big deal.

- Be sure to emphasize the benefits of being a VBS Assistant Investigator: a chance to gain experience working with and caring for younger children, an opportunity to assist your church in reaching out to others in your community, a fun way to learn more about God and the Bible.

MAKING IT FUN

If you make participation as a VBS Assistant Investigator an opportunity that offers both responsibility and fun, the youth will show more commitment and better attitudes. Consider some of these ideas:

- Using the VBS *Good News Clues™* logo, design a badge, T-shirt, or vest for the VBS Assistant Investigators to wear. This will help the younger children identify who the responsible helpers are when they need help.

- Assign various job titles similar to the titles used by the adults helping in the program: Detective Assistant; Craft Assistant; Game Assistant, etc.

- Include them in the Discovery Site planning meetings so they feel the responsibility and inclusion in the program.

TRAINING THE ASSISTANT INVESTIGATORS

Training is essential if you want your VBS Assistant Investigators to be effective helpers during the VBS program. It doesn't have to be long—and it can be fun! Here are some suggested ways to train.

- Plan a time that is convenient for both the youth and their parents. Consider a time that is just before or after another youth activity. It wouldn't have to take longer than 30 minutes.

- Call the training session a "party." Keep the kids thinking, moving, and participating during most of the training. Use a lot of visuals.

- Walk the kids through one of the Discovery Sites. At each section of the Discovery Site, explain what the Site Investigator might need help with. *(See the complete list below.)*

There are two main areas to stress during your training: responsibility and kindness.

Responsibility: The VBS Assistant Investigators need to show responsibility to the Site Investigator by arriving on time, paying attention during class, remembering and carrying out duties, and looking for extra *(unasked for)* ways to help as they arise.

Kindness: The VBS Assistant Investigators need to be kind to the younger children they are helping. Kindness includes patience and being a good example at all times. If a discipline problem arises with the younger children, the Assistant Investigators should show kindness as they take the problem to an adult.

JOBS OF THE ASSISTANT INVESTIGATORS

The responsibilities you choose for the VBS Assistant Investigators will depend on your specific church and class needs. Here are ideas for how the youth in your church can help, serve, and learn during the *Good News Clues*™ VBS program.

- Help set up the classroom and gather supplies before the children arrive.

- Welcome the children—make sure they have a name tag and get to the right group.

- Welcome visitors—help them find a "buddy" to guide them during the day's activities.

- Take part in the skits or role-playing as assigned by the Site Investigator.

- Lead the children from one activity to another as directed by the Site Investigator.

- Help with the CD player or other audio visual equipment as needed.

- Participate with and/or help lead the singing.

- Help non-readers with writing/reading activities.

- For snacks: Wash and wipe tables before and after snack time, gather supplies and set up the snacks, help with hand-washing, refill cups, etc.

- For games: Do preparation, gather supplies, help the children understand the rules, be a partner to reluctant children, etc.

- For crafts: Arrange supplies, help younger children with assembly or writing on crafts, check to be sure all crafts have names on them, move completed crafts to a safe area until the end of class, clean up craft tables.

- Oversee classroom cleanup.

- Pass out take-home papers and crafts at the end of each day.

TIPS FOR PROBLEM SOLVING

Discipline problems, emergencies, and unexpected incidents are bound to arise. A responsible and well-trained VBS Assistant Investigator can be a big help during these times. Be sure your training session includes a time to cover this.

DISCIPLINE

The VBS Assistant Investigators should know that all discipline is handled by adults. However, the Assistant Investigators can be a big help in setting a good example for the younger children and by helping in the following ways:

- When a child loses attention or starts to play or talk during the lesson, the VBS Assistant Investigator can quietly go and sit by that child. Usually that is all that will be needed to draw the child's attention back to the lesson, along with an occasional "shhh" or cheery reminder to "let's not miss what the teacher's saying!"

- If a child becomes unruly or wants to wander off during transitions, the VBS Assistant Investigator can gently hold the child's hand and walk alongside.

- If a child becomes disruptive during a craft or game, it may be because the child doesn't understand what to do, has finished early, or is frustrated. The VBS Assistant Investigator can sit by the child and offer encouragement, instruction, or a friendly conversation that focuses the child back on the task.

EMERGENCIES

Even with every detail planned and everything in place, emergencies do occur. How these emergencies are handled can make the difference between a slight inconvenience and a major upset in the classroom.

Make sure the VBS Assistant Investigators know where the nearest first-aid kit is kept so they can retrieve it for the Site Investigator. Be sure to have a plan so that VBS Assistant Investigators know how to find the staff member in charge of VBS in case a parent needs to be contacted.

VBS Assistant Investigators should walk through your church's fire escape procedures so they could help lead the children outdoors in the event of a fire alarm.

EXPECTING THE UNEXPECTED

Younger children may need to use the restroom at any point during the lesson. Instruct the VBS Assistant Investigators to be on the lookout for any children with this need and to be prepared to quietly lead the child to and from the restroom. Boys should always escort boys and girls should always escort girls.

Some children may be unwilling to leave their parents when they arrive for VBS. They may cry or show stubbornness. A VBS Assistant Investigator can join the child with a smile, offer to be a friend or buddy, and help the child get started on a transitional activity. Sometimes a VBS Assistant Investigator may need to be assigned to one child for the whole class.

Visitors feel better when they have a friend, so a VBS Assistant Investigator can take on that role. He or she can show the visitor where activities take place and explain what is happening during each part of the lesson.

TRAINING YOUR CHURCH'S YOUTH LEADERS

The youth who participate as your VBS Assistant Investigators will be your church's future adults and leaders in the next few years. You have a wonderful opportunity, not just to have useful helpers in the classroom, but to make an important spiritual impression on these young people. Now is the time to help them form connections with your church, build relationships with Christian adults (like yourself), and develop a commitment to God that goes beyond their parents' responsibility to bring them to the church doors each week. By having useful and age-appropriate responsibilities, these VBS Assistant Investigators will recognize and have an outlet for their God-given talents and interests. They will learn what it means to be part of the Body of Christ. Their participation as VBS Assistant Investigators will develop spiritual maturity that will help them understand and draw closer to the Lord.

With this in mind, plan to meet with your VBS Assistant Investigators. Listen to their interests and concerns. Try to assign them duties that fit with their personalities and interests. Be sure they understand and are comfortable with their assignments and know who to contact during the VBS program in case of illness or unforeseen difficulties that could prevent them from participating. Pray with them about this opportunity for service.

Team Building

Help your VeBS staff grow into a team of people who share a common goal and purpose. Use these team building activities during staff training meetings, before each VeBS session, or any other time your staff will be together. Have fun!

Get-to-Know-You Map

Designate the four walls of your room north, south, east, and west. Invite the group to move to spots in the room that correspond to the place where each was born. For example, someone born in Maryland would stand near the middle of the east wall; someone from Kansas would stand in about the center of the room. If you have people who were born outside of the country, be sure they find an appropriate geographical spot to claim. If most of your group is from your state, you could limit the "map" to represent just your state. See how fast the group can get themselves oriented on the map. Then take a minute to encourage people to look around and see where the others hail from.

Team Message Challenge

Divide the staff into small teams. Give each team a set of messages on index cards, prepared ahead of time, but don't let the teams read the cards yet. The messages you write on the index cards should each give a simple instruction, for example:

> *Get a Bible and open to Psalm 1.*
> *Untie and retie someone's shoe in this room.*
> *Give the VeBS director a high five.*
> *Draw a smiley face on the board.*
> *Sing one verse of a familiar hymn.*

Have each team choose one person to begin. The others on the team draw one card and figure out how to give their player the message on that card—without making any sounds or touching the player.

Through motions and facial expressions, the team must communicate with their player what task he or she is supposed to accomplish. The player is allowed to talk and ask questions. As soon as the player figures it out and completes the task, another team member gets a turn while the rest of the team draws another card and works together to communicate the message.

Kids Are Like . . . Mural

Hang a long sheet of butcher paper on the wall and have colored markers or chalks available. Title the paper "Kids Are Like . . ." Invite the staff to think about what metaphors or symbols remind them of kids. For example, someone might feel kids are like trees because they are always growing and changing. Or someone might think kids are like puppies because they are active and enthusiastic. Encourage the group to think of a wide variety of things that represent something positive about children to them. Then invite the group to the butcher paper to create a mural that will define a wide variety of kids' characteristics. Have the staff sketch *(with any ability level)* their symbols for kids.

Bible Story Partner Charades

Divide the staff into pairs. *(If your group is large, divide them into groups of three.)* Have each pair choose a favorite Bible story and decide how they could best act it out without using words. *(For this version of charades, sound effects are encouraged.)* Then let each pair have a turn acting out their Bible story for the rest of the group until someone guesses what it is.

Teamwork Treasure Hunt

If you have outdoor space and good weather, try a treasure hunt that is most successful when done as a team. Ahead of time, make up the instruction lists. You can put the instructions in a different order for each team's list—so that they're not just following the others—and still use the same verses.

Adjust the instructions to fit your surroundings.

Example instructions *(be sure to exclude the correct answer on the copies you give out):*

Starting at the door, walk east to the _____ (Ps. 1:3). [tree]

Turn south and go to the _____ (Ex. 3:2). [bush]

Go to the nearest group of _____ (1 Pet. 1:24) and look among them. [flowers]

Walk west and look under the _____ (Acts 20:9). [window]

Walk past the _____ (Matt. 3:9) and look down. [stones]

Climb over the big _____ (Ps. 61:2) to your left and look behind it. [rock]

Plan to hide a "treasure" at the last location, such as gold-foil-wrapped chocolate bars or a bookmark for each player. Or you could hide a small "treasure" at every location. Another option, depending on your surroundings, would be to give each team only the first direction and hide the subsequent directions at the stops along the way; a team would find its next direction only by correctly following its first one.

What I Like Best

Give each person an index card and pencil. Ask everyone to silently consider how they would complete this thought: "What I like best about kids is . . . ." Then challenge the group to write down only three words on their index cards that would somehow describe what they enjoy most about children. When everyone has their three words written, collect the cards, mix them up, and pass them out. Have everyone start to wander around the room, looking for the person whose card they are holding. When found, have the pairs briefly share with each other why they wanted to work with VeBS this year.

Devotions

The devotions on the following pages provide an opportunity for you and the leaders to learn about and experience the love of Jesus so that you can show that love to the precious children at your VBS. They can be easily used during a prayer time before each VBS session or in the training meeting before VBS begins. Whether you do these devotions as a group or as individuals in preparation for VBS, we encourage you to do them! Take the time to allow God to speak to your heart, to fill you with the hope that is in Jesus Christ so that hope may overflow to the children.

Be sensitive to the fact that there may be workers in your own group who have never received eternal life by believing in Christ for themselves or who, through this time working with the kids, realize their desire to recommit their lives to Him. If you sense that there may be someone like that in your staff, be sure to make some time to spend with that person alone, outside of VBS. God can use VBS to touch the lives of adults and children alike!

These devotional pages can be used as personal reflection and/or to facilitate group discussions. If you hold corporate devotions with all the volunteers, you will need to photocopy the devotions for volunteers.

Color—Dark

"Or despisest thou the riches of his goodness and forbearance and longsuffering; not knowing that the goodness of God leadeth thee to repentance?" —Romans 2:4

Darkness is what we think of when the lights are out. When the moon is new and the city's glow is far away. When we can't see where we're going, either literally or figuratively. Darkness can remind us of our sin, our unworthiness before God. When Adam and Eve sinned, they hid—not out in the bright sunlight where they would be easily seen, but in the shade, under the trees, somewhere dark. Did they really hope that God wouldn't be able to find them? The darkness is as light to Him *(Ps. 139:11-12)*.

Of course, the Lord knew. How did He respond to this very first sin and the sinners' hiding in darkness? He responded immediately with mercy, with kindness. He gave them the chance to come to Him. His first words were not a condemnation, but an invitation in the form of a rhetorical question, "Where art thou?" *(Gen. 3:9)*. He wanted them to come out and seek Him. Even after Adam and Eve crept out, the Lord still did not accuse; rather, He asked. His questions encouraged them to think through what they had done and why; His questions opened the opportunity for them to ask forgiveness.

When we sin, why do we try to "hide" from God? Sometimes we stay in the "dark," avoiding our prayer times, keeping unfocused during worship. We forget the kindness and mercy of our loving Lord. He doesn't want guilt to drive a wedge between us. He wants His kindness to lead us to repentance, our memories of His compassion to lead us to confession *(Micah 7:18-19)*.

When King David had committed a set of unconscionable sins—murder, adultery, scheming, and utter self-centeredness—he knew to run *to* his God. He was drawn to God's mercy, unfailing love, and great compassion *(2 Sam. 11—12; Ps. 51; Prov. 18:10)*.

No matter how huge our sin, no matter how deep our darkness, God is there (Ps. 139:7-8). He knows, He cares, He desires to draw us out of darkness and back into His light *(Ps. 18:28)*.

Whenever you do something that puts you in that proverbial darkness, remember that God is your refuge, your safe spot, your devoted Father. Seek him out and trust his kindness and mercy, for he loves you.

Personal Reflection

Reflect on ways you have seen God's love for you despite your sin. How have you tried to hide in the "dark" from God, and how has he drawn you to himself?

NOTES

GOOD NEWS CLUES™

Color–Red

"In whom we have redemption through his blood, the forgiveness of sins, according to the riches of his grace." –Ephesians 1:7

What does the color red represent in our culture? It can symbolize anger or a bad temper. It can be used to add vibrancy or dramatic flare or warmth to a room or painting. It has been used to represent immoral sins.

From the Bible we get the symbolism of red representing death as a sacrifice, for when someone bleeds, their blood exposed to oxygen turns bright red. This can be a scary color to see on someone we love.

The blood of Jesus, shed on the cross for our sins, changed history, both in heaven and on earth. Yet many people don't really grasp how essential it was for Jesus— God incarnate—to suffer and die. Just what does the blood of Christ cover? Whose sins are forgiven, and which sins? When a member of a cult or non-Christian religion hands you a tract or knocks on your door, let the color red as defined in the Bible be your truth and comfort.

Why did Christ need to shed His blood on the cross? Beginning in the Book of Genesis and through Revelation, God clearly calls for sin to be paid for by the shedding of blood—the sacrifice of a life. While the Old Testament animal sacrifices were only a symbol of paid-for sin *(Heb. 10:11)*, God promised that His "perfect lamb" would actually pay the debt for all mankind *(Isaiah 53:5-7, 1 Pet. 1:18-19)*. Then He sent Jesus to be that perfect Lamb *(John 1:29)*. His death alone opened the way for a relationship with God *(Mark 15:37-38, Col. 1:19-20; Heb. 10:19-22)*. And when we get to heaven, we will know that we are there because of the blood of Christ *(Rev. 1:5)*.

How many sins does Christ's blood cover? Some groups that claim to be Christian accept His sacrifice to pay for original sin—the sinful nature we are born with—but they believe that consciously-committed sins must be made up for through good works. Yet the Bible teaches that Jesus' shed blood covers *all* our sins *(1 John 1:7)*. Scripture makes crystal clear that good works do not do one iota of good toward earning or keeping our salvation *(Rom. 3:22-25; Eph. 2:8-9)*.

So rejoice! The Lord covers us with a "robe of righteousness," washed clean with His blood, which was shed for us *(Isa. 61:10; Rev. 7:14)*. Your debt has been paid in full!

Personal Reflection

Read chapters 9 and 10 of Hebrews, looking for how Christ's death fulfilled the Old Testament system of sacrifices. Write your reflections here.

Write a "psalm" praising God for what the color red represents—your salvation through faith in Christ's blood.

NOTES

_____

_____

_____

_____

_____

_____

_____

_____

_____

_____

_____

_____

Color—White

"Let us draw near with a true heart in full assurance of faith, having our hearts sprinkled from an evil conscience. . . ." –Hebrews 10:22

Think of a time that you ran into an old friend, someone you hadn't seen for a while. How good it felt to see that wide grin on your friend's face! We are energized by the joy and familiarity of an old friend. It's a great feeling to get together with someone who really knows you and likes you, isn't it?

As Christians going to meet the Lord in prayer, we sometimes have an opposite reaction. Aware of our sin and unworthiness, some of us shuffle into God's presence, fearful of a reprimand, hoping He's not too disappointed in us. We begin with apologies and even self-criticism, sometimes never getting around to the joy and friendship. While it's important to never forget God's awesome holiness, we also need to keep in mind His awesome affection for us. Our sin weighs us down, but is that what God sees when He looks at us?

The story of the prodigal son is a great example of how God sees us. When the son returned home, he hung his head, weighed down with the knowledge of his sin. But the father ran to his son and greeted him with genuine joy *(Luke 15:20).* The father loved his son deep-down and wanted to celebrate the relationship.

When God meets you at your prayer time, He also comes with joy. That's because when He looks at you, He sees the cleansing blood of Jesus *(1 John 1:7),* He sees the holiness He gave you *(1 Cor. 1:30),* He sees the friend He loves *(John 15:15).* If we can picture the Lord greeting us with a smile, then we, like the psalmist, can go eagerly into our prayer times *(Ps. 16:11; 18:1; 28:7).*

If you have committed your life to Jesus and asked Him to be your Savior and Lord, then He has made you clean from sin *(Ps. 51:7).* He wants you to draw near to Him with confidence and joy *(Heb. 4:16),* as if you were meeting an old friend. Because, after all, the Lord really does know you and like you.

Personal Reflection

Reflect on how your conversations with the Lord would be different if you approached them with this truth in mind: Because God has cleansed you from your sin, He welcomes you like an old friend.

Ponder these verses as you contemplate God's affection for you:

1 John 3:1a

Psalm 103:11-13

Hebrews 4:15

NOTES

Color—Green

"Confirming the souls of the disciples, and exhorting them to continue in the faith, and that we must through much tribulation enter into the kingdom of God." —Acts 14:22

Green is a color that represents life, a reminder of the new shoots springing back from the dormancy of winter each spring. Green can represent our growth as Christians, our strengthening spiritual maturity, our deepening walk with God.

How do we grow spiritually? What elements impact the maturing of your faith?

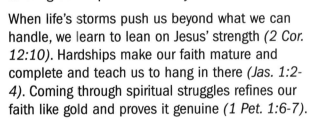

Along with Bible study, prayer, fellowship, worship, serving, and outreach, comes another factor that many of us would sometimes like to forget—trials! God uses trials, hardships, and struggles to bring us to spiritual maturity.

When life's storms push us beyond what we can handle, we learn to lean on Jesus' strength *(2 Cor. 12:10)*. Hardships make our faith mature and complete and teach us to hang in there *(Jas. 1:2-4)*. Coming through spiritual struggles refines our faith like gold and proves it genuine *(1 Pet. 1:6-7)*.

Take an example from life: Any athlete knows that to build a stronger body, workouts are necessary. Muscles grow by being used—and by being used hard. Muscle tissue builds by first being torn. As an athlete pushes a muscle past its point of comfort, past any point it has reached before, small tears occur in the muscle. The body rushes to heal the tear, and as the days go by, the spot that was torn grows back stronger, the muscle bigger. An athlete's workout is, in effect, a trial that the body is put through. When the "trial" is over, the athlete can see the results, though at the time of the workout, nothing was felt but discomfort and even pain *(Heb. 12:11)*.

In a similar way, the Lord, in His goodness, pushes us beyond the point where we can rely on ourselves so that we must learn to rely on Him *(2 Cor. 12:9)*.

It's unpleasant to get out of our comfort zone, but that's one way God builds strong spirits. We can expect trials, not fear them, as we desire to see growth in our spiritual lives *(1 Pet. 4:12)*.

If we've prepared ourselves with Bible study, a deepening relationship with the Lord, and the other elements that assist spiritual growth, then when trials assail us, we will be equipped to come through to the end *(Jas. 1:12)*.

Personal Reflection

What are some trials you've been through, and how did they mature your faith? What trials are you going through now that might be deepening your walk with God?

NOTES

Color—Gold

"Ye were sealed with that holy Spirit of promise, which is the earnest of our inheritance until the redemption of the purchased possession. . . ." —Ephesians 1:13b-14a

"**The street of the city** [heaven] was pure gold . . . " *(Rev. 21:21)*. This is one well-known feature of heaven. Gold is a memorable symbol of the majesty and brightness of the future home of believers. But the physical beauty of heaven is probably not as important to us as the emotional burdens that will be lifted from us—no more sorrow, pain, or physical suffering *(Rev. 7:16; 21:4)*. How much we look forward to that part of heaven! But even more significant will be our uninterrupted and completed relationship with the Lord *(Rev. 7:17; 21:3)*. We will finally be able to see our friend Jesus face to face *(1 Cor. 13:12; Rev. 22:4)*.

But we don't have to wait until we die before we can experience some of heaven's "gold." When the Lord sent His Spirit to live in us, that was His "deposit" of heaven: "Now he which stablisheth us with you in Christ, and hath anointed us, is God; who hath also sealed us, and given the earnest of the Spirit in our hearts" *(2 Cor. 1:21-22)*.

When you make a large purchase, it's not unusual to place a deposit to hold that purchase. This money is just a small portion of what will come later, but it obligates both the seller and the buyer to keep that commitment. It also gives the seller a very real taste of the rest of the expected money. When the Apostle Paul referred to the Spirit as a deposit, he meant that God's Spirit living in us—guiding, helping, comforting, and restoring us—is just a small portion of what's waiting for us when we reach heaven *(1 Pet. 1:3-5; Rom. 8:11)*.

Yet isn't it hard some days to see God's kingdom within ourselves? Remember that faith is a key ingredient to all deposit transactions. When you accept a monetary deposit on a purchase, you take it in faith that the buyer will eventually fulfill the remainder of the payment. How much more will the God of the universe honor his deposit in us and bring us home!

Whenever you doubt your future in heaven, look to the deposit the Lord left—His very own Spirit residing inside your heart. Look at His work in your life. We don't have the streets of gold right now, but we do have the treasure of His constant love and help.

Personal Reflection

Reflect on ways you see the golden "deposit" of God's Spirit in your life.

NOTES

Appreciate Your Staff!

VBS could never happen without all the volunteers. Let them know that they are appreciated and that the time and effort they put in is valued. Here are some ideas to get you started. There's no such thing as too much appreciation, so plan a number of ways to say thanks throughout VBS!

- Arrange a full Saturday or an evening when high school kids babysit for leaders' kids so the leaders can have some free time.

- Take your leaders out for a team lunch.

- Purchase small baskets and fill them with fruit and an encouraging note for each leader.

- Create a snack pack with chocolates, candies, and other treats.

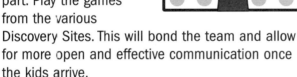

- Do something crazy, challenging, team-building, and adventurous with your team of leaders: have your own game day where the leaders take part. Play the games from the various Discovery Sites. This will bond the team and allow for more open and effective communication once the kids arrive.

- Place a colorful plant or flower in each classroom to brighten the leaders' day.

- At the beginning of VBS, give each leader a "survival kit" with notes of encouragement, treats, fun gifts, uplifting verses, and so on, that they can dive into anytime they need a lift during VBS.

- Give out gift certificates from a favorite restaurant, ice-cream shop, or coffee house.

- Have volunteers from the church cook and deliver dinner for each leader and his or her family one night during VBS.

- Give each leader an inexpensive fanny pack, backpack, or bag to carry their supplies to and from VBS.

- Create a *Good News Clues*™ team of adults who, for some reason, can't be present at VBS but want to be part of it. Have this team be in charge of coordinating prayer partners, making encouraging phone calls, and writing notes of encouragement to the leaders and volunteers for your VBS.

- Throughout VBS, have a rope that you bring to leader meetings. Have a few minutes set aside where leaders can share encouraging and exciting things that are happening in their groups of kids. Each time they tell a story, have them tie a knot in the rope. At the end of VBS, schedule a time when volunteers can stand up in church, show the rope, and tell one of the stories that is represented by the knots. leaders will appreciate the opportunity to share how God worked as well as the opportunity to be recognized by the congregation.

- Give a pack of candy with a verse to encourage leaders to hang in there through the adventure.

- Give a "night at the movies" with a package containing a movie rental gift certificate and a bag of microwave popcorn.

- Acknowledge your leaders in front of the entire church. Display in a prominent area pictures of each leader with a quote from a child about how much that leader meant to them during VBS.

- Print the *Good News Clues*™ logo or a favorite Key Verse on a water bottle or coffee mug for each leader.

- Print Ephesians 6:10 on some colorful paper and put it in an inexpensive frame for each leader.

- If you know each of your leaders well, select different gifts, appropriate for each person (*a favorite candy bar would work*). The fact that you thought of each one individually will mean a lot to the leaders.

Promote

Promoting your VBS is an important part of your planning. The ways that you choose to promote VBS will partly determine who and how many attend *Good News Clues*™. Before you decide on methods of promotion, you may want to meet with your committee and determine the goals you have. How many children do you want to attend? How much money is in the budget for promotion?

Do you want to reach kids in your church first, kids in other churches, kids throughout the community, or all of the above?

Clarifying these things in the beginning will help promotion to run smoothly.

Included in the Reproducible Resources section is artwork for promotional posters. There is also a full-color poster available on the *Good News Clues*™ CD. Place these posters in prominent places in your church and community to let people know that the *Good News Clues*™ VBS will be taking place at your church. Be sure to fill in the details—dates of your VBS, the time VBS will be held each day, and the name and location of your church.

Use any of the ideas listed here and the resources in the Reproducible Resources section and the *Good News Clues*™ CD. Feel free to customize them to fit your VBS.

Involve the Kids...

Print copies of the full-color poster found on the *Good News Clues*™ CD, or the black and white Event Poster provided on page R·8. Allow children to take the posters with them and hang them somewhere in their neighborhood, school, store, and so on.

- Use the postcard design to send out invitations to children in the church and the community. You may want to have extra copies of the postcard available for members of the church who would like to take them and give them to parents of children in their neighborhoods. Be sure the postcard includes information about when and where parents can register their children. *(See the postcard invitation on page R·10 or on the Good News Clues*™ *CD.)* Point out that although a child is invited by a friend, the parent must still register their child for VBS. *(See Registration Form on page R·4.)*

- The art images in the Reproducible Resources section, and the electronic clip art on the *Good News Clues*™ CD can be used in many different ways. Use it on water bottles, T-shirts, hats, and bookmarks to add fun to any of the promotional activities that you do!

Involve the Church...

Designate a certain Sunday as VBS Sunday to introduce your program. Be sure to include the bulletin insert *(page R·42 or on the CD)*. This will launch the VBS for this year and get people familiar with the theme and excited about the outreach potential for VBS.

- As soon as you launch VBS, be sure to have plenty of registration cards *(page R·4)* available for people to fill out.

- Even as early as a couple of months before VBS, start including flyers and information in the bulletins at your church. You may want to start with the flyer encouraging people to pray for VBS. *(See page R·11.)*

- As it gets closer to VBS, hand out the volunteer flyer *(see page R·11)* to encourage volunteers to sign up for all areas of VBS.

- All flyers and bulletin inserts will be most effective if supplemented by an announcement or skit during the service.

- Make magnets or bookmarks out of the prayer reminders *(page R·11)* and send them to each person who has agreed to be a prayer partner. You may also want to have them available at worship services so people can take them home.

- If you want to save some money by having some of the supplies and props for VBS donated, distribute a flyer to let people know what you need. Be sure to include information about whom they can contact and where they can leave the supplies. You will want to do this close enough to VBS that you do not have to store the materials for too long, but far enough in advance so you know what additional supplies need to be purchased. Use the complete supply lists on pages D·18-26 and P·4-10 as a guide.

- Make T-shirts using the T-shirt pattern and sell them before VBS begins *(or as part of pre-registration)* so that the kids can wear them and share the news about VBS with their friends and neighbors. *(Use the transfer art on the CD, or use other art images to create your own T-shirt design.)*

- Use art images provided on the CD to create other items *(inexpensive plastic cups or water bottles, stickers, bookmarks, and so on)* for the kids to take home from VBS as a reminder of what they have learned.

- Hang a large banner inviting neighborhood children to *Good News Clues*™ in a prominent place in your church or over the registration table. Be sure to fill in the correct information for the dates, time, and place on the poster.

Involve the Community...

Many radio stations provide air time for public service announcements or community events. Let your local radio stations know about the upcoming VBS at your church. Use the Press Release *(see page R·43)* to provide the necessary information. You may also want to ask station managers to let you call in and talk live on the radio about your VBS. If your church has audio production capabilities, you might record a short *(15-second)* radio spot to advertise VBS. Use the Press Release information as your guide.

- Some cable TV companies offer free advertising for local groups in the form of scrolling ads during off-time. Check with your local cable company for what they offer and what they require from you.

- Host a *Good News Clues*™ Day in a park or nearby public area. Use this day to attract attention to VBS and to provide registration for people in the community who are not regularly involved in the church.

More Promotional Ideas...

Hand out balloons at church one Sunday with a Postcard Invitation *(page R·10)* attached to the bottom of the balloon.

- Have a race or walk where members of the church without kids can contribute to VBS through this fund-raiser.

- Create one of the VBS Discovery Sites in advance and have it set up in the church where people can get information about VBS and register their kids.

- Make magnetic reminders by printing the *Good News Clues*™ logo pattern on colorful cardstock and add the dates and times of your VBS. Put a magnetic strip on the back. Give the magnets to kids along with an extra to give to a friend with an invitation. You may also want to give them as reminders for people to pray for VBS.

- Instead of including all the flyers as bulletin inserts *(page R·42)*, have some of the kids dress up in Bible-time outfits and hand out the flyers at the worship services.

- Sell raffle tickets and give the winners gifts. *(T-shirt, gift certificate, stuffed animal, mini-golf tickets, and so on.)*

- For one of your VBS announcement times, sing a song instead of speaking. You may want to use one of the songs from the VBS CD or put the information you need to communicate to a familiar tune.

- Make a short video clip to show on Sunday morning to introduce VBS. One idea is to ask a number of kids in your church this question and videotape their response. ***What's the most exciting news you have ever been given?***

- If your VBS schedule is other than five consecutive sessions, do a mid-VBS report for the church. Be sure to include some kids!

- Print copies of the full-color promotional poster found on the *Good News Clues*™ CD to display around your church and in legal public notice areas in your community. Be sure to fill in the correct information for the date, place, and time on the poster.

- There are many excellent Bible resources on the Internet. You may want to use these in addition to the promotional aids available through our VBS site at **www.cookvbs.com.**

Follow-up on Kids

Give each of your kids a Bible or New Testament so they can learn more on how to study and grow in their new life in Jesus.

- Take your VBS kids to visit a children's hospital, or a nursing home and share with the people the love that they have found in Jesus. Sing some of the VBS songs.

- Encourage the Assistant Investigators who went to each of the five Discovery Sites with their groups to sponsor an activity just for their kids. This will help to maintain the relationship that was established in VBS and may give visiting kids just the contact and the encouragement they need to start attending church regularly.

- Find out if there are any sports competitions in your area and take the kids to see one. Even an outing to a college or community sporting event will be fun for the kids. This will give you a chance to spend time with those kids who may need extra encouragement.

- Make a list of the kids that attended VBS and send them a postcard one month after VBS ends, encouraging them to continue studying and growing in their Christian life as they finish out the summer and head back to school.

- Make a *Good News Clues*™ certificate for each child using the certificate sample on page R·9, or the color version from the *Good News Clues*™ CD, or create your own original certificate.

Follow-up on Leaders

Put together a slide show of pictures or video taken during VBS. Host a fellowship gathering for your staff. Show your slides or video to let them see the wonderful job they did for the kids.

- Make the time over the next six months to have lunch with your volunteers *(you may want to do it one on one or in small groups)*. This will not only help them feel appreciated, it will keep you in touch with them for next year—and they will probably have great ideas and suggestions for VBS in the future.

- Be sure you have accurate mailing and phone lists of all the leaders so that you can contact them easily in the future. Encourage them to let you know if any of their information changes.

- Have kids make thank-you notes for people who donated time, supplies, prayer, and so on.

Follow-up on Families

If possible, plan a reunion a few weeks after VBS is over so kids and families can play games, enjoy refreshments, and catch up with one another.

- Invite families to take part in a day-long "field trip" together, such as a day hike, a bike ride, or a tour of a local establishment.

- Arrange a time in a worship service where the kids from VBS can sing some VBS songs for the congregation. Be sure to have this arranged by the end of VBS so that you can let all the parents know. This will be an excellent way to get kids and parents who do not attend church to come visit.

- You may want to arrange host families that you can match up with non-church kids and their families after VBS is over. This will encourage those families to come visit church, get answers to questions they have, and help them feel comfortable coming to church.

Follow-up on the Church

Let the church know how VBS went by showing a videotape of the highlights of *Good News Clues*.™

- Present the Project Share God's Treasure mission project to the church. Let them know what the kids have learned and how they have given of their money to help provide *New Testament Picture Bibles* for children in South America, Africa, the Middle East, Asia, and India. Challenge the church body to match the amount that the kids gave.

- Ask a few kids to tell their favorite things about VBS in front of the church.

- Schedule a time when kids from VBS can sing the songs they learned during VBS.

- Invite all those in the church who prayed for VBS or who participated in any way to be part of the intergenerational closing program.

- Put together a video, a slide show, or a picture collage to present to the church to let them know all about the exciting things that happened during VBS.

NOTES

project
SHARE GOD'S TREASURE

Children sharing the treasure of Jesus with children of the world

As your VeBS children excitedly hunt for clues that point them to the treasure of new life in Jesus, there are many children who don't even have *hints* about salvation. These are the children from the slums of India, the kids in isolated villages along the Amazon, or little ones in remote Asian countries like the Philippines and Vietnam. They have no clues about Jesus. No Bibles of their very own to treasure.

Give your VeBS kids the opportunity to share God's treasure, the *New Testament Picture Bible*, with these children so that they, too, can find Jesus.

Project Share God's Treasure lets VeBS children meaningfully spread the Good News by giving of their treasure—their nickels and dimes—and the knowledge that the Bible leads to Jesus.

Cook Communications Ministries International (CCMI) has mission projects around the globe. In **Project Share God's Treasure**, CCMI and kids in VeBS programs nationwide, can give the Bible to children who are without the hope of Jesus. CCMI will print, bind, and distribute colorfully illustrated Bibles that have evangelized children all over the world. For as little as $5, four children who are eager to find Jesus will have their own *New Testament Picture Bible*. For many, it will be the first book they've ever had.

"For where your TREASURE is, there will your heart be also."
—*Matt. 6:21*

MORE CLUES ABOUT THE URGENT NEED

Each day talk about **Project Share God's Treasure** during the opening assemblies. Make copies of the flyer on the next page for kids to show their parents. Post flyers around your church to get others involved. Use a world map or globe to show kids where India, Asia, the Middle East, Africa, and South America are located.

Before your program begins, get a **FREE** *New Testament Picture Bible* from CCMI to explain how the pictures and words give clues to Jesus. During each opening assembly, collect an offering. Each *New Testament Picture Bible* costs only $1.25, about the price of a candy bar. Every penny of the contributions goes to **Project Share God's Treasure**.

Call 1-800-323-7543 to receive one *New Testament Picture Bible* (#69906 VEBS PNT OFFER - SPANISH; #103329 VEBS PNT OFFER - ENGLISH) per VeBS program. Please specify to the service representative that this is Special Offer VBS0000 and provide the item number.

OTHER IDEAS TO SHARE GOD'S TREASURE

Coin Drive: Kids may not think they have much to give, but they will be amazed at how quickly their pocket change adds up! Use a clear container with a Bible or a map of the world painted on it. Or, use a box painted to look like a treasure chest.

All-Church Challenge: After the VeBS kids raise money, have them present **Project Share God's Treasure** to the rest of the church and ask members to match the amount the children have raised.

NOTES

CREATION Adam and Eve

"For all have sinned, and come short of the glory of God."
Romans 3:23

Why Kids Need to Discover That They've Sinned and Are Separated from God

Every child who comes to VBS will know that there is a distinction between right and wrong. However, their concept of right and wrong, and what sin is, may be very skewed from God's definition. Some children have come to believe that wrong is only bad if you get caught. Others may think what's right and wrong changes depending on the situation. You might also meet children who haven't experienced forgiveness and a close relationship with their parent(s), which will influence their understanding a loving heavenly Father.

Here's one way to define sin: wanting to do things our own way and choosing to disobey God's rules. When you have the children share real-life examples of sin, they all will begin to realize they are sinners. Showing them the actual memory verse in the Bible can also help them understand their own state of sinfulness.

Once children recognize they are indeed sinful, you can illustrate the truth that they are separated from God by teaching them that God is without sin. Just

relate to. Teach the Bible story in a way that puts them in Adam and Eve's shoes—sinful, separated, needy for forgiveness. But don't leave kids in the despair of their sin and separation. Be sure that within this site you also clue them in that there is a way to close the gap between them and God.

Getting More from the Bible Story

This Bible story begins as God's awesome act of creation is finished. In Genesis 2 God commissions Adam to be the caretaker and have dominion *(absolute control and authority)* over the Garden and the animals that inhabit it. Eden was a paradise that would have been like living in heaven. It was perfect, without the effects of sin, full of only good things. God gave Adam responsibility both for the garden and for his own choices while living there.

When Eve and Adam chose to eat the fruit of the tree of the knowledge of good and evil they ultimately chose to disobey God. This was sin. Eve and Adam's choice to disobey God produced the same result: death. Their sin separated them from the tree of life and thus from eternal life. The tree of life is also described in Revelation 22:2 as having 12 kinds of fruit to be enjoyed by those who spend eternity in heaven with God.

The serpent that successfully tempted Eve was Satan in disguise. Satan had been an angel who rebelled against God and was thrown out of heaven. In this first temptation, just as when he tempted Jesus in the wilderness *(Matt. 4:1-11),* Satan used God's own words, but warped them, to lure his victim away from obedience to the Father. Like every sin, choosing one's own way leads to disobedience and death.

factoid

Fingerprints are often useful clues for detectives. The science of fingerprinting—dermatoglyphics—was first practiced by the ancient Chinese who fingerprinted on wax seals to close important documents. Every individual's fingerprints, made of whorls, arches, and loops, are unique. Today's fingerprint identification system was founded by Sir Edward Henry who created the first fingerprinting department for Scotland Yard in 1900.

like oil and water separate, a sinner is separated from God by his sin.

Taking the truth of sin and salvation down to its most simple, basic bones will make it easier to teach and easier to grasp. Help each child own his own sin by being sure your students have examples they can

Creation

"For all have sinned, and come short of the glory of God."

Site Mission

Children will learn that sin separates us from God who love us.

Key Bible Verse

"For all have sinned, and come short of the glory of God." — **Romans 3:23**

Site Coordinators

- **Green Thumb Gerty**
- **Doc Diggit**

Both are avid gardeners who can depict their roles by wearing garden hats, shorts, garden clogs, having dirty hands and smudges on their faces, carrying garden tools and seed packets.

Puppet Option

Investigator #2 or an Assistant Investigator can operate BOSWORTH to help lead the children to different areas and interact spontaneously with the teacher and children. *(See puppet pattern for BOSWORTH on pages R · 55-59.)*

Bible Passage

Genesis 1:26-31; 2:4—3:23

setting the scene

The Garden should be like someone's own home garden. Use large potted plants, silk trees, and containers of vegetable and fruit plants for the background. A green piece of carpet or artificial grass can be laid out under the garden scene, or use green butcher paper. A potting cart *(that gardeners use to pot up plants)* can add more life to the scene, or stand a garden gate or shed door against the wall as a backdrop. Add stacks of terra cotta pots, bags of compost and soil *(or a mound of dirt)*, watering can, fertilizer bags/boxes, and a coiled hose. Bring in hand tools: trowel, shears, hoe, rake, etc.

More life can be added by attaching fake butterflies to the trees or plants, putting a few plastic bugs around, and playing a tape of birds, crickets, water trickling in a brook, etc.

Investigator's Inventory

General

- [ ] Garden mural
- [ ] *Good News Clues*™ CD or tape copy
- [ ] CD player or cassette tape player
- [ ] Copy of "The Quest Continues" student take-home paper *(page E1 · 14)* for each child
- [ ] Copy of the "Detective's Diary" for each child *(pages R · 61-68)*. Note the two age levels and use accordingly.

Games and Activities

- [ ] Dead plant in pot of dry dirt
- [ ] Broken garden tool
- [ ] Clues written on dark paper
- [ ] Fragrant flower
- [ ] Inflated balloons
- [ ] Small pieces of paper with 1–2 words of Bible verse to insert into balloons
- [ ] Key Verse poster
- [ ] Key Verse Cards *(page R · 60)*
- [ ] Copy of song lyrics for each child or have the words on an overhead transparency *(pages R · 21-26)*
- [ ] Overhead projector
- [ ] Ball
- [ ] Dirt or potting soil
- [ ] Buckets *(two for each five to eight kids)*
- [ ] Plastic spoons
- [ ] Plastic cups
- [ ] Puppet *(optional)*
- [ ] Dark beads *(one per child)*
- [ ] Lacing

- [ ] *Emily's Bracelet (optional)*
- [ ] Treasure basket and sliced apples

Snacks

- [ ] Healthy veggies to dip *(carrot sticks, celery sticks, cucumber slices, etc.)*
- [ ] One or two soft dips, such as ranch dip *(already prepared or use your own recipe)* or vegetable dip
- [ ] Small paper plates
- [ ] Spoons for dip
- [ ] Red crepe paper
- [ ] Pretzels, small crackers, or candy
- [ ] Green floral tape or green twist ties
- [ ] Bushel baskets
- [ ] Paper cups and napkins

Crafts

- [ ] Scratch paper *(art paper that has multicolors underneath a layer of black)*
- [ ] Satin ribbon, 12" lengths
- [ ] Wooden scratching tools or paperclips
- [ ] Hole punch
- [ ] Gel pens or markers for drawing on dark paper
- [ ] Dark-colored paper cups *(option: cover a standard paper cup with dark construction paper)*
- [ ] Potting Soil
- [ ] Scoop for potting soil
- [ ] Small annual flowers or nontoxic houseplants
- [ ] Clear self-adhesive paper

Procedures of the Day

10 minutes: Preparing to Search

15–20 minutes: Focus on the Bible

10 minutes: Bible Memorization

5 minutes: Music Time

15 minutes: Gumshoe Grub

20 minutes: Case-Cracking Games

20 minutes: Putting the Pieces Together

10 minutes: Elementary Deduction

10 minutes: Detectives' Departure

Detective Preparation

- Have craft samples prepared in advance to show Detectives.

- Be sure all supplies are gathered and your site is ready each day for Detectives to arrive.

- Post the Procedures of the Day where Investigators and helpers (called *Assistant Investigators*) can refer to it.

- Address each other by site titles. Children should be referred to as Detectives. The helpers that go with them from camp to camp are called Assistant Investigators—Assistant Investigator Jim or Assistant Investigator Sharon.

- After taking attendance, an Assistant Investigator should tell those responsible for refreshments how many Detectives are present to be prepared for snack time.

- In advance, write all the clues for the day's hidden treasure onto the color of paper indicated.

- You may wish to do some background research into the Bible story. Refer to Bible commentaries, encyclopedias, and dictionaries for additional information.

PREPARING TO SEARCH

(A1) Supplies:

- Actual dead plant in a pot of dry dirt

- Broken garden tool

 **Clue 1 on dark paper:** "It's red or green."

Greet the Detectives as they enter. Introduce yourselves as Green Thumb Gerty and Doc Diggit. This section serves as an introduction to the Bible story and is best handled as a dialogue between the two leaders, but can be done by one leader if desired.

GERTY: **Howdy! It's great to have you visiting our garden today! Doc Diggit and I were just cleaning out the garden shed.** *(Point to props: bag of soil, fertilizer, tools, and other garden things.)*

DOC: **Indeed. How I love getting down into the dirt and making something grow. Whoever thought of all the kinds of plants and flowers and vines and . . . well, it's all so beautiful and creative, don't you think?**

GERTY: *(Nods)* **But Doc Diggit, there are a few things that are mysteries to me. I've been thinking we need to get a Detective involved here, to help us figure out some very mysterious problems.**

(Leader clears throat and announces that all the kids are Detectives, and are willing to solve mysteries.)

(Gerty and Doc are excited, jump up and down, hug each other, etc.)

DOC: *(displays the dead plant)* **Here's the first mystery. What's wrong with this lovely specimen of** _____*(name of plant being held)*? **Not long ago it had the most colorful flowers that smelled good. Now look at it! Any ideas, Detectives, what's happened here?**

(Call on kids. Encourage them to look for clues by touching, looking, etc. Congratulate them for answer: It died for lack of water.)

GERTY: I knew these Detectives could help us out! I have another mystery for you. *(Shows a broken tool, such as a trowel, shovel, pruners, etc.)* **I've tried and tried to make this work. I really, really need to dig some weeds** *(or whatever you'd do with the chosen tool).* **You should see all the weeds that are coming up. But this tool won't work! Any clues from you Detectives about what the problem is?** *(Let children offer ideas.)*

DOC: Yes, that's it! This *(trowel/ whatever)* **is broken!** *(Picks up* **Clue 1,** *which is laying on the ground in front of him, reads it silently, then says:)* **Here's another mystery. I just found**

this strange clue. It says, "It's red or green." I wonder what that means? *(Looks around group for ideas, shrugs, then puts clue aside.)*

GERTY: Well, we need to get this tool fixed. I'll take it to the tool shop. Seeing this broken tool and talking about how much Doc and I need to weed reminded me of a story about another garden. Wait 'til you hear about it. It has snakes and fruit and . . . well, why don't we just tell you the story. How about it, Doc?

FOCUS ON THE BIBLE

Genesis 1:26-31; 2:4—3:23

(A2) Supplies:

- Bible
- Fragrant flower

Both site coordinators should tell the story, alternating back and forth. While they don't need to memorize the script word for word, the main points of the Scripture text should be given.

GERTY: *(Passes around a fragrant flower so kids can smell it.)* **I want you to imagine the most lovely garden that ever existed. It must have smelled sweeter than this flower you're passing around. This garden was not only perfect, it was the very first one ever made. God created it when He made the earth and all the animals. The Bible says God made this garden and named it Eden. It had so many wonderful flowers and trees that looked so beautiful. And it had tasty fruit to eat.** *(Smacks her lips.)* **Yum.**

DOC: I don't think we can really imagine how beautiful and wonderful Eden was. And it was always green and lush, never dried out, because God made rivers running through it. Now this wasn't a show garden, either. This was home for the first man and woman that God created. After He made Adam and Eve, the first people, He put them in charge over the garden and the animals. Wow. What a fun job—being a zookeeper over every kind of animal, and living in the perfect garden!

GERTY: *(Sighs.)* Sounds too good to be true. Adam and Eve not only got to live in this paradise and take care of the animals, they could eat almost everything God had put into the garden. What kinds of things do you think they had to eat from the garden? *(Let kids contribute ideas of types of produce.)* Oh, that sounds good! I wish I had a juicy peach right now!

DOC: But you couldn't eat it, because we're getting into the heart of this story now. Adam and Eve must have had such a special time in the Garden of Eden that God had made. Just about everything was theirs. All except one thing. There was one tree in the center of the garden that was different. God said, "You can eat from any tree in the garden, but you can't eat the fruit of the tree of the knowledge of good and evil. If you do that, you'll die."

GERTY: That's sounds fine, doesn't it? But then there was a problem. One day as Eve was enjoying the garden, a serpent, which is sort of like a snake, talked to her. This serpent was tricky and crafty, and it wanted Eve to break God's one rule. The serpent tried to confuse her and he told her a lie. Tell them what the serpent said, Doc.

DOC: The Bible says this serpent was crafty; he was sneaky. He asked Eve if God had said not to eat from any of the trees in the garden. Eve knew that wasn't right. She said that God told them they could eat from any tree except the one in the middle of the garden. "You won't die," said the serpent. "God knows if you eat the fruit on that tree, you'll become just like Him and know good and evil." That was a lie! But Eve believed it. She looked at the fruit and thought how yummy it might taste. It sure looked good. So she picked one and ate it. She even gave one to Adam and he ate it too.

GERTY: That was totally the wrong thing to do. Choosing to disobey God brought something new to the garden. Any clues what that might be? *(Let kids guess.)* It was sin. Sin is when you do something to disobey God. Sin made Adam and Eve feel ashamed. They didn't want God to know what they'd done, because they knew it was wrong. But they couldn't hide it.

DOC: That's right. That night, God Himself was walking in the garden. Adam and Eve didn't want God to know they had sinned, so they hid. God called, "Where are you?" God knew they were there. Adam and Eve felt even worse. God asked them what they'd done, and they had to admit that they had done the one thing God had said not to do. Everything was ruined in the garden for Adam and Eve. The sin had broken their friendship with God.

GERTY: Adam and Eve's sin couldn't be washed off with soap or buried like a rotten potato. Because of their sinfulness, God had to send them out of the garden forever. They had to work and sweat—just like we do today—because they weren't in the perfect garden anymore. God even put an angel with a flaming sword in front of the entrance to Eden so they could never get back in.

DOC: *(hold up broken tool)* **This broken tool is actually a clue, you know. What happened to this trowel has also happened to us. It's broken like our friendship with God is broken. Here's a clue why: S-I-N. Just like Adam and Eve's doing wrong broke their friendship with God, we've all sinned. We're separated from God too. We all need our sin taken care of. There's more to this story, because God made a way for us to have our sin taken care of. Because God loves you and me so much, because we're His creations just like Adam and Eve, God sent His only Son, Jesus, to earth. Jesus had never sinned. But Jesus took the punishment for our sins, so that we wouldn't have to be separated from God always. Jesus paid the price for our sins. You and I can** have our sin cleaned away by asking Jesus to forgive us for doing wrong. Then we won't have to be separated from God. We can enjoy His love and friendship.

GERTY: Every Detective can figure out the clues to how to have his or her sins forgiven, can't they, Doc? *(He nods.)* Asking Jesus to forgive us fixes our sin problem. I'm really glad God loves us enough to make a way to fix the sin problem we have. If any of you detectives are wondering about your sin and asking Jesus to forgive you, you can talk to one of the Investigators today. They'll help you understand it.

DOC: That's right. Well, we'd better fix this tool problem now, Gert, or the weeds will be even worse tomorrow. Let's get going to the tool shop. *(They leave.)*

Gather the Detectives and guide them to the area for the Bible memory activity.

BIBLE MEMORIZATION

(A3) Supplies:

- Small pieces of paper with 1 or 2 words of the verse printed on each.
- Inflated balloons, each with 1–2 words of the verse inside *(tape balloons into flower shapes)*. Have one "flower" for every 4–5 kids.

Clue 2 on dark paper: "Crunchy and sweet."

- Key Verse poster
- Key Verse Cards *(found on page R·60 in Resources)*
- Detective's Diaries *(found on page R·61-68 in Resources)*
- Tape

In Advance: Letter the verse on poster board so it's easily readable.

Early and Upper Elementary Verse

"For all have sinned, and come short of the glory of God." —**Romans 3:23**

Point to the words on the Key Verse poster as you lead the kids to read with you in unison. Ask: **Who does it say has sinned?** *(All, everyone.)* **What is sin?** *(Disobeying God; anything that goes against God's Word, the Bible.)* **Name some examples of sin.** *(Try to get everyone to contribute one idea; correct mistakes, add other sins the kids can relate to if they don't say them. These may include lying, stealing, cheating, etc.)* **According to this verse, what happens because each one of us has sinned?** *(We fall short of the glory of God. By doing things our way instead of God's we separate ourselves from God. God hasn't sinned, but when we do, we aren't able to be friends with God anymore.)*

This verse is really important. It tells us we have a major problem in our lives. But God knows this. He gave us a solution to this problem by letting Jesus take the punishment for our sins.

Explain that this game will help kids learn the verse while they use their detective skills. Inside the "petals" of each "flower" are parts of Romans 3:23. Each group needs to pop the balloons to get out the verse parts, and then put them in order. Tell kids they can use the poster to help know the order for the words.

Give a "balloon flower" to each group of four to 5 kids. Let kids go to work popping the balloons however they choose, then figuring out the verse order. When someone discovers **Clue 2**, let them read it *(with help if necessary)* and see if anyone can solve the mystery. If not, put the clue aside for later.

When the activity is done, have the groups stand in clusters around the area. Have each group shout out a word of the verse as you point to them, so that the verse is shouted in proper order. When done, lead everyone in clapping and cheering.

Before moving on to the Music Time, tape each child's Key Verse Card in his or her Detective's Diary.

MUSIC TIME

It Is No Mystery

(A4) Supplies:

- Copy of song lyrics for each child or have the words on an overhead transparency *(pages R · 21-26)*
- *Good News Clues*™ CD or tape copy of "It Is No Mystery" *(Track 2)*
- CD or tape player
- Overhead projector
- Puppet *(optional)*

Have the children listen to the song for this site, "It Is No Mystery." Play the song again and have the kids join in with the singing. Allow them to stand and move around if you have the space. If age-appropriate, project the words of the song onto a screen for the children to follow along as they sing. You may want to have BOSWORTH help teach the song.

GUMSHOE GRUB

Gardener's Delight

(S1) Supplies:

- Healthy veggies to dip, such as carrot sticks, celery sticks, cucumber slices, and other vegetables

- One or two soft dips, such as ranch dip *(already prepared or use your own recipe)* or vegetable dip

- Small paper plates

- Spoons for dip

Directions: Place small containers of the dips on tables where all the children can reach them. Explain what flavors the dips are. Have children spoon some dip on a small paper plate and take a few vegetables for dipping. Serve with juice or water. **NOTE: Beware of dairy allergies.**

Crepe Paper Apples

(S2) Supplies:

- Red crepe paper cut into 10-inch circles, one per child

- Pretzels, small crackers, or candy

- Green floral tape or green twist ties

- Bushel baskets

Directions: Cut the red crepe paper into 10-inch circles. Place a handful of pretzels, small crackers, or candy in center of crepe paper circles. Gather the crepe paper to form a ball, securing with

green floral tape or green twist ties. Place your "apples" in bushel baskets to serve. Also serve juice or water.

CASE-CRACKING GAMES

Produce Stand

(G1) Supplies:

- Ball

Any size group from six kids and up can play this game. Whisper a type of fruit or vegetable to each player, using a master list of produce on a board for everyone's reference. Tell them they need to remember their fruit or veggie. One player starts with the ball, while others cluster around that player. The ball holder throws the ball straight up into the air as far as possible and calls out a fruit or vegetable. Whoever has that name runs to get the ball while everyone else scatters. Once the player catches the ball, he shouts "garden time." Everyone freezes wherever they are. The ball holder can take 3 large steps *(adjust for playing area and kids)* and then throws or rolls the ball to hit someone below the waist. If successful, the hit person takes the ball and is the next to toss it and call a fruit/vegetable name. If the thrower misses, he remains the ball tosser for the next round. Play until kids are tired or time's up.

Dig It

(G2) Supplies:

- Dirt/potting soil

- Buckets *(two per five to eight kids)*

- Plastic spoons

- Plastic cups

Half fill half of the buckets with soil. Put a

plastic spoon and cup in each soil bucket. Place one soil bucket and one empty bucket at one end of the play area, with groups lined up at the opposite end. Divide into groups of five to eight. Kids will take turns racing to the bucket and spooning dirt into the cup. When you blow the whistle or yell "time," the players dump their cups into the empty bucket then race back, and the next player runs to the bucket. Add variety by varying the amount of time players have to get dirt into the cup. At the end of the playing time *(after everyone goes twice, or after a certain length of time)*, the group with the most dirt in their bucket wins. *(Expect lots of ties, and congratulate everyone all around.)*

PUTTING THE PIECES TOGETHER

Scratch Paper Bookmarks

(C1) Supplies:

- Scratch paper *(art paper that has multicolors underneath a layer of black)* cut into 1-3/4" x 8" strips, one per child

- Satin ribbon cut into 12" lengths, one per child

- Wooden scratching tools or paperclips, one per child

- Hole punch

In Advance: Cut scratch paper into 1-3/4" x 8" strips. Punch a hole in the top. *(Note: Scratch paper can be found in art supply stores or online.)*

Directions: Using a wooden scratching tool or paperclip, have students create a garden scene of flowers on the bookmark by

scratching off the top black layer. The Bible memory verse can also be scratched onto the bookmark if desired. Attach one piece of ribbon to the bookmark by folding the ribbon in half, pulling the folded end of the ribbon through the hole, then pulling the ribbon ends through the ribbon loop.

Garden Flower Pots

(C2) Supplies:

- Gel pens or markers made to draw on dark paper

- Dark-colored paper cups *(If unavailable, use another cup and cover it with dark construction paper.)*

- Potting Soil

- Scoop for potting soil

- Small annual flowers or nontoxic houseplants, one per child

- Clear self-adhesive paper

Directions: Using the gel pens, have students decorate the dark paper cups with a floral design and the Key Bible Verse. When the decorating is complete, have students *(assisted by Investigator's Assistants)* cover the outside of the cups with clear self-adhesive paper for protection from water damage. Allow students to scoop about 3/4 cups of potting soil into the cups. Place one small flower on top of the soil. Then add more soil to fill the cup to about a half-inch from the top of the cup.

ELEMENTARY DEDUCTION

(A5) Supplies:

- Dark beads
- Lacing or cord
- Detective's Diaries *(found on page R·61-68 in Resources)*
- Crayons, colored pencils, markers
- *Emily's Bracelet (optional)*
- Treasure Basket

Clue 3 on dark paper: "They grow on trees and are a favorite snack. You'll find this treasure in a basket in the garden."

Remind kids of the broken tool Gerty and Doc showed them. Ask: **How is the broken tool like their relationship with God?** *(Clarify that because we all have done wrong, we've sinned. Our sin made us become separated from God.)* Ask: **How did God make it possible for our friendship with Him to be fixed?** *(Summarize that Jesus, God's Son who never sinned, died in our place and took the punishment for our sin.)* **When we ask His forgiveness for doing wrong, our relationship with God is restored. God loves us so much He doesn't want us to be separated from Him.**

Hand out a bead to each child along with plastic lace. Explain that each day they'll be adding a bead onto their choker or bracelet *(see directions in Resources, page R·69)* that reminds them what they learned from the Bible that day. This site's bead is dark, which stands for sin.

Next hand out the Detective's Diaries. As you're doing so, let **Clue 3** flutter to the ground. Look surprised as you pick it up. Read the first part aloud: **"They grow on trees and are a favorite snack."** Ask children to help you solve the mystery.

Then read the last part of the clue, **"You'll find this treasure in a basket in the garden,"** so they can find the treasure. They can eat at an apple slice while working on their Detective's Diaries.

Have the Detectives turn to the page for The Garden. Read the directions together. Allow the Detectives to work with a friend while completing this page. Be available to help answer questions and talk about the activity as needed. Assistant Investigators should also be available to assist with this part of the lesson.

When the children have finished working in their diaries, gather them together into a large group. If you have time, you may want to read the book *Emily's Bracelet (©2004, available from Cook Communications Ministries, 1-800-323-7543)* and talk about the story. It will help the children begin to understand more about the colors used in each of the sites. It will also help them get a grasp of the choker or bracelet that they are making throughout the week.

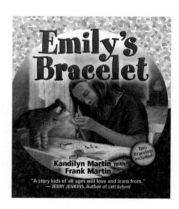

DETECTIVES' DEPARTURE

(A6) Supplies:

- "The Quest Continues" take-home paper, one per child

- Craft projects from the day

Conclude the time in the site with singing a rousing version of "It Is No Mystery" *(Site One song)*. Ask everyone to close their eyes while you pray that each will discover this week that they can have their friendship with God fixed and their sins forgiven. Have the kids collect their crafts and personal items to take home. Be sure each child has a copy of "The Quest Continues" to take home.

Today your child visited a lovely garden and found out that Adam and Eve sinned when they disobeyed God (*Genesis 1:26-31; 2:4—3:23*). Their sin separated them from God, so their friendship with Him was broken. This matters because the Bible says every person has sinned and has a broken relationship with God. God has made a way for our relationship with Him to be fixed and our sins forgiven, through trusting in Jesus Christ.

For more information about *Good News Clues*™ VBS and what your child is learning, go online to **www.CookVBS.com**. This site will help you and your child better understand how to restore your relationship to God and enjoy the life He's given you.

TALK IT OUT

Why does disobedience hurt your relationships in your home?

How does doing wrong (sinning) **make you feel? Now how do you feel when you've resisted a temptation and not sinned?**

FAMILY STUFF

A Bite of Temptation

Point: Sin ends up disappointing you.

Supplies:

- An excellent looking apple. Cut a wedge from the back of the apple and hollow it out as much as possible without breaking the skin. Replace the apple flesh with as many cotton balls as possible, then replace the wedge, "gluing" it closed with a few dabs of honey or peanut butter.

- A blindfold

- A sharp knife

Activity: Set the apple on a table, placed so the cut side is in back and out of view of the kids.

Explain that this activity teaches about how sin disappoints us. Ask for a volunteer to eat an apple. Tell the volunteer that you'll cut the apple for them to eat. Expect surprise and dismay when the apple is sliced and the cotton is found inside.

Talk about how sin is like this activity.

How does sin disappoint you? (*When you disobey you end up getting in trouble. Sometimes the sin isn't worth the punishment. A guilty conscience also results and gives lots of anxiety and stress.*)

What are some of the temptations that are hardest for you to resist? (*Let everyone share their ideas. Adults should contribute too.*)

How does your sin affect others? (*Again, let family members share their thoughts. You might take an example of a sin they can relate to, and have everyone contribute to describing how that sin affects others in your home and even outside it.*)

God's Word tells us every person has sinned. That means we've all broken our friendship with Him. But we can be very thankful that God didn't leave us in our sin. He made a way that we can fix our friendship with him. That way is through Jesus. Read Romans 3:23, then Romans 6:23.

BIBLE VERSE

"For all have sinned, and come short of the glory of God."
– Romans 3:23

site2

PASSION WEEK
Last Supper

*"While we were yet sinners,
Christ died for us."*

Romans 5:8

Why Kids Need to Know
That Jesus Is the Only Way of Salvation

In contemporary socio-political society, tolerance for everyone's view is expected and even legislated in some instances. The view that there is one way to forgiveness of sin and eternity in heaven could be considered exclusionary and narrow-minded. Many children may have been exposed to mindsets such as there are many roads to God, or as long as you're a good person God will receive you into heaven. Rather than debate and argue with an outspoken child, pray silently for the Holy Spirit to show each child the truth.

Especially when working with children unfamiliar to a church setting, stay away from "church language" and use more familiar, common wording for biblical truths. Children will more readily understand the principles of sin and salvation if they hear words, word pictures, and examples they can relate to.

factoid

Invisible inks have been used since A.D. 600. George Washington used invisible ink to send secret military communications during the British occupation of New York in 1776. Invisible inks fall into two categories: sympathetic and organic. Sympathetic inks are visible when applied, then disappear when dry. To read these inked messages, a chemical is applied to the paper to cause the ink to show up again. Organic inks, made from substances like vinegar, milk, or fruit juice, become visible again when the writing surface is heated.

The topic of Jesus' death can be upsetting for younger children and draw questions about the fairness of it from older kids. Many children will have experienced the death of someone they know, and will connect that experience with Jesus' death. While it's a central and essential fact in our salvation, you can teach it without dwelling too long on it. Be willing to answer questions during the session or afterward.

Getting More from the Bible Story

A large, hefty serving of Scripture is covered in Site Two, the Dining Room—the final week of Christ's life, culminating in His death, burial, and resurrection. Many children may not have heard this story in its entirety, or might know just some of the facts and details you'll be relating.

Christ's entrance into Jerusalem at the start of the Passover is in stark contrast to the events a week later. His riding into the city on a donkey's colt was itself a clear announcement of His kingship and fulfilled Zechariah's prophecy of 500 years earlier (*Zech. 9:9*). This is one of the rare recorded instances when Jesus' kingship and majesty were recognized on earth.

Jerusalem was crowded with Jewish people, since all Jewish males age 12 and older had to go to Jerusalem for the Passover festival and the weeklong festival of unleavened bread which followed. Four days after entering the city on the donkey's colt, Christ shares with His closest friends His last meal before His death.

In the upstairs room, Jesus and the disciples shared what was both a ritual meal and a symbolic event. Jesus used two parts of the meal—passing around bread and drinking wine—to demonstrate the significance of what would soon be happening.

In Matthew 26:28, Jesus states that the fruit of the vine represents His blood of the covenant. Until His crucifixion, people had to approach God and have their sins forgiven through a priest and animal sacrifices. The new covenant means that individuals can approach God directly through the sacrifice of Christ.

The Last Supper

"While we were yet sinners, Christ died for us."

This is the **Dining Room**, with mice who would be small in relation to human furnishings. You can create a wall scene of a dining table and chairs larger than life, or make fake furniture from cardboard. An alternative is to have mouse-sized furnishings—table, chairs, dishes, etc., where the mice are seated.

Site Mission

Children will learn that Jesus died, was buried, and rose again to forgive their sins and provide the way for salvation.

Key Bible Verses

Early Elementary

"While we were yet sinners, Christ died for us." —**Romans 5:8**

Upper Elementary

"But God commendeth his love toward us, in that, while we were yet sinners, Christ died for us."
—**Romans 5:8**

Site Coordinators

■ **Maxie**

■ **Marshall**

Maxie and Marshall Mouse, two mice that live in the dining room, eating the scraps and crumbs humans leave behind. Portray the characters by wearing gray or brown clothing. Make some large ears and long tails; add whiskers.

Puppet Option

Investigator #2 or an Assistant Investigator can operate

BOSWORTH to help lead the children to different areas and interact spontaneously with the teacher and children. *(See puppet pattern for BOSWORTH on pages R·55-59.)*

Bible Passage

Matthew 21:1-11; 26:17-29; 26:47—28:10

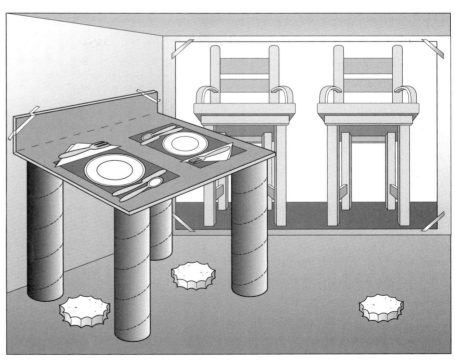

Investigator's Inventory

General

- [ ] Dining Room mural
- [ ] *Good News Clues*™ CD or tape copy
- [ ] CD player or cassette tape player
- [ ] Copy of "The Quest Continues" student take-home paper *(page E2 · 14)* for each child
- [ ] Copy of the "Detective's Diary" for each child *(pages R · 61-68)*. Note the two age levels and use accordingly.

Games and Activities

- [ ] Two large bread rolls
- [ ] Plate of bite-size crackers or bread pieces spread with grape jelly
- [ ] Clues written on red paper
- [ ] Dining table shapes *(spoon, knife, fork, plate, and napkin)*
- [ ] Key Verse poster
- [ ] Key Verse Cards *(page R · 60)*
- [ ] Copy of song lyrics for each child or have the words on an overhead transparency *(pages R · 21-26)*
- [ ] Overhead projector
- [ ] Puppet *(optional)*
- [ ] White towel or cloth *(one per team)*
- [ ] Tray *(one per team)*
- [ ] Plastic plate and cup *(one set per team)*
- [ ] Knife, fork, spoon *(one set per team)*
- [ ] Napkin *(one per team)*
- [ ] An assortment of crackers, cheese cubes, apple wedges, juice or milk, carrot sticks
- [ ] Index cards, numbered 1 through 6

- [ ] Bleach
- [ ] Red food coloring
- [ ] Measuring spoons
- [ ] Water in 2 clear glass cups
- [ ] Red beads
- [ ] Lacing
- [ ] *Emily's Bracelet*
- [ ] Clusters of grapes on a plate

Snacks

- [ ] A variety of pieces of red fruit, such as cherries, watermelon balls, or strawberries
- [ ] A variety of red candies such as red licorice, red sour balls, red hots, etc.
- [ ] Small paper cups
- [ ] Matzo crackers or other crackers
- [ ] Cheese slices *(American, Swiss, cheddar, etc.)*
- [ ] Knife for slicing cheese

Crafts

- [ ] Clear photo key chains, one per child
- [ ] White and red drawing paper, one each per child
- [ ] Thin-line markers
- [ ] Inexpensive white fabric placemats or white fabric cut to the size of placemats and hemmed
- [ ] Fabric markers

Procedures of the Day

10 minutes: Preparing to Search

15–20 minutes: Focus on the Bible

10 minutes: Bible Memorization

5 minutes: Music Time

15 minutes: Gumshoe Grub

20 minutes: Case-Cracking Games

20 minutes: Putting the Pieces Together

10 minutes: Elementary Deduction

10 minutes: Detectives' Departure

Detective Preparation

- Have craft samples prepared in advance to show Detectives.

- Be sure all supplies are gathered and your site is ready each day for Detectives to arrive.

- Post the Procedures of the Day where Investigators and helpers (called Assistant Investigators) can refer to it.

- Address each other by site titles. Children should be referred to as Detectives. The helpers that go with them from camp to camp are called Assistant Investigators—Assistant Investigator Jim or Assistant Investigator Sharon.

- After taking attendance, an Assistant Investigator should tell those responsible for refreshments how many Detectives are present to be prepared for snack time.

- In advance, write all the clues for the day's hidden treasure onto the color of paper indicated.

- You may wish to do some background research into the Bible story. Refer to Bible commentaries, encyclopedias, and dictionaries for additional information.

 **PREPARING TO SEARCH**

(A7) Supplies:

- Two large bread rolls

- Plate of bite-size crackers or bread pieces spread with grape jelly

- Napkins (just in case)

 Clue 1 written on red paper: "You'll find them in clusters."

Maxie and Marshall are nibbling in mouse-like fashion on pieces of bread when children enter. Don't acknowledge kids until an Investigator clears throat or other prearranged signal.

MARSHALL: Oh! (Startled.) Uh, Maxie, did you see that we have company?

Maxie is enjoying her food, looks up, and is astonished. Both greet the group, welcome them to the Dining Room and introduce themselves, then continue gnawing now and then.

MARSHALL: Excuse us for eating while you're here, but we've been hungry for days. The family who lives here has been on vacation, and their dining room's been empty until this morning.

MAXIE: I sure liked that bread they had this morning. It tastes so good!

MARSHALL: And you got the biggest crumbs, Maxie. I was under the other side of the table. (Sighs.)

MAXIE: But you were in the perfect spot to get that bread with . . . well, whatever it was.

MARSHALL: (Makes a puzzled face.) I still can't figure out what it is. It doesn't taste like filling from a toaster pastry. It's not ketchup, or honey. It's . . . oh I don't know how to describe it. And I'm not sure I should even eat it.

MAXIE: Why not? It's good even if what it's called is a mystery.

LEADER: A mystery? Did you say this food you found is a mystery? Do I have news for you! These **kids** *(gestures toward the children)* **are not just your ordinary bunch of children. These are Detectives, and they're always on the lookout for mysteries to solve. Right, kids?** *(Lead kids to nod, say yes.)*

MARSHALL: **You mean you all like to solve mysteries? Do you know how to do that?** *(Kids should nod and agree.)*

MAXIE AND MARSHALL:
(Smile at each other and say together.): **Cool!**

MAXIE: **Here's one clue about this mysterious food that**

someone at the dining room table left behind for us. **"It's purple!"**

MARSHALL: **And it's sticky. I had to clean my paws every time I touched it.**

MAXIE: **Marsh, we should just let these Detectives try it for themselves. The taste of this mysterious stuff is the best clue.**

MARSHALL: **Well, ok. As long as they don't eat it all. I want to keep some.**

*(Mice confer with backs turned, like they're getting something ready. When they turn around, they'll have a plate or tray of small crackers or small squares of bread spread with grape jelly. Also put on the tray the red paper with **Clue 1**. Leaders can pass the tray around, notice clue, and ask a child to read it. Tell the kids that until you have more information, you can save the clue for now.)*

MARSHALL: Now smell it first.

MAXIE: And touch it! It's sticky, I tell you. After you have clues about the smell and feel, try it.

(Let kids give their conclusions about the mysterious substance—grape jelly.)

MARSHALL: Grape jelly? Is that it? I've had strawberry jam and maple syrup. I sure like those. But I've never had grape jelly. What can I say? Thanks for helping us figure this out. I hope they have this again. I like it.

MAXIE: Speaking of supper, didn't you say you were going

to tell me about some famous supper somewhere? Now that I'm full *(Stretches, settles self comfortably.),* I'm ready for a good story. These detectives might like to hear it too.

Investigators should have kids stretch for a moment, then find a comfortable position to listen to the story.

FOCUS ON THE BIBLE

Matthew 21:1-11; 26:17-29; 26:47—28:10

(A8) Supplies:

■ Bible

Both site coordinators should tell the story, alternating back and forth. While they don't need to memorize the script word for word, the main points of the Scripture text should be given.

MAXIE: Marshall, I think you might have heard this story about the Last Supper before. It's not a made-up story. It's the story of the last meal Jesus had with His disciples before He died on the cross.

MARSHALL: I do know that one. It starts when Jesus came to Jerusalem at the beginning of the Jewish festival called Passover. Jesus actually rode into the city on a donkey, and a crowd of people came out to welcome Him. It was like a parade! People called out "Hosanna: Blessed is the King of Israel that cometh in the name of Lord!" Jesus, God's Son, was the main attraction of this parade.

MAXIE: Yes, people were excited to welcome Him. That week Jesus and His disciples, the 12 men who were Jesus' closest friends, ate the Passover dinner together. It was a very special dinner. Jesus did some things that the disciples thought were mysterious, because they didn't understand what was going to happen in the next few days. At this special Passover dinner, Jesus took some bread. He thanked God for it and broke it into pieces and said that the bread was an example of His own body. He gave it to the disciples to eat.

MARSHALL: I wonder what they were thinking, because then Jesus took a cup. He did the same thing with the cup. He thanked God for it, and then passed the cup around for each of them to take a drink. While they were each having a sip, Jesus told them that what they were drinking was an example of His own blood. He said that His blood would pay for the sins of many people. And then He said He wouldn't be drinking again until He would drink it with them in His Father's kingdom. The disciples must have been even more surprised by these mysterious words.

MAXIE: That was only the beginning of the surprises that night. After Jesus and His 12 friends ate this last supper, they went to a garden. Soldiers rushed into the garden and arrested Jesus. They took Him to the house of a religious ruler. All through the night, different rulers asked Jesus if He was really God's Son. He was treated very badly. Finally one of the rulers said that Jesus would be killed because He said He was God's Son.

MARSHALL: It was awful. Jesus had never sinned, or done anything wrong. He didn't deserve to die. But He knew that was God's plan. Jesus let Himself be killed on the cross so His blood would be the payment for everyone's sins. God let people kill Jesus, His Son, because it was the only way for people to be able to be free of their own sins. Jesus took the place of people who are sinners—that's you, me, and everyone.

MAXIE: You're right, Marshall, but the story isn't done yet. The best part is still to come. After Jesus died, He was buried in a tomb, sort of a cave. The rulers wanted to be sure no one got into the tomb. There was already a big rock that had been put over the opening. So soldiers were ordered to seal the stone in place and guard the tomb. But those things didn't matter at all. Since God is more powerful than any ruler or group of soldiers, or any huge boulder, there was a big surprise waiting two days later.

MARSHALL: I want to tell them this part. It's so awesome. On the third day after He had been buried in the tomb, Jesus came back to life. God is more powerful even than death! His plan all along had been for Jesus to die and

His blood to be the payment for people's sins. Then by coming back to life, Jesus proved that He was God's Son, and that God was all powerful. Because He came back to life, He proved He's the only way we can have our sins forgiven. Then we can have a friendship with God and one day live in heaven with Him.

MAXIE: I think the next thing you get to do helps you understand this even better. But at any time today if you want to talk to a grown-up about your sins and Jesus dying for you, just tell one of the Investigators.

Gather the Detectives and guide them to the area for the Bible memory activity.

BIBLE MEMORIZATION

(A9) Supplies:

■ Dining table shapes *(spoon, knife, fork, plate, and napkin—patterns found on page R · 54 in Resources)*

■ Key Verse poster

■ Key Verse Cards *(found on page R · 60 in Resources)*

■ Detective's Diary *(found on page R · 61-68 in Resources)*

■ Tape

Clue 2 on red paper: "They come in green, purple, and even black colors."

In Advance: Write the Key Verse in segments on large cardboard cut-out shapes of a spoon, knife, fork, plate, and napkin. On the back of one of the shapes, tape the red **Clue 2.** Write the verse on a poster.

Early Elementary

"While we were yet sinners, Christ died for us." —**Romans 5:8**

Upper Elementary

"But God commendeth his love toward us, in that, while we were yet sinners, Christ died for us." —**Romans 5:8**

Teach the children the verse by reading it slowly together while you point to the words. Say it at least three times together. Then have kids take turns practicing this way: Choose five kids and give each one of the cardboard shapes. Have them "set the table" in order so they spell out the verse. Ask everyone else to read it as they've created it, then scramble them up and have another five kids do it. Vary the activity by having kids hold shapes and line up in correct order. Conclude this activity by reciting the verse in unison as a group.

Note: When a child discovers **Clue 2**, have the child read it *(with help if needed)*. Ask if anyone has discovered what the clues mean. If not, tell kids you can put the clue aside until you find out more.

Tape Key Verse cards in Detective's Diaries before children go to the game time.

MUSIC TIME

Be Brave and Tell

(A10) Supplies:

- Copy of song lyrics for each child or have the words on an overhead transparency *(pages R·21-26)*
- *Good New Clues*™ CD or tape copy of "Be Brave and Tell" *(Track 3)*
- CD or tape player
- Overhead projector
- Puppet *(optional)*

Teach "Be Brave and Tell" by playing the CD and having the children listen. Then encourage the children to sing along the next time you play it. If age-appropriate, project the words of the song onto a screen for the children to follow along as they sing. If you are using the puppet option, have BOSWORTH help teach the song.

GUMSHOE GRUB

Red Hot Snacks

(S3) Supplies:

- A variety of pieces of red fruit such as cherries, watermelon balls, or strawberries
- A variety of red candies such as red licorice, red sour balls, red hots, etc.
- Small paper cups
- Napkins

In Advance: If serving cherries, you may want to remove the seeds prior to serving. Wash and prepare all fruit into bite sized pieces.

Directions: Allow the children to spoon a few different pieces of fruit or candy into a small cup. **NOTE: Be aware of allergies to strawberries or red food coloring. If serving to younger children, be sure to remove all seeds. Do not serve small, hard candies to young children.**

Passover Feast

(S4) Supplies

- Matzo crackers or other crackers
- Cheese Slices *(American, Swiss, cheddar, etc.)*
- Napkins
- Sharp knife for slicing cheese

In Advance: Slice cheese into small pieces. Arrange on a plate or tray by kinds so that children can select two or three pieces to eat on their crackers.

Directions: Explain to the children that Matzo crackers are used today by many Jewish people to celebrate the Passover. In Jesus' day, the bread that they used for Passover was made without leaven *(yeast)*. Matzo crackers are also made without leaven.

Let children select a few crackers and pieces of cheese for their snack today. **NOTE: Be aware of dairy allergies.**

CASE CRACKING GAMES

In Advance: Write **Clue 3** on red paper *(see below)* and put it into the game you choose, attached to a prop or within the playing area. When found, read it aloud and ask if anyone has solved the mystery. If not, save the clue for the end of the day.

Clue 3 written on red paper: "Sweet juices flow from these round shapes."

Waiter Relay

(G3) Supplies

- White towel or cloth *(one per team)*
- Tray *(one per team)*
- Plastic cup *(one per team)*
- Plastic plate *(one per team)*
- Plastic knife, fork, spoon *(one set per team)*
- Napkin *(one per team)*

This game can be played in a large circle or a long line. Divide kids into groups of five. Besides the starting line, there will be four other areas where group members will stand. Teams break up so that each of the five stations *(starting line plus four others)* has a member of each team there. Station each group an equal distance from each other, either in a circle or line. At each station, there is one relay item *(in this*

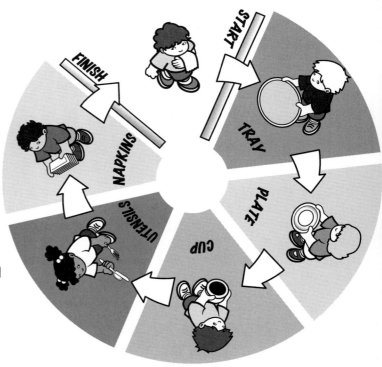

order: tray, plate, cup, utensils, napkin). At the starting signal, players at station one place the towel over their arms, "waiter" style, and race walk to next station, handing towel to next player on their team. That player, with towel in place, picks up a tray and race-walks to next station, hands off both to third player who adds a plate. Relay continues until each team's final players are racewalking back to starting point with tray of dining items, towel over their arm. First to arrive with all items intact wins. Play again the same way, or have players walk backward.

Eat Your Dinner

(G4) Supplies:

- An assortment of crackers, cheese cubes, apple wedges, juice or milk, and carrot sticks
- Table, placemats, candlesticks, place settings
- Index cards numbered 1 through 6

This is also a relay. Set up a dining room table *(make it as simple or elegant as you desire)* with placemats, candlesticks, place settings, etc. Each team needs at least six players *(if fewer, some can take two turns)*. Set the table with enough place settings and chairs so each team has a place. Set each place with a numbered card and one item of food on each card *(crackers #1, apple #2, etc.)*. Teams line up at other end of play space from the table. At starting signal, first players of each team run *(or your choice of movement, such as hopping, etc.)* to table, sit down, and eat first item. The whole thing has to be chewed and swallowed before player leaves table, runs back and tags next player who eats #2 item.

If you want to, add bonus points for the neatest team or one with best manners.

Note: Be aware of any food allergies.

PUTTING THE PIECES TOGETHER

Key Chains

(C3) Supplies:

- Clear photo key chains, one per child
- White drawing paper, one per child
- Red drawing paper, one per child
- Thin-line markers

In Advance: Cut the drawing paper into 2-1/4" x 3-1/4" pieces or a size that fits into the clear key chains. On the red drawing paper, type or print the Key Bible Verse for the day.

Directions: On the precut white drawing paper, have students draw a self-portrait using the thin line markers. Give each student a piece of the red drawing paper with the Key Bible Verse. Have them put the plain sides of the white and red pieces back-to-back. Then, have students insert the two pieces into the photo holder on the key chain. One side should show the drawing they made while the other side shows the Key Bible Verse.

Fabric Placemats

(C4) Supplies:

- Inexpensive white fabric placemats or white fabric cut to the size of placemats and hemmed
- Fabric markers
- Scissors and sewing machines if making placemats *(optional)*

In Advance: If using white fabric, cut into individual pieces the size of average placemats and hem.

Directions: Using fabric markers, have students decorate their placemats by illustrating the Bible story or today's Key Bible Verse. They can draw one symbol that will remind them of the story or draw a more elaborate illustration.

To preserve the drawings, have an adult iron the placemats according to the directions on the marker box.

ELEMENTARY DEDUCTION

(A11) Supplies:

- Bleach
- Red food coloring
- Measuring spoons
- Water, 2 clear glass cups
- Red beads
- Lacing
- Detective's Diary *(found on page R·61-68 in Resources)*
- Crayons, colored pencils, markers
- *Emily's Bracelet (optional)*
- Clusters of grapes on a plate

Clue 4 on red paper: "Its juice was part of the last supper Jesus shared with His disciples. You'll find some of these fruits _____" *(add a location where you've placed a couple of clusters of grapes.)*

Hand out a red bead to each child along with plastic lace or cord. *(See Resources, page R·69, for directions.)*

This site's bead is red. What did you learn today that gave you clues about what red stands for? *(Learned about the Last Supper, the death and resurrection of Jesus, His blood paying for our sins, etc.)* As they put on the bead, review:

Today you found out about the Last Supper Jesus shared with His closest friends. Then Jesus died and was buried. And because He's God He came back to life. He did this because it's the only way for any person, including you and me, to be able to have our sins forgiven. We've all done wrong things. Those wrong things have broken the friendship we could have with God, who loves us. Jesus' dying and coming back to life has given us a chance to be forgiven. Then we can look forward to being in heaven forever.

Jesus died in our place. His blood paid the punishment we deserve for our sins. The red bead you're adding stands for Jesus' blood.

Now here's a mysterious experiment to help you understand this even better.

Have both of the glasses not more than 1/3 full of water. Make sure all the kids can see as you add 3 drops of red food coloring to one glass and stir. To the second glass, add one tablespoon of bleach and stir *(separate spoon)*. Then pour the red water into the glass of clear water. **In a while you'll see a change in the color of this red water. We'll keep our eye on it while you work on your Detective's Diaries.**

Hand out diaries so children can do the activity on the Dining Room page. When they're done, have them check the water glass. It should be mostly or completely clear. **When you tell Jesus you're sorry for your sins, He'll forgive you. Like the red water was changed to clear, Jesus' blood cleans the sin you've done. Every one of us needs our sins taken care of, and only Jesus can do that, because He died on the cross for us.**

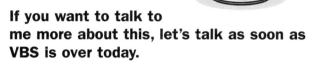

If you want to talk to me more about this, let's talk as soon as VBS is over today.

Before concluding the day, "find" the last clue as you clean up the experiment you just did. Before you read it, bring out the other three red clues and reread them in order, then add the last one. Don't read the line about the location until children have had a chance to solve the mystery. Once they do, read where they'll find the grapes. If the children don't solve the mystery, help them by going over the main points of the Bible story up to where Jesus passes the cup.

If you have time, you may want to read the book *Emily's Bracelet* (©2004, available from Cook Communications Ministries, 1-800-323-7543) and talk about the story. It will help the children begin to understand more about the colors used in each of the sites. It will also help them get

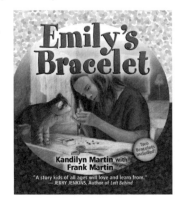

a grasp of the choker or bracelet that they are making throughout the week.

DETECTIVES' DEPARTURE

(A12) Supplies:

- "The Quest Continues" take-home paper, one per child
- Craft projects from the day

Collect the Detective's Diaries and chokers/bracelets. Gather in a circle. Ask children to show you with their expressions how they feel about Jesus dying. Have them show you how they would feel if they were the first ones to find the tomb empty. Then they can show you expressions of how it feels to have their sins forgiven.

Ask children to say the memory verse for you or with you. Pray briefly, thanking God that He allowed His Son, Jesus, to die so that each child there can be forgiven and have a friendship with God. Dismiss children, giving out crafts and "The Quest Continues" take-home papers to take home.

Today your child got the inside story about the week of Jesus' life leading up to His resurrection. They learned about the last supper Christ shared with His closest friends, how His death means we can have our sins forgiven because of His sacrifice, and how Jesus came back to life, proving He is God.

Go online to **www.CookVBS.com** for more information about *Good News Clues*™ VBS and what your child is experiencing each day.

TALK IT OUT

Has someone else ever taken the punishment that you deserved? How did that feel?

What difference does it make that Jesus came back to life?

FAMILY STUFF

Only One Way

Point: Jesus is the only way of salvation.

Supplies:

- Variety of keys and one lock—padlock, door, etc. *(Keep the one key that unlocks it separate until later in the activity.)*

Activity: Bring out or direct the family to the lock and ask **How many ways are there to open this lock?** Challenge family members to unlock the lock using the keys you've collected *(but not the one that actually works)*, as well as a paper clip, hair pin, or other items they think will work. Let them keep trying until they give up. Then produce the correct key and allow someone to unlock the lock.

How many ways did you try to get this lock open? *(Together, count how many different attempts they made.)*

How many keys actually opened the lock? *(One.)*

Before continuing your discussion, you may want to move to another area and have everyone sit down. **There were lots of useful keys here. But even a beautiful antique key or a very strong one wouldn't have been able to do the job. Only one key can open the lock. That's an example of Jesus being the only way of salvation. People have many ideas of how they can have their sins forgiven, or how they will one day live in heaven. Jesus says He's the one and only way, just like there's only one key to unlock this lock.** Open your Bible and read John 14:1-6. Explain that Jesus was speaking to His disciples, telling them that there is only one way to have eternal life—through Jesus. This is the same way that you and I can receive Jesus as Savior and know that we will live in heaven for eternity. You may want to review the passages studied in Matthew 21:1-11; 26:17-29; 26:47—28:10.

Encourage all family members to read and memorize the Bible verse listed below. For young children, have them memorize the part of the verse that is in bold print.

BIBLE VERSE

*(Early-elementary verse in **bold** type.)*

*"But God commendeth his love toward us, in that, **while we were yet sinners, Christ died for us.**"*
—**Romans 5:8**

Prodigal Son

"For God so loved the world, that he gave his only begotten Son, that whosoever believeth in him should not perish, but have everlasting life." **John 3:16**

Why Kids Need to Discover That They Can Be Forgiven and Know Jesus as Their Savior

Even with the range of ages in your VBS, every child can relate to his or her need and desire for forgiveness. All your students know they have done wrong and that it causes problems in their family relationships. Many younger children may not be able to verbalize or even consciously understand how sin affects their relationships at home. But each one will certainly be able to identify with the prodigal son in some way, if only in wistfulness for the way the father lovingly and unconditionally welcomed his son home. This act of forgiveness will help every child envision the picture of how the heavenly Father has open arms, inviting each child to come to Him for full forgiveness.

Some children may not have experienced the unconditional forgiveness that God offers. It might seem impossible or unrealistic

Getting More from the Bible Story

The prodigal son parable is an illustration of a sinner's relationship with God. This willful, selfish son demanded his inheritance—one third of the estate—early *(Deut. 21:17)*. Typically he would have received it at the father's death. His request also showed great disrespect of his father's authority. The son's experiences after leaving home signify how far one can plunge when left to one's own worldly choices. Where he was once a rich young man, he became a slave of another. Just like before knowing Christ, we're all slaves to sin. Often it takes sorrow and failure to bring us to realize our need for God.

Upon his return to his father, repentant and aware of his need for help, the son receives grace and mercy, just as God offers to us. The father was quick to hug and physically welcome his son, even though the boy had been living with pigs and probably smelled vile.

The robe the father takes to clothe his son symbolizes how we as sinners are clothed with Christ's righteousness.

factoid

The magnifying glass was invented by the Romans. Experimenting with different glass shapes, they discovered that glass that's thicker in the middle and thinner on the edges magnified objects they saw through the glass. The name 'magnifier' or 'burning glasses' stuck after it was discovered that the glass's shape could focus, or magnify, the sun's rays so intensely as to start a fire. Magnifying lenses weren't used commonly until the 13th century when they became used for eyeglasses. Eventually magnifying lenses led to the discovery and use of microscopes.

to them. If you sense this is true, you can point out that God is able to forgive them no matter what their sin is, and His love for them is greater than their wrongs. Be prepared and expect the Holy Spirit to move children to acknowledge their need for Christ during this site, and have workers ready to talk one-on-one with children who express the need or have questions and concerns.

Isaiah 61:10 describes the robe of righteousness as the garment of salvation. Then the father calls for a feast and a celebration. When a sinner turns to God and repents, there is singing and celebration in heaven in a similar fashion.

This parable differs a bit from the parables of the lost coin and the lost sheep in that in those two examples, the owner actively seeks the lost item. In this parable, the lost one must choose to return of his own accord, where he will find the father patiently, lovingly waiting for him.

Prodigal Son

"For God so loved the world, that he gave his only begotten Son. . . ."

Site Mission

Children will learn that they can ask forgiveness for their sins and accept Jesus as their personal Savior.

Key Bible Verse

"For God so loved the world, that he gave his only begotten Son, that whosoever believeth in him should not perish, but have everlasting life." —**John 3:16**

Site Coordinators

■ **Shirley**

■ **Holmes**

Shirley and Holmes are teenagers. They should be dressed in typical clothing of their age group (*Holmes should be wearing all white as part of the mystery*) and use language and actions common to that age. Older teens or young adults might best portray these characters.

Puppet Option

Investigator #2 or an Assistant Investigator can operate BOSWORTH to help lead the children to different areas and

Setting the Scene

A casual Family Room setting: recliners or beanbag chairs, video player and tapes, TV, stereo, casual décor, a lamp, bowl of popcorn or 2 cans of soda, with a jigsaw puzzle on a table. Add reality with a throw rug, afghan, a coffee table, a Sunday newspaper with the comics on top, whatever gives the flavor of a lived-in, relaxed room. A wall hanging or poster might be on a wall.

interact spontaneously with the teacher and children. (*See puppet pattern for BOSWORTH on pages R · 55-59.*)

Bible Passage

Luke 15:11-32

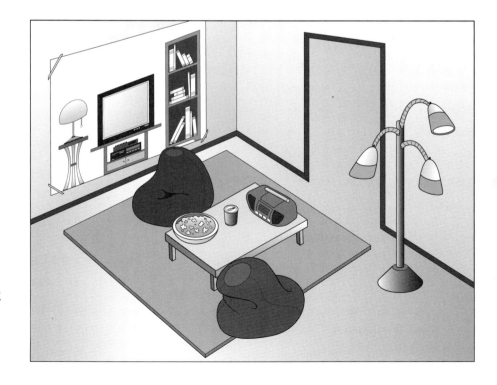

Investigator's Inventory

General

- ☐ Family Room mural
- ☐ *Good News Clues*™ CD or tape copy
- ☐ CD player or cassette tape player
- ☐ Copy of "The Quest Continues" student take-home paper *(page E3 · 15)* for each child
- ☐ Copy of the "Detective's Diary" for each child *(pages R · 61-68)*. Note the two age levels and use accordingly.

Games and Activities

- ☐ Jigsaw puzzle *(see pg. E3 · 5 for details)*
- ☐ Large mirror
- ☐ Clues written on white paper
- ☐ Regal-looking robe
- ☐ Large costume jewelry ring
- ☐ Sandals
- ☐ Fabric bag of coins
- ☐ Ragged clothing
- ☐ Key Verse poster
- ☐ Key Verse Cards *(page R · 60)*
- ☐ Card stock puzzle pieces with verse phrases
- ☐ Copy of song lyrics for each child or have the words on an overhead transparency *(pages R · 21-26)*
- ☐ Overhead projector
- ☐ Puppet *(optional)*
- ☐ Taped or chalked shapes *(circles, squares, rectangles)* on the floor
- ☐ Scissors
- ☐ Glue sticks
- ☐ Lacing or cording
- ☐ White beads

Snacks

- ☐ Regular or microwave popcorn in a variety of flavors, such as kettle corn, cheese popcorn, buttered popcorn
- ☐ Large serving bowls
- ☐ Scoops
- ☐ Small paper bowls
- ☐ Napkins
- ☐ White cake mix, eggs, and oil
- ☐ Cupcake tin and cupcake liners
- ☐ Canned or homemade white frosting
- ☐ White sprinkles

Crafts

- ☐ Magnet strips with adhesive on one side
- ☐ Puzzle pieces
- ☐ White spray paint
- ☐ Cardboard frames
- ☐ Craft glue
- ☐ Newspapers
- ☐ Tempera paint, variety of colors
- ☐ Photo insert paper *(See page R · 53)*
- ☐ Yarn
- ☐ Cotton fabric
- ☐ Sewing machine, thread
- ☐ Safety pins
- ☐ Shiny pennies
- ☐ Fabric paint
- ☐ Paint Shirts

Procedures of the Day

10 minutes: Preparing to Search

15–20 minutes: Focus on the Bible

10 minutes: Bible Memorization

5 minutes: Music Time

15 minutes: Gumshoe Grub

20 minutes: Case-Cracking Games

20 minutes: Putting the Pieces Together

10 minutes: Elementary Deduction

10 minutes: Detectives' Departure

Detective Preparation

- Have craft samples prepared in advance to show Detectives.

- Be sure all supplies are gathered and your site is ready each day for Detectives to arrive.

- Post the Procedures of the Day where Investigators and helpers (called *Assistant Investigators*) can refer to it.

- Address each other by site titles. Children should be referred to as Detectives. The helpers that go with them from camp to camp are called Assistant Investigators—Assistant Investigator Jim or Assistant Investigator Sharon.

- After taking attendance, an Assistant Investigator should tell those responsible for refreshments how many Detectives are present to be prepared for snack time.

- In advance, write all the clues for the day's hidden treasure onto the color of paper indicated.

- You may wish to do some background research into the Bible story. Refer to Bible commentaries, encyclopedias, and dictionaries for additional information.

PREPARING TO SEARCH

(A13) Supplies:

- Jigsaw puzzle that's been altered so that a message reads backward. Message is **4 GIVE N**.

- Large mirror *(placed so that it faces the audience of kids)*

 **White paper with Clue 1:** "I'm all ears."

Shirley and Holmes are sprawled in the recliners, on a couch, or on bean bag chairs, working on a puzzle. Detectives come in while they are working. Shirley keeps trying to get Holmes to tell her something.

SHIRLEY: **So what is the big mystery, Holmes? I don't get it.**

HOLMES: *(Smiles benignly.)* **I don't know what you're talking about, Shirley.**

SHIRLEY: **Well, look at you. Everything you're wearing is white. You look like an advertisement for Extra Clean Laundry Soap or**

something. I've never seen you look that spotless.

HOLMES: Maybe for a change, the way I look on the outside is a lot like how I am on the inside.

(Shirley shrugs; they work silently for several seconds.)

HOLMES: *(Looking around.)* Are you sure you don't know where the box is for this puzzle? It would help a lot to know what the picture is that we're supposed to be putting together.

SHIRLEY: No, I don't have any idea. The puzzle was in a plastic bag in the closet. But it's more challenging to put it together without knowing just what it will turn out like.

(Holmes grunts and keeps looking for pieces. When they find a piece, they make a big deal of it. Holmes puts in the last piece, and then they both look at the finished puzzle, then look at each other with confused expressions.)

SHIRLEY: What is it, anyway? Do you know what this is supposed to be?

HOLMES: It looks like a message, but I can't read it. I think it's a big-time mystery. Maybe it's like some unusual foreign language. *(Gets excited.)* Or it could be a strange dialect of an Amazonian rain forest Indian tribe. Or even a super secret code to a long lost pirate treasure.

SHIRLEY: *(Skeptical.)* Or maybe we just put some pieces in the wrong places and we made a complete mess of the whole thing! Let's pick it up and see if these kids can make any sense of it. *(They move the puzzle to a vertical position, facing the mirror, which is facing the kids. The message "4 GIVE N" will be readable when read in the mirror, but backward when read straight on. Leader can help kids see the message in the mirror.)*

HOLMES: No, it's no use, Shirley. This is one mystery I really can't figure out. Let's just take it apart. Unless someone else has any ideas . . . . *(Let kids offer their ideas.)*

(Both exclaim and praise the kids for solving the mystery of the puzzle.)

SHIRLEY: There's another mystery solved! There's just one more mystery we haven't figured out yet. Holmes, where is that white paper you found with the puzzle pieces?

*(Holmes fishes around in his pockets and comes up with white paper with **Clue 1** and reads it.)*

HOLMES: It says, "I'm all ears." Just what does that mean?

(He and Shirley shrug.)

SHIRLEY: Even if we can't decipher that little mystery, we do have a cool story for you. Wait until you hear it.

(Give kids a chance to resettle and pay attention as silent actors come in and arrange props.)

FOCUS ON THE BIBLE

Luke 15:11-32

This Bible story can be done in one of two ways. Two male actors can be silent players as the narrator reads the story and they use facial expressions and movement to portray the characterizations. Or one of the site coordinators can tell the story as written.

If using the actors, have one serve as the father and one as the younger *(prodigal)* son. Lay props to the side of the actors for easy access, but where they're not in the way nor too obvious. At appropriate times, the actors use the props as the narrator reads.

(A14) Supplies:

(If using actors, you'll need the following.)

- Bible
- Regal-looking robe
- Large costume jewelry ring
- Sandals
- Fabric bag of coins
- Ragged clothing

SHIRLEY: This story comes from the Bible in the Book of Luke. It's called a parable, because it's a story Jesus told people to show them something important. In this parable, there was a father and two sons. They all worked in the family business. One day the younger son came to his father and said, "I want my share of the family business." This wasn't how things were usually done, but the father gave him his share of the money from the family.

It wasn't long before this younger son decided he wanted to go out into the world and have a good time. So he got the money his father had given him, and his other possessions and went to have a fun time. He did all kinds of wild things. But all the wild times he had used up all the money from his father.

That was bad enough, but then there was a famine. The country had a very hard time and people couldn't get enough food, even if they had money to buy it. This son didn't have any more money, and he got very hungry. The only way he could get money was to go to work. So he got a job working for a farmer. His job was to feed the pigs. It was dirty, yukky work. But he was hungry. In fact, he was so hungry even the food he was feeding to the pigs looked tasty to him.

His life wasn't anything like it used to be. One day he realized how much he had lost by leaving his father and his home. The son said to himself, "Even the employees in my father's business have food to eat, and I'm starving. I'm going to make the long trip back home."

As he walked and walked back to his home, the son thought about what he would tell his father. He expected his father would be very upset, maybe even mad at what he had done. The son decided he would say this to his father, to try to apologize. "Father, I've sinned and done wrong against you and against God. I don't deserve to be called your son anymore. Would you just let me work for you so I can have a place to live and food to eat?"

The son kept walking, and wondered what his father would say when he saw him. He was still a long ways off one day when his father spotted him. The father had been waiting for the son, and keeping a watch for him. He saw him coming and was so glad to see him. He felt bad that his son was so ragged and dirty and thin. He ran right out of his yard and went to give his son a big hug and a kiss.

The son was ready with his apology. "Father, I've sinned and done wrong against you and against God. I don't deserve to be called your son anymore."

The father wasn't even listening! He was calling to his servants. "Quick! Bring my best robe. Put a ring on my son's finger. Get some sandals for his bare feet. And get a big dinner ready—let's celebrate in a big way. This son of mine was as good as dead, and now he's alive again! He was lost and now he's been found." And they had a big party because the son had come back and the father had forgiven him and welcomed him.

HOLMES: That is such an amazing story, Shirley. It's a mystery to me that the father could be so ready to forgive the son, even though that son had really messed up.

SHIRLEY: Well, that son is no different from you or me. Just like him, you and I and everyone else in the world are sinners. We've all done things wrong.

HOLMES: I know. And that's broken our relationship with God, just like the son broke his relationship with his dad. But when the son came back and was ready to admit how wrong he was, the father was ready to forgive him.

SHIRLEY: God is ready to forgive every person who realizes he or she has sinned. When someone asks God to forgive his sins, then Jesus can be their Lord and Savior. It's like getting all your sins washed away and starting a new life with Jesus.

HOLMES: Don't forget how God promises us that when we have a new life with Jesus, we'll be living forever in heaven too!

SHIRLEY: If any of you detectives have questions about God forgiving your sins or what receiving Jesus is about, tell one of the Investigators today. They can help you understand it all better.

Holmes and Shirley say good-bye and leave. Investigators direct kids to the Bible verse memorization activity.

BIBLE MEMORIZATION

(A15) Supplies:

- Key Verse poster
- Card stock puzzle pieces with verse phrases on them
- Detective's Diaries

Clue 2: white paper with words, "Sometimes yellow, sometimes white, but always best with butter and salt."

Early and Older Elementary:

"For God so loved the world, that he gave his only begotten Son, that whosoever believeth in him should not perish, but have everlasting life." —**John 3:16**

> **For God so loved the world, that he gave his only begotten Son, that whosoever believeth in him should not perish, but have everlasting life.**

In Advance: Design and cut out the extra large puzzle pieces and write phrases of the memory verse on them so the verse will be complete when the puzzle is assembled. *(See pattern piece suggestions in Resources, page R · 49.)* Also write the verse on a poster or whiteboard.

Explain to children that it's no mystery how God made a way for us to have our sins forgiven and be friends with Him. God showed us how much He loved us by letting His only Son, Jesus, come to earth and die for us. Jesus came back to life, which only He could do because He's God's Son. When He died, He took the punishment we deserve for our sins. When we ask Him to forgive our sins, He cleans away our sin. Then we have a friendship with God and we'll be able to live forever in heaven with God. Point to and say the verse together twice.

Divide the group in two. One group will go elsewhere while the other hides the puzzle pieces. Tuck **Clue 2** in a hiding place with one of the puzzle pieces when no one's looking. *(When it's found, take time out of the activity to read the clue and see if anyone can unravel the mystery.)* After one group hides the puzzle pieces, the second group has to discover the puzzle pieces and assemble the puzzle, then read the verse aloud. They should be able to refer to the poster or whiteboard for reference. Switch roles and do the activity again.

Before Music Time, have kids tape a Key Verse Card in their Detective's Diaries.

MUSIC TIME

Coming Back to You

(A16) Supplies:

- Copy of song lyrics for each child or have the words on an overhead transparency *(pages R · 21-26)*

- *Good News Clues*™ CD or tape copy of "Coming Back to You" *(Track 4)*

- CD or tape player

- Overhead projector

- Puppet *(optional)*

Have the children stand and stretch before playing today's song, "Coming Back to You." As the song plays, have children try to learn the words. If age-appropriate, project the words of the song onto a screen for the children to follow along as they sing. If you are using the puppet option, have BOSWORTH help teach the song. If you have time, you may want to sing other songs the children know that fit with the story.

GUMSHOE GRUB

Popcorn Day Treats

(S5) Supplies:

- Regular or microwave popcorn in a variety of flavors, such as kettle corn, cheese popcorn, buttered popcorn

- Large serving bowls

- Scoops

- Small paper bowls

- Napkins

Directions: Prepare the popcorn and put into large serving bowls. Allow the children to scoop the popcorn they would like to eat into their bowls. Be sure to remind the children that the Prodigal Son was feeding corn to the pigs before he came home. However, the corn used to make this popcorn is special corn grown just for this purpose. Serve with juice or water. **NOTE: Be aware of any allergies when choosing and serving the different popcorn flavors.**

White-as-Snow Cupcakes

(S6) Supplies:

- White cake mix *(24 cupcakes/ mix)*

- Eggs

- Oil

- Cupcake tin

- Cupcake liners

- Canned or homemade white frosting

- White sprinkles

- Napkins

Directions: Prepare and bake cupcakes according to the cake mix directions. Frost with white icing and top with white sprinkles. Remind the children that when God forgives us it is as if our sins become white as snow *(Ps. 51:7)*. Allow each child to select a cupcake to eat for his or her snack. Serve with juice or water.

CASE-CRACKING GAMES

Forgiven Tag

(G5) Supplies:

- None needed

Directions: This is a version of freeze tag. Have a wide playing area with clearly defined boundaries. Appoint one or more children "It" *(for large groups or wide playing areas, have at least two)*. "It" chases the other players to tag them. When tagged, a player kneels on the floor and must remain that way until everyone's been tagged. Once all the kids are kneeling, "It" goes around and touches each player on the shoulder and says, "You're forgiven." After everyone's been forgiven, the game can start over with a new "It."

Chair Share

(G6) Supplies:

- Taped or chalked shapes *(circles, squares, rectangles)* on the floor
- Music *(CD or video)*

Just like many people race to get into their favorite chair in the family room before someone else grabs it, this game is about squeezing as many people as possible into a small space. Mark out two or more shapes on the floor, small enough so that the expected number of players will have to really squeeze to fit in the spaces. Explain that you'll play music while kids jump or otherwise move around the area *(outside*

the shapes). When you turn off the music, everyone must try to crowd into one of the shapes. This will take teamwork and cooperation so kids can get all their body parts inside the boundaries. To make it more challenging, have everyone sing a

short song *(from the VBS program or a common one like "Twinkle, Twinkle" or "Happy Birthday")* before they can be released from the shape.

PUTTING THE PIECES TOGETHER

Puzzle Piece Frame

(C5) Supplies:

- Magnet strips with adhesive on one side
- Puzzle pieces
- White spray paint
- Cardboard frames
- Craft glue
- Newspapers
- Different colors of tempera paint
- Photo insert paper *(on page R · 53 in Resources)*

In Advance: Find old 500-piece puzzles at garage sales or a thrift store. Spray paint the puzzle pieces white. Cut frames out of cardboard or from cereal boxes. See diagram for the size. Cut magnet strips 2–3 inches long. Photocopy the photo insert paper from Resources *(one per child)*.

Directions: Cover the tables with newspaper. Have each student glue white puzzle pieces on the cardboard frame so that all the frame is covered. The pieces need to overlap so that there are two layers of puzzle pieces. When all the gluing is completed, allow students to "drizzle" different paint colors over the frame. **Note:** You may want to do this project before your game time so that the frames will have sufficient time to dry. When the frames are dry, adhere two magnet strips *(one on the top, one on the bottom)* to the back of each frame. Have each student fill in the information on the photo insert sheet and tape it to the back of the frame with the words facing the front of the frame.

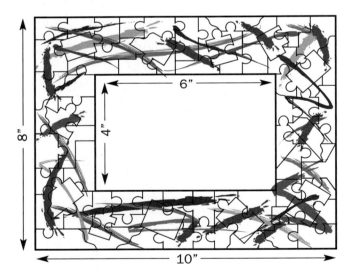

Penny Pouch

(C6) Supplies:

- Yarn cut to 15" lengths, two per child
- Cotton fabric cut into 12" x 6" rectangles, one per child
- Sewing machine, thread
- Safety pins
- Shiny pennies for each word of the Bible memory verse, per child
- Fabric paint
- Newspapers
- Paint Shirts

In Advance: Cut fabric into 12" x 6" rectangles. Fold a 1" hem on each 6" end and sew in place. Fold the fabric in half so that hems are on same end and right sides of the fabric are together. Sew a seam on each side of the pouch up to the hem. DO NOT sew through the hem on either side. Cut enough yarn into 15" lengths so that you have two pieces per child. Clean the pennies by soaking in an acidic substance (cola, lemon juice, etc., all work well).

Directions: Cover tables with newspaper prior to starting this project. Have students insert safety pin into one end of a piece of yarn. String the yarn through one side and then through the other side. Knot the ends together. Use the other piece of yarn. Begin at the opposite side of the bag and repeat. You will have a knot in each side. Pull on the knots to close the bag. When the yarn step is completed, have the children lay their bags flat on the table and decorate them with the fabric paint. Be sure they are wearing paint shirts to protect their clothing. When the paint is dry, give the children the pennies to place inside their pouches.

ELEMENTARY DEDUCTION

(A17) Supplies:

- Detective's Diaries *(see page R · 61-68 in Resources)*

- Supplies for Older Elementary Detective's Diaries: paintbrush or toothpick for each child and invisible ink made from the recipe on The Family Room page in the Detective's Diary.

- Scissors

- Glue sticks

- Pens/pencils

- Key Verse poster from Bible Memorization activity

- White beads and lacing or cord *(See directions on page R · 69 in Resources.)*

- **White paper with Clue 3:** "Sounds corny, but after humans eat my kernels, pigs eat my cob. You'll find me _____." *(Write location where you'll hide an ear of corn and a bag of popped corn, which everyone can sample.)*

Let's think for a minute about the Bible story of the son who came back to his father. How do you think the son felt when he knew his father had forgiven him? *(Let kids offer suggestions.)* **That's how I felt when I asked God to forgive my sins and told Jesus I wanted Him to be my personal Savior. I knew my sins were cleaned up and my broken relationship with God was fixed. That's how each of us can feel when we ask Jesus to be our personal Savior.**

Hand out Detective's Diaries and any other materials you may need for the correct age level. Read the directions together as a group. Be sure to answer any questions the children may have about completing this page. Be available to answer questions or help the Detectives as they work.

The Bible verse you learned today isn't just a nice thought. God meant it just for you. On the blank line in your verse, write your own name. Then let's read it together.

After kids have written their names, say the verse with each child's name inserted.

That's how much God loves each of you! Some of you may want to talk to an Investigator about what this verse means to you, or about having your sins forgiven. You can do that right now, or as soon as the group is dismissed. Allow children to find a leader/helper to talk with.

Hand out white beads and lacing or cord. **What do you think the white bead you're adding today stands for?** Review the meaning of the other colors. Let children offer ideas about the white color. *(White stands for Jesus cleansing our sin.)*

Ask Detectives to think back to Shirley and Holmes before the Bible story. **Can you figure out the mystery of Holmes's white clothes?** *(He asked Jesus into his heart, had his sins forgiven.)*

As kids are adding beads, "suddenly" discover **Clue 3** among the beads and lacings. Read it to the kids and let them figure out that the treasure is an ear of corn. When one has found the corn, let them share the popcorn.

White stands for how clean your heart is when you've asked Jesus to forgive your sins. Kids will add the beads.

If you have time, you may want to read the book *Emily's Bracelet* *(©2004, available from Cook Communications Ministries, 1-800-323-7543)* and talk about the story. It will help the children begin

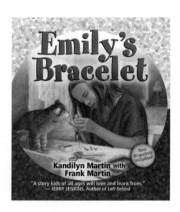

to understand more about the colors used in each of the sites. It will also help them get a grasp of the meaning of the choker or bracelet that they are making throughout the week.

 DETECTIVES' DEPARTURE

(A18) Supplies:

- "The Quest Continues" take-home paper, one per child
- Craft projects from the day

Make today's departure a celebratory one, letting children know that because we can have our sins forgiven, we can celebrate. Sing an appropriate song. Pray with praise and thanksgiving. Be sure children collect their crafts and "The Quest Continues" take-home paper.

Today your child had a tour through the family room where we uncovered the parable of the prodigal son (*Luke 15:11-32*) who squanders his inheritance and returns to his father poor and needy. His father lovingly forgives and welcomes him. We discovered that this is exactly how it is with us: as humans we're sinful, but when we approach God with a repentant attitude, he lovingly forgives and accepts us.

Find more information about *Good News Clues™* VBS and what your child is learning by going online to **www.CookVBS.com**.

TALK IT OUT

What are ways you can ask forgiveness when you've done wrong or hurt someone?

How should we respond to each other when someone asks our forgiveness?

FAMILY STUFF

Dirty/Shiny Penny Experiment

Point: God cleanses us of our sin when we ask His forgiveness.

Supplies:
- Old and very dirty pennies (*one per person, plus one extra*)
- Small glass bowl
- Measuring cup
- Teaspoon measuring spoon
- White vinegar
- Salt
- Soft cloth

Give each person one old, tarnished penny. Save one. **Pretend this penny is you, when you're full of sin. Think of the wrong things you've done this week. Each time you sin it's like you get a little dirtier. After a while all those sins make you as dirty and unclean as your penny. Let's find out what changes when we decide to change and ask God's forgiveness for our sin.**

Only with adult supervision, mix 1/4 cup white vinegar and 1 teaspoon salt in the bowl and stir well. Each person drops his penny in the bowl and watches to see how it changes. Let the pennies remain until they're clean and shiny. Have an adult take each one out, rinse, and dry it with a cloth. Compare these to the still-dirty penny.

How is this an example of what God does when we come to Him as a sinner and ask His forgiveness? (*He cleanses us of our sin the same way the vinegar and salt water cleaned the tarnish from the pennies.*)

How does it feel when you know you've done wrong? (*Guilty, bad, uncomfortable, afraid of getting in trouble.*)

What does it feel like to be forgiven? (*Relieved, light and free, happy, pleased, clean.*)

Read the parable of the prodigal son from Luke 15:11-32. Let each family member share what the son and father must have felt like at different times in the story. Remind them that they too can have this happy ending when they choose to trust Jesus as their personal Savior.

BIBLE VERSE

"For God so loved the world, that he gave his only begotten Son, that whosoever believeth in him should not perish, but have everlasting life." —**John 3:16**

Parables Mustard Seed and Yeast

"Grow in grace, and in the knowledge of our Lord and Saviour Jesus Christ."

2 Peter 3:18

Why Kids Need to Know That Once They Trust in Jesus, They Should Seek to Grow as Believers

Many of the children who attend VBS will be in the concrete stage of thinking and learning. Grasping the realities of a spiritual life and what follows a decision to trust in Jesus are abstract concepts for many of these youngsters. Because kids can't see the God they're learning to love, it takes a gigantic leap of understanding to figure out how to grow in their relationship with Him.

As you teach them the practical, day-by-day ways they can learn, understand, and mature in their faith in Christ, you'll be helping them connect spiritual growth with physical growth, which they more readily comprehend. Tangible examples of how to manage worship, Bible reading, and prayer are best accomplished by showing them how to do it. Help them find a Bible verse, let them listen to simple prayers they can imitate or model their own prayers after, invite them to church and see that they get there.

adult (6 feet or more), and can be perched upon by large flocks of birds. The birds are attracted to the mustard bush for its tiny black seeds.

This parable and the one following give word pictures of the growth of the kingdom of God: It starts from the smallest beginning and grows to immense size, beyond imagining. In the Middle East and in New Testament times, a great empire was pictured as a great tree, with birds using the tree f or shelter and rest (see Ezek. 31:6).

Jesus told this parable to encourage believers to grow in their faith and thus grow the church. This message would have been very stimulating to the disciples, who were a small group with an immense mandate, facing such formidable opposition.

The parable of the yeast is another one describing a transformation that emerges from the smallest of beginnings. The making of daily bread in the home was a common way of life in New Testament times. While a farmer or field worker could understand the mustard seed parable, a woman who kept house could easily comprehend this one. The leaven was a small piece of dough kept from the previous day's bread-making; it fermented until it was used in the new dough to create the next day's bread.

factoid

Codes: The science of writing in code is called cryptography. Secret codes were created thousands of years ago. Ancient Jewish writers sometimes hid sacred texts by reversing the alphabet. This type of code, called a cipher, appears in the Bible. One instance is Jeremiah 25:26, in which "Sheshach" is written for "Babel" (Babylon), using the second and twelfth letters from the end of the Hebrew alphabet instead of from the beginning. Greek and Spartan military men communicated by sending messages written across the edges of parchment strips wrapped around a staff. The message was read by unrolling the strip and wrapping it onto an identical size staff.

Getting More from the Bible Story

The parable of the mustard seed uses something very familiar in the Middle Eastern culture to share an important truth. Mustard plants were very common in the part of the world where Jesus walked. Mustard plants can grow higher than a tall

Unleavened bread was like a cracker, while leavened bread was light, airy, and tasty. Jesus compared the way leaven works in bread to grow and transform it to the way His light in one's life transforms that life and those around it. As the leaven changes bread dough, so Christ changes one's life.

Parables 1

"Grow in grace, and in the knowledge of our Lord and Saviour Jesus Christ."

Site Mission

Children will learn that Jesus wants them to grow to be stronger Christians.

Key Bible Verses
Early elementary

"Grow . . . in the knowledge of our Lord and Saviour Jesus Christ." —**2 Peter 3:18**

Upper elementary

"Grow in grace, and in the knowledge of our Lord and Saviour Jesus Christ." —**2 Peter 3:18**

Site Coordinators

- **Chef Breadly**
- **Rollo the Baker**

Both should be wearing clothing and accessories that fit professional kitchen workers, such as aprons, white shirts with sleeves rolled up, and even chef's hats.

Puppet Option

Investigator #2 or an Assistant Investigator can operate BOSWORTH to help lead the children to different areas and interact spontaneously with the teacher and children. *(See puppet pattern for BOSWORTH on pages R · 55-59.)*

Setting the Scene

Create a working Kitchen as much as possible. Have a large table at center stage, with a mixer, mixing bowls, spatula, wooden spoon, recipe book, some baking ingredients *(sugar, flour, baking powder, etc.)*. The background could be an actual baker's shelf or some cabinets and a counter with other kitchen items such as a crock of utensils, coffee maker, more recipe books, boxes of cereal, a fruit bowl, a knife block, some pans, a tea kettle, etc. A real or pretend window can be mounted above the counter in the background with a red and white checked curtain. The mural can be enlarged for this purpose too.

Bible Passage
Matthew 13:31-33

Investigator's Inventory

General

- [ ] Kitchen mural
- [ ] *Good News Clues*™ CD or tape copy
- [ ] CD player or cassette tape player
- [ ] Copy of "The Quest Continues" student take-home paper *(page E4·14)* for each child
- [ ] Copy of the "Detective's Diary" for each child *(pages R·61-68)*. Note the two age levels and use accordingly.

Games and Activities

- [ ] Yeast dough *(prepared; ready to knead)*
- [ ] Wet wipes or basins with water, soap, and paper towels
- [ ] Tables *(space for all kids to work)*
- [ ] Flour
- [ ] Baking sheets
- [ ] Loaf of homemade bread without yeast
- [ ] Clues written on green paper
- [ ] Yeast
- [ ] Box or bag of mustard seed
- [ ] Key Verse poster
- [ ] Key Verse Cards *(page R·60)*
- [ ] Copy of song lyrics for each child or have the words on an overhead transparency *(pages R·21-26)*
- [ ] Overhead projector
- [ ] Puppet *(optional)*
- [ ] Inflated balloons
- [ ] Hardboiled eggs *(one per team)*
- [ ] Kitchen items—skillets, spoons, tongs, plates, bowls, mugs, cookie sheets
- [ ] Index cards

- [ ] Sample recipe cards
- [ ] Green beads
- [ ] *Emily's Bracelet (optional)*
- [ ] Treasure basket and yeast rolls

Snacks

- [ ] Small hot dogs *(one or two per child)*
- [ ] Refrigerated crescent roll dough
- [ ] Ketchup
- [ ] Mustard
- [ ] Multi-colored fish crackers
- [ ] Baking sheets
- [ ] Small plates
- [ ] Lime green gelatin *(prepared in advance)*
- [ ] clear cups, 8-oz. size *(one per child)*
- [ ] Whipped topping
- [ ] Plastic spoons
- [ ] Paper cups and napkins

Crafts

- [ ] Copy of bird pattern *(page R·48 in Resources)*
- [ ] Utility knife
- [ ] Drawing paper
- [ ] Hole punch
- [ ] String
- [ ] Pictures of various types of birds *(available at your local library)*
- [ ] Yellow foam board
- [ ] Inexpensive measuring tapes *(or pattern from page R·47 in Resources)*
- [ ] Stickers of flowers *(about 10–12/child)*
- [ ] Red craft foam
- [ ] Black markers
- [ ] Tacky material to attach pieces
- [ ] Utility Knife

Procedures of the Day

10 minutes: Preparing to Search

15–20 minutes: Focus on the Bible

10 minutes: Bible Memorization

5 minutes: Music Time

15 minutes: Gumshoe Grub

20 minutes: Case-Cracking Games

20 minutes: Putting the Pieces Together

10 minutes: Elementary Deduction

10 minutes: Detectives' Departure

Detective Preparation

- Have craft samples prepared in advance to show Detectives.

- Be sure all supplies are gathered and your site is ready each day for Detectives to arrive.

- Post the Procedures of the Day where Investigators and helpers (called Assistant Investigators) can refer to it.

- Address each other by site titles. Children should be referred to as Detectives. The helpers that go with them from camp to camp are called Assistant Investigators—Assistant Investigator Jim or Assistant Investigator Sharon.

- After taking attendance, an Assistant Investigator should tell those responsible for refreshments how many Detectives are present to be prepared for snack time.

- In advance, write all the clues for the day's hidden treasure onto the color of paper indicated.

- You may wish to do some background research into the Bible story. Refer to Bible commentaries, encyclopedias, and dictionaries for additional information.

PREPARING TO SEARCH

(A19) Supplies:

- Yeast dough that is prepared and ready to be kneaded *(enough for each child to have a small handful)*

- Wet wipes; basins with water, soap, and paper towels; or a place for kids to wash and dry their hands

- Tables *(space for all kids to work)*

- Flour

- Baking sheets

- One loaf of homemade bread baked with the yeast left out so that it's hard and hasn't risen.

Green paper with Clue 1: "Good cold, best warm." Hide clue under recipe card Baker will refer to in this scene.

In Advance: Set up enough tables so the kids can knead dough all at the same time. Sprinkle flour on the tables beforehand.

As kids come in, Chef Breadly and Rollo the Baker are working in the kitchen. They can be kneading dough, mixing up ingredients, reading the recipe book, etc. They introduce themselves and welcome the Detectives as the kids are settling in.

BAKER: You're just in time to help us with a very big meal. We don't have nearly enough hands to get everything ready, so we hope you can help us.

CHEF: That's right. The first thing all kitchen workers need to do is wash their hands. *(Kids should clean their hands now.)*

Invite kids to the tables that are floured. Baker and Chef spoon out a handful of dough for each child. Baker and Chef should demonstrate kneading technique so each child can observe.

CHEF: So now we need you to knead! That's right, knead your piece of dough. Baker and Chef should keep enough flour on the tables to keep dough from sticking, and help kids who are in need. After several minutes, have kids stop.

CHEF: Well done! Now we need to let the dough rest. Each of you can put your kneaded dough on a baking sheet.

Once that's done, Baker and Chef cover the sheets with towels to rise.

Settle kids back to listen.

CHEF: I'm so glad you all came along when you did. Our dinner

wouldn't have been anywhere near ready if you hadn't helped get that dough kneaded. Some of you show real talent for this.

BAKER: But these kids already have a job. In fact, I think they've come here today to investigate the mystery you and I are working on.

CHEF: I surely hope they can figure out what's happened. *(He takes out a loaf pan with a baked, unrisen loaf of bread.)*

See what you think of this bread we made today.

Pass it around and encourage them to smell and see it. After they've all done so, turn the pan upside down over the table and let the heavy, unrisen loaf fall out with a thud.

BAKER: There is something very wrong with this bread. I was planning to use it for lunch, but as you can see, it's terrible. *(Poke at it and make a face.)*

CHEF: I'd like to know if any of you detectives might have an idea what happened to our bread, why it's like this?

FLOUR

(Let volunteers offer ideas. The answer is that it didn't rise because it had no yeast.) If no one guesses, read them the recipe with the title "Best Yeast Bread." Have the ingredients sitting out: flour, salt, water, but no yeast.

Once someone has guessed, thank them for solving the mystery of why the bread didn't rise.

BAKER: **Here's a second mystery. I found this scrap of paper under my recipe card just now. It says, "Good cold, best warm." I wonder what that means?**

He and Chef puzzle over it for a moment, wait to see if the kids have any ideas, then agree to put it aside for the time being.

CHEF: **Since we've been talking about yeast today, I think you'd like to hear a story about yeast. There's also a story about another interesting kitchen item, mustard seeds.**

FOCUS ON THE BIBLE

(A20) Supplies:

- Bible
- Container of yeast
- Box or bag of mustard seed

One of the site coordinators can tell the Bible story since it's short, while the other hands around the yeast and mustard for the kids to see.

CHEF: **This story is one that Jesus told. It's in the Book of Matthew. This is a parable. That's a story that Jesus told that is an example to** **help people understand something important.**

Jesus was talking to a crowd of people. He told them that the kingdom of heaven is like a mustard seed. *(Baker hands around small containers of mustard seeds for children to inspect.)* **That's pretty tiny, isn't it? In the parable, Jesus said a man took one mustard seed and planted it in his field. These are one of the smallest types of seeds, but when it grows, it becomes a very big plant. In fact, it can grow to be like a tree. The tree might be so big that birds can perch on the branches.**

(Baker collects mustard seeds.)

Then Jesus told the people another parable. He said that the kingdom of heaven is like yeast. *(Baker passes around a bowl or jar of yeast.)* **A woman took a little bit of this yeast and mixed it into a large amount of flour, just like Baker and I do when we make bread. But in the parable, she had a huge bowl of flour, yet the yeast was able to be worked into the dough and cause it to rise for good bread.**

BAKER: **Now what do you think Jesus was trying to help people understand with these two short parables?** *(Let kids give you their ideas.)* **The one thing yeast and a mustard seed both can do is grow. They both are very small, but when they are used for their intended purpose, they grow something**

large and useful. The mustard seed grows into a large bush or a tree. The yeast creates a big loaf of tasty bread.

CHEF: Jesus told such good parables. They help us learn things we might not understand. Jesus wants us to be like the mustard seed and the yeast. Once we know Him as our Savior, He wants us to grow in our spiritual lives and become strong. Just like the yeast and mustard, we start out small. When we first accept Jesus as our Savior, we're like baby Christians. What are ways we can grow into bigger, stronger Christians? *(Listen to God in the Bible, learn more about Him, practice living the way He tells us, talk to God by praying, and be a part of His family in a church.)*

BAKER: This growing only happens, though, after you've learned that you've sinned. The Bible says every person on earth has sinned, or done wrong. That sin has broken our friendship with God. The only way to have our sins forgiven is through Jesus. Because God loves us, He let His Son, Jesus, die for our sins. Jesus came back to life and proved He is God. He died and took the punishment we deserve. So when we ask Him to forgive us for our sins, we can become friends with God again. And one day we'll be living in heaven with Him. If you would like to know more about receiving Jesus as your Savior, you can talk to one of the Investigators or leaders here in our room.

Move children to the Bible memory activity.

BIBLE MEMORIZATION

(A21) Supplies:

- Key Verse poster *(made in advance)*
- Key Verse Cards
- Detective's Diary *(one for each child)*
- Tape

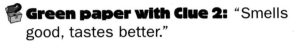

Green paper with Clue 2: "Smells good, tastes better."

In Advance: Write the Key Bible Verse on poster board.

Early Elementary

"Grow . . . in the knowledge of our Lord and Saviour Jesus Christ." —**2 Peter 3:18**

Upper Elementary

"Grow in grace, and in the knowledge of our Lord and Saviour Jesus Christ." —**2 Peter 3:18**

Use an echo game that grows in volume to help children learn the key verse and reinforce the theme of growth.

Divide everyone into two groups who will face each other. One group should be able to read the Key Verse poster. They'll whisper the verse, one phrase at a time, which the second group will echo. After one time through, the voices should grow in volume. With each repetition of the verse, both groups should also "grow" by moving from their low crouching position to kneeling, squatting, standing, and then standing on tiptoe. By the fourth or fifth repeat of the verse, voices should be very loud. If you want, you can reverse the echo and repeat the activity.

Review with the kids how we grow in our lives as Christians. Have them brainstorm with you various avenues such as prayer, memorizing Scripture, worshiping with other believers, Bible study, listening to sermons, singing praise songs, etc.

Pass out each child's Detective's Diary and today's Key Verse Cards so each child can tape a card into his or her diary. While passing out the cards and diaries, "discover" **Clue 2**. Get everyone's attention and ask a volunteer to read the clue: **"Smells good, tastes better."** Let kids try to guess what the clue means. If no one does, tell them they can work on it after playing games.

Before moving along to the game time, have kids return to the scene of the Bible story to see how the dough has grown *(risen)*. Rollo the Baker and Chef Breadly can then bake the bread if possible. If not, refrigerate the risen dough until it can be baked after the session.

Grow in Grace and Wisdom

(A22) Supplies:

- Copy of song lyrics for each child or have the words on an overhead transparency *(pages R · 21-26)*
- *Good News Clues*™ CD or tape copy of "Grow in Grace and Wisdom" *(Track 5)*
- CD or tape player
- Overhead projector
- Puppet *(optional)*

After listening to "Grow in Grace and Wisdom," have the children join in to sing along with the music. If age-appropriate, project the words of the song onto a screen for the children to follow along as they sing. If you are using the puppet option, have BOSWORTH help teach the song.

Hot Dog in a Blanket

(S7) Supplies:

- Small hot dogs *(one or two per child)*
- Refrigerated crescent roll dough
- Ketchup
- Mustard
- Multi-colored fish crackers *(if desired)*

Hot Dogs in a Blanket

(serves 4–6 children)

1 8-oz. tube refrigerated crescent rolls

8 hot dogs

Preheat oven to 400 degrees. Separate the crescent dough into eight triangles. Place one hot dog on the wide end of each triangle and roll up. Place, with the dough tip down, on an ungreased baking sheet. Bake at 400 degrees for 10–15 minutes or until golden brown. Hot dogs can be cut into two pieces to make smaller pieces if desired.

- Baking sheet(s)
- Small plates
- Napkins
- Cups

In Advance: Prepare the hot dogs in a blanket following the recipe above. Provide one or two small hot dogs per child.

Directions: Place hot dogs on small plates. All children take a small amount of ketchup or mustard to dip their hot dogs into. Allow the children to take a scoop of fish crackers to put on their plates. Serve with juice or water.

Gelatin Parfaits

(S8) Supplies:

- Lime green gelatin
- Clear cups, 8-ounce size
- Whipped topping
- Spoons

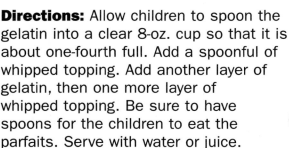

In Advance: Make lime green gelatin in a shallow pan the day before serving. Cut gelatin into cubes.

Directions: Allow children to spoon the gelatin into a clear 8-oz. cup so that it is about one-fourth full. Add a spoonful of whipped topping. Add another layer of gelatin, then one more layer of whipped topping. Be sure to have spoons for the children to eat the parfaits. Serve with water or juice.

CASE-CRACKING GAMES

Expanding Yeast Tag

(G7) Supplies:

- None needed

Directions: This is a version of tag. Choose one or two "Its" who'll move around the play area trying to tag other kids. Those who are tagged will hold hands or link arms *(your choice)* with "It" and try to tag others. In this way, "It" grows until everyone is a part of "It." Play again with the last two people who were tagged becoming "It."

Popcorn

(G8) Supplies:

- Inflated balloons *(same or greater number as there are kids)*

Directions: Let the kids imitate being a gigantic popcorn maker. Kids lie on their backs on the ground within a designated area, an arm's distance from each other. Leaders and helpers should stand around the edges of the group. At the "go" signal, leaders toss in all the balloons *(popcorn kernels)*, which the kids have to keep in the air using their feet and hands. Try not to let any hit the ground. Leaders and helpers around the perimeter punch back to the center balloons that float away from the group of kids.

Egg Relay

(G9) Supplies:

- Hardboiled eggs *(1 per team)*
- Kitchen items such as skillets, serving spoons, tongs, plates, bowls, mugs, cookie sheets *(one set of items per team)*

Directions: Divide into 2 or more teams, depending on size of the group. Each team

will divide in half and line up on opposite sides of the playing area facing each other from across the play space. Divide the kitchen items in half also, putting half in front of one half of the team, the other half in front of the rest of the team. The game consists of team members carrying an egg on one of the kitchen items over to the other side where the other half of the team waits. Upon arriving there with the egg, the player gives the egg to a teammate waiting there, who will pick up a kitchen item and use it to carry the egg back to the other side. Each player must use a different carrier. Try to have older kids use the harder items (skillet, plate) so younger kids can use easier ones (mug, bowl). First team to have the egg carried back and forth by all the players, using all the items, wins.

PUTTING THE PIECES TOGETHER

Flying Birds

(C7) Supplies:

- Copy of bird pattern (see page R • 48 in Resources)
- Utility knife
- Drawing paper
- Hole punch
- String
- Markers
- Scissors
- Pictures of various types of birds (available at your local library, etc.)

In Advance: Photocopy the bird pattern onto drawing paper (one for each child). With a utility knife, cut the slit for placement of wings. Cut drawing paper into rectangles that are 6" X 4" to use for wings. Cut string into 24" pieces (one per child).

Directions: Show students various birds from books explaining that God created birds with a variety of colors. Then have students cut out their birds and decorate them with markers on both sides. Then have students color the 6" x 4" wings on both sides as well. Accordion fold the 6" x 4" paper lengthwise into about 1/2" folds. Fold the accordion folded paper in half. Slide the folded paper through the slit on the bird's body. Bring the wings above the bird's body and hole punch through the first fold of the right and left wing. Tie string through holes. Hole punch the eye. Let kids twirl birds on string in  a circle over their heads. Birds can be displayed in an artificial tree before students take home their art project.

Growth Chart

(C8) Supplies:

- Yellow foam board
- Inexpensive measuring tape *(or use measuring tape pattern from page R·47 in Resources)*
- Stickers of flowers *(about 10–12 per child)*
- Red craft foam
- Black markers
- Tacky material to attach pieces
- Utility knife

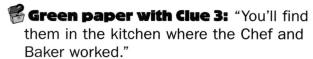

In Advance: Cut foam board into 6" wide pieces *(enough pieces per child to match their height plus 12")*. Use a purchased measuring tape or photocopy the sections of the measuring tape found on page R·47 in Resources. Cut red craft foam into lady bugs *(see pattern on page R·53 in Resources)*. Younger children may need the tape measure glued to the center of the foam board for them.

Directions: Students decorate the lady bugs with black markers after being shown an example of a completed lady bug. Older students can glue the tape measure to the center of the foam board *(running vertically up the center)*. Students may decorate one side of the growth chart with flower stickers. Attach the tacky material to the back of the lady bugs to be the growth marker. Place the lady bug on the growth chart to identify the height of each child.

ELEMENTARY DEDUCTION

(A23) Supplies:

- Index cards
- Markers or colored pencils
- Sample recipe cards *(any kind)*
- Detective's Diaries
- Plain white copy paper cut into 5-1/2" x 8-1/2" pieces, two per child
- Pencils
- Green beads
- Lacing or cording
- *Emily's Bracelet (optional)*
- Treasure of the day: yeast rolls

🗑 **Green paper with Clue 3:** "You'll find them in the kitchen where the Chef and Baker worked."

Hand out index cards and instruct the kids to create a recipe for growing a Christian. Older children can write ways they can grow, younger kids can draw pictures of the ways. *(Refer to the suggestions given during the Bible story and Bible memorization times, and think up more if necessary.)* The children can be as creative as they want. Have some sample recipe cards so children can see how recipes are written. On the back, have kids draw a picture of themselves as growing believers as an example of the product of following their recipe.

Jesus gave us the parables of the yeast and the mustard seed as examples of how we should grow once we know Him as our Savior. God wants us to become strong followers of His so we can encourage others, serve Him, and stay strong when hard things happen.

After creating their recipe cards, pass out the Detective's Diaries. Read through the

directions and help the kids complete the activity for today.

You're like the yeast or the mustard seed Jesus talked about. If you follow the ideas on the cards you wrote, you can grow in your understanding of God and how to follow Him.

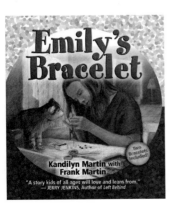

Hand out the green beads and lacing. While doing that, "find" **Clue 3** and show kids what you found. Read them the clue: **"You'll find them in the kitchen where the Chef and Baker worked."** If kids are struggling to unravel the mystery, reread the other clues and help children figure out that the treasure is yeast rolls. After they discover the treasure, let them enjoy a roll while they put a green bead on their lacing or cording to continue working to make their bracelet or choker.

If you have time, you may want to read the book *Emily's Bracelet (©2004, available from Cook Communications Ministries, 1-800-323-7543)* and talk about the story. It will help the children begin to understand more about the colors used in each of the sites. It will also help them get a grasp of the meaning of the choker or bracelet that they are making throughout the week.

DETECTIVES' DEPARTURE

(A24) Supplies:

- "The Quest Continues" take-home paper, one per child
- Craft projects from the day

What does a mustard seed do when it's planted? *(Grow.)* **How does yeast act to help bread rise?** *(It grows.)* **What are we to do as Christians?** *(Grow.)* Tell kids to crouch and begin saying the memory verse, moving to a standing position as they finish. Sing "Grow in Grace and Wisdom" together, then pray briefly, thanking God for His help as each child grows in his or her faith.

Dismiss the children, having them collect their crafts and "The Quest Continues" take-home papers. If the bread they kneaded has been baked, hand out a wrapped roll to each child to take home.

Today your child investigated two parables Jesus told. In one, they learned how bread rises through the action of yeast; in the second they found that a tiny mustard seed grows into a large tree. These examples of growth are in Matthew 13:31-33. Though short, the parables pack valuable truth about growing as a follower of Jesus.

Go online at **www.CookVBS.com** to find out more about *Good News Clues*™ VBS and other materials that can help you and your child grow in your Christian faith.

TALK IT OUT

What would it be like if babies or toddlers never grew up?

How do the things we read and watch influence how we grow, even when we're adults?

FAMILY STUFF

I Remember When...

Point: Even grown-ups were kids once. Just like we grow physically, we should work to grow spiritually.

Supplies:

- Family photo albums
- Scrapbooks
- Videos
- Mementos
- Drawing paper, crayons (*optional*)
- Camera (*optional*)

Activity: Make a time to share family memories with each other. Parents can talk about events in their lives—from the minor to the major ones—when they were children and teens. Tell about how you learned to ride a bike, or the first time you slept away from home. Kids can share their earliest memories of their own lives and their siblings' growing up, from their first lost tooth to funny experiences of trying new foods or learning to walk.

After sharing and laughing over these memories, bring out photo albums and other records of growth—yearbooks, videos, scrapbooks, etc. Look at how each family member has changed over time.

Finish the time of family interaction by talking about how each person can grow spiritually in the next year. Read the parables of the yeast and the mustard seed in Matthew 13:31-33. Help each other think about specific goals, such as memorizing a portion of Scripture, getting involved in a service project that uses a spiritual gift, studying a particular aspect of the Bible, joining a church or Bible-based kids' club, etc. Pray for God's help in growing as His children. Record the goals on a calendar or notebook and make a reminder tool so you can revisit these goals in a year's time.

You may want to ask each family member to make a drawing or take a photograph of the family or each individual to record this particular day and time. Then you can again notice the changes and growth when you check back in one year.

BIBLE VERSE

*(Early-elementary verse in **bold** type.)*

"Grow in grace, and **in the knowledge of our Lord and Saviour Jesus Christ."**
—2 Peter 3:18

site 5

Parables Hidden Treasure and Pearl

"But lay up for yourselves treasures in heaven. . . ."

Matthew 6:20

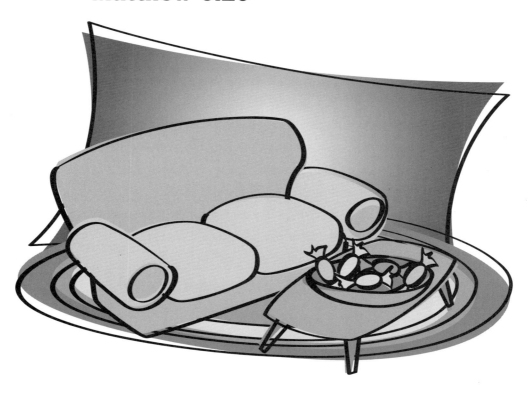

Why Kids Need to Know
That Heaven Can Be Their Eternal Home

Current society is more transient than just 25 years ago. Families move more often, neighborhoods aren't the safe haven they once were, and a sense of community is harder to find in most places. Children can't count on knowing they'll finish their education in the same location, or that life as they know it will be the same a year from now.

That absence of certainty often creates insecurity and anxiety, especially for younger children. That's one reason the certainty of a future in heaven is so important for children to know and understand.

The concept of heaven is vague, intangible, and often webbed with misconceptions and myths. Kids develop all types of imaginative images of heaven, from the belief that everyone there becomes an angel to what heaven is like and what God requires

to enter heaven. This lesson offers children a solid foundation of truth about heaven, the God who inhabits it, and the promise of the future it holds for each of us. Let this lesson be a wellspring of hope and a firm handhold for kids who are often coping with fearful images about the future.

Getting More from the Bible Story

The setting for these two parables would have seemed very common to listeners in Jesus' day. Banks and safety deposit boxes didn't exist in those times, so people typically hid their most valuable possessions by burying them. *(See Matthew 25 for another parable in which someone buries a valuable item.)*

In Jesus' time, Jewish rabbinic law stated that if someone found money, it belonged to him. Those hearing this first parable from Jesus would have known that the man who found the treasure had the right to keep it under this Jewish law. The main point of this parable and the following one is that both individuals received such joy from their discoveries that they were willing to give up all else to possess them. Jesus used these word pictures to teach that the person who realizes the invaluable worth of heaven will want to go to any length to attain that goal.

The parable of the found pearl also relates closely to the life of listeners in Jesus' time. Back then, people considered pearls as very desirable both for the monetary value and for the beauty of the pearl. A gem merchant was continually in search the most valuable pearl. In this story, a merchant finds such a pearl and is willing to do whatever it takes to acquire and keep it.

Both these parables illustrate how significant it is for a person to gain knowledge of Christ and the surety of heaven, and that it's worth any sacrifice to securely anticipate eternity with God.

factoid

Sherlock Holmes—Author Sir Arthur Conan Doyle's introduction of his character Sherlock Holmes greatly influenced detective fiction. Sherlock Holmes first appeared in *Beeton's Christmas Annual* in Doyle's story "A Study in Scarlet" in 1887. Most of the Holmes tales were short stories printed in magazines. Over 40 years, Sir Arthur Conan Doyle wrote 56 short stories and four novels about the fictional detective. The character expanded in the public's imagination when first Sidney Paget and then Frederic Dorr Steele drew illustrations of Holmes. Eventually Sherlock Holmes became a literary character, a folk hero, and a cultural icon.

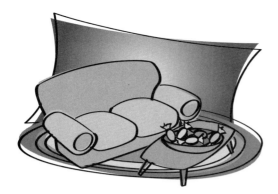

Parables 2

"But lay up for yourselves treasures in heaven. . . ."

Site Mission

Children will learn that if they trust in Jesus as their Savior, heaven will be their eternal home.

Key Bible Verses

Early Elementary

"But lay up for yourselves treasures in heaven. . . . For where your treasure is, there will your heart be also." —**Matthew 6:20-21**

Upper Elementary

"But lay up for yourselves treasures in heaven, where neither moth nor rust doth corrupt, and where thieves do not break through nor steal: For where your treasure is, there will your heart be also." —**Matthew 6:20-21**

Site Coordinators

- **Goldy, an interior decorator** *(If a man is handling this role, he could be called Mr. Gold.)*

- **Dusty, a housecleaner**

The designer would be dressed in contemporary, stylish clothes with a modern hair style. This person's accessories might be a measuring tape, clipboard, some fabric samples, and decorating magazines. The housecleaner would wear work clothes, maybe a bandana around his/her hair, and have a bucket of cleaning supplies (dusting cloth, furniture polish, etc.).

Puppet Option

Investigator #2 or an Assistant Investigator can operate BOSWORTH to help lead the children to different areas and interact spontaneously with the teacher and children. *(See puppet pattern for BOSWORTH on pages R · 55-59.)*

Bible Passage

Matthew 13:44-45

Investigator's Inventory

General

☐ Living Room mural

☐ *Good News Clues*™ CD or tape copy

☐ CD player or cassette tape player

☐ Copy of "The Quest Continues" student take-home paper *(page E5 · 14)* for each child

☐ Copy of the "Detective's Diary" for each child *(pages R · 61-68)*. Note the two age levels and use accordingly.

Games and Activities

☐ Small treasure chest with lock and key

☐ Clues written on yellow or gold paper

☐ King-size white bedsheet

☐ Two to four bright lights

☐ Shovel

☐ Small ball *(smaller than a golf ball)*

☐ Treasure box

☐ Boxes, bags, clothing

☐ Cloth bag of jingling coins

☐ Seven poster board placards with writing as instructed on page E5 · 7

☐ Key Verse posters

☐ Poster board, one sheet/4 children

☐ Key Verse Cards *(page R · 60)*

☐ Copy of song lyrics for each child or have the words on an overhead transparency *(pages R · 21-26)*

☐ Overhead projector

☐ Puppet *(optional)*

☐ Yellow or gold beads *(one per child)*

☐ Lacing or cording

☐ *Emily's Bracelet (optional)*

☐ Couch or lounge chair

☐ Two chairs

☐ Two carpet squares

☐ Two or more end tables

☐ Two or more small lamp shades

☐ Garbage bags filled with paper wads

☐ Cotton balls or foam packing peanuts

☐ Grocery bags, paper or plastic

Snacks

☐ Pudding *(store bought or homemade)*

☐ Clear 8-oz. cups

☐ Spoons

☐ Chocolate chips, butterscotch chips, or mini marshmallows

☐ Small decorated cookies *(store bought or homemade)*

☐ Juice

☐ Doilies and serving plate

☐ Fancy napkins

☐ Paper cups

Crafts

☐ Small boxes *(purchased or made with the pattern in Resources, page R · 50)*

☐ Gold spray paint

- ☐ Old newspapers
- ☐ Pasta—variety of kinds
- ☐ Needles *(one per child)*
- ☐ Thread—white or gold
- ☐ Pearl-like beads of various sizes
- ☐ 1-1/2" wide, wired gold ribbon
- ☐ Spring clothespins *(one per child)*

Procedures of the Day

10 minutes: Preparing to Search

15–20 minutes: Focus on the Bible

10 minutes: Bible Memorization

5 minutes: Music Time

15 minutes: Gumshoe Grub

20 minutes: Case-Cracking Games

20 minutes: Putting the Pieces Together

10 minutes: Elementary Deduction

10 minutes: Detectives' Departure

Detective Preparation

- Have craft samples prepared in advance to show Detectives.

- Be sure all supplies are gathered and your site is ready each day for Detectives to arrive.

- Post the Procedures of the Day where Investigators and helpers *(called Assistant Investigators)* can refer to it.

- Address each other by site titles. Children should be referred to as Detectives. The helpers that go with them from camp to camp are called Assistant Investigators—Assistant Investigator Jim or Assistant Investigator Sharon.

- After taking attendance, an Assistant Investigator should tell those responsible for refreshments how many Detectives are present to be prepared for snack time.

- In advance, write all the clues for the day's hidden treasure onto the color of paper indicated.

- You may wish to do some background research into the Bible story. Refer to Bible commentaries, encyclopedias, and dictionaries for additional information.

PREPARING TO SEARCH

(A25) Supplies:

- A small tabletop size treasure chest with a secure, working lock and key. Set box in a prominent place in the room.

 Prepare Clue 1 on yellow paper:
"A sweet fortune."

When the children enter, Goldy will be taking and writing down measurements for drapes or furniture coverings while Dusty is cleaning. One can be humming or whistling while working.

Once children are seated, Goldy turns to Dusty.

GOLDY: *(Looking at swatches of upholstery fabric.)* **I'm still not certain what fabric would be best for re-covering this furniture. Which of these do you think fits best in this room?**

DUSTY: *(Looks at the fabric and surveys the room.)* **Hmm. This is a very fancy room. Not the kind of place where the kids will be hanging out and watching videos or playing games. You don't need to worry about purple grape juice stains, do you?**

GOLDY: *(Shakes her head "no.")* **No, this living room is meant to be a place to welcome guests. You could have a formal tea here, or**

take wedding pictures in this room. I expect at Christmas this family has a fancy Christmas tree with gold and silver ornaments in here—something very expensive and beautiful.

DUSTY: *(Points at the treasure box.)* **This box is something very expensive and beautiful, don't you think? It looks like it might have held a treasure once upon a time.**

GOLDY: I've wondered about it too. *(Turns to kids.)* **What do you Detectives think? Is this some kind of treasure box that holds a valuable treasure?**

Let kids offer their thoughts. *(She picks up the box and looks at it from different angles.)*

DUSTY: I'd love to know what's inside. *(She takes the box and looks at it, tries to open it, but it's locked.)* **Since you are all experienced detectives, would you be willing to figure out what's inside this treasure box?** *(After kids agree, she can pass the box to the kids.)* **Each of you hold the box and then pass it on. I'd like to know if you have any clues about what's inside.**

GOLDY: Or how it could be opened.

As children examine the box briefly

and pass it on—an Investigator may want to help expedite this process—Dusty and Goldy resume their tasks. When the box returns to them, they can set it again in its place. As Goldy sets it down, she sees **clue 1** on yellow paper, picks it up and reads it silently with a frown on her face.

GOLDY: What could this be for? It says, "A sweet fortune." Do any of you detectives have an idea what that means? When she gets no answers, she hands it to an Investigator and says, **Why don't you keep it, so you can work on it some more?**

DUSTY: I don't know what that clue means, but it does make me think of a couple of parables Jesus told. They were both about fortunes that people found. Why don't I tell you the story and see if it helps work out the meaning of the clue?

FOCUS ON THE BIBLE

Matthew 13:44-45

(A26) Supplies:

- King-size white bedsheet strung up a few feet from a wall as a screen.

- 2–4 bright lights *(photographic lights or strong work lights)*

- Shovel

- Small ball (smaller than a golf ball)
- Treasure box
- Armload of "stuff" such as boxes, bags, and clothing
- Cloth bag of jingling coins
- Seven poster board placards, each with a phrase about heaven:
  1. No sadness or tears
  2. No sickness or death
  3. God lives there
  4. No sun—God is the light
  5. Streets of gold
  6. Gates made of single pearls
  7. Walls of precious, sparkling gems.

Set up the sheet to act as a screen upon which children will see shadows acting out the Bible story. The lights should be positioned a few feet behind the sheet and pointing toward it. Two actors—one at a time—will be behind the sheet (out of sight of the kids) with the lights behind him/her, creating a shadow play. Each will make movements that visualize the Bible text as it is narrated. The actor for the first parable will come in from one side, while the actor for the second comes from the other; this will distinguish the two parables from each other. The lights can be turned off briefly between parables also to help separate them from one another.

The narrator can direct children's attention to the sheet screen, then stand off to the side to read the script with expression.

NARRATOR:
> This is a parable Jesus told about heaven. Heaven is where God lives. It's a place where every person who knows Jesus as their Savior will be able to live forever. Heaven is such a special,

wonderful place! Jesus used two parables to help people understand it better.

(Actor for parable one enters and performs actions concurrent with script.)

In this first parable, Jesus said that the kingdom of heaven is like a treasure. This treasure was hidden underground in a field. *(Actor "digs" with shovel.)*

A man found the treasure under the ground. *(Actor drops shovel and bends to pick up treasure.)*

He was so excited and overjoyed. *(Actor jumps up and down, throws up hands in delight, acts thrilled.)*

He wanted to keep the treasure safe. *(Actor looks around furtively while holding treasure close to chest.)*

So he hid it in the ground again. *(Quickly digs a hole and buries treasure, and pats it down with hands.)*

Finding this amazing treasure was so thrilling, that the man wanted to do anything he could to keep it. So he collected everything he had. *(Goes off "stage" and comes back with arms full of stuff—boxes, clothes—and walks off other side.)*

He took the money he got for selling his things. *(Comes back holding money bag.)*

And he bought that field where the treasure was hidden. That's how very important this treasure was.

(Stands over treasure with shovel in hand in a proud stance.)

Extinguish lights for 15–30 seconds, then turn them back on.

Second actor enters from opposite side.

Jesus wanted His listeners, and you and me, to know how special heaven is, so He told this second parable about heaven. Jesus said that the kingdom of heaven is like a merchant, or businessman, who wanted to buy very good pearls. Pearls are valuable and expensive and beautiful. The merchant searched for the best pearls.

(Actor acts as if he's inspecting pearls.)

When he found the most valuable pearl there was, he knew he wanted to have it.

(Holds up small ball as pearl, clutches it to himself, jumps up and down, twirls around to show excitement.)

So just like the first man, this merchant went home and collected all his things.

(Goes off stage, comes back holding "stuff," exits opposite side.)

He sold everything.

(Returns with empty arms, holding money bag.)

Then with the money he got, he went right away and bought that priceless pearl. It was that special.

(Hands away money off stage and takes pearl, walks around holding and admiring it.)

Turn off light. Narrator comes to stand in front of kids.

NARRATOR:

Do you know what heaven is like? Jesus used these two stories to help us understand that heaven is more special than anything we have on earth. It's worth more than all we own now. Here's what the Bible says about heaven.

Ask seven kids to come up front and stand shoulder to shoulder. As narrator names each description, he hands that card to a child to hold and show the group.

Heaven is a place where there is no sadness. God says no one will ever cry there.

No one is sick, or ever dies in heaven.

God Himself lives in heaven. When we trust Jesus as our Savior, we'll know for sure that one day heaven will be our home, and we'll be right there where God is.

Do you know that heaven doesn't need a sun or light bulbs for light? God Himself is the light of heaven. And it will only be daytime, never nighttime there.

Heaven is like a treasure because its streets are made of pure gold, shiny like glass.

The gates of heaven are made of a single pearl. Just one giant, perfect pearl makes a gate.

The walls around heaven are made of precious gems. They sparkle and shine.

Heaven isn't like anything on earth. It's a treasure God has to share with us one day. He will share heaven with all who have realized that they've sinned and know that they need their sins forgiven. When we ask Jesus to forgive our sins, and to be our Savior, Jesus washes our sin away. And He promises that heaven will

be our home one day. If you have questions about this, or aren't sure if heaven is going to be your home one day, you can talk to one of the leaders today before you go home. They want to answer your questions and help you understand how you can be sure heaven will be your home one day.

Thank kids and dismiss them to the Bible Memorization activity.

BIBLE MEMORIZATION

(A27) Supplies:

- Two Key Verse posters *(one for early-elementary verse version, one for upper elementary)*
- Poster board, one sheet per 4 kids
- Markers
- Detective's Diaries *(see page R · 61-68 in Resources)*
- Pencils
- Key Verse Cards
- Tape

In Advance: Write each Key Verse on a separate poster board.

Early Elementary

"But lay up for yourselves treasures in heaven. . . . For where your treasure is, there will your heart be also." —Matthew 6:20-21

Upper Elementary

"But lay up for yourselves treasures in heaven, where neither moth nor rust doth corrupt, and where thieves do not break through nor steal: For where your treasure is, there will your heart be also." —Matthew 6:20-21

If you are working with multiple age levels, divide children into early- and upper-elementary groups, since their verses are significantly different. Then break into groups of three to four children. Have leaders and helpers work with younger groups. Give each group a poster board and some markers and ask them to come up with a rebus for the verse, putting drawings and symbols in place of as many words as they can. Have them write and draw the verse on the poster board, using large letters. Encourage groups to illustrate and decorate the edges of their poster.

After sufficient time has passed, ask each group to present its poster to the others, reading the verse aloud in unison. Display the posters around the room.

Hand out the Detective's Diaries and pencils or markers. Read the directions together on the Living Room page and let the children do the activity. Assist them as needed. Tape a Key Verse Card in each child's diary as well.

MUSIC TIME

Treasures in Heaven

(A28) Supplies:

- Copy of song lyrics for each child or have the words on an overhead transparency *(pages R · 21-26)*
- *Good News Clues*™ CD or tape copy of "Treasures in Heaven" *(Track 6)*
- CD or tape player
- Overhead projector
- Puppet *(optional)*

This is a good time to have the children move around. First, have them listen to the song for this site, "Treasures in Heaven." Then play the song again and have the kids join in with the singing. Allow them to stand and move around if you have the space. If age-appropriate, project the words of the song onto a screen for the children to follow along as they sing. You may want to have BOSWORTH help teach the song.

 **GUMSHOE GRUB**

Treasure in a Cup

(S9) Supplies:

- Pudding—can be store bought in large containers or make your own

- Clear cups—8-ounce size

- Spoons

- Chocolate chips, butterscotch chips, or mini marshmallows

In Advance: Prepare the pudding according to the directions if you are making your own.

Directions: Spoon pudding into a clear cup about one-half full. Spread the pudding up the sides of the cup, leaving a space in the middle of the pudding. Add about a tablespoon of the chips or mini marshmallows in the space. Top with a spoonful of pudding to hide the surprise!

NOTE: Be aware of any allergies to chocolate or dairy products.

Tea Party

(S10) Supplies:

- Small decorated cookies, store-bought or homemade

- Juice, such as apple juice

- Doilies and serving plate

- Fancy Napkins

- Cups

In Advance: If you are preparing homemade cookies, plan ahead to have time to make and decorate them. Children enjoy simple cookies like sugar cookies or chocolate chip cookies which can still be decorated.

Directions: Have a "tea" party with apple juice (or water) and fancy cookies. Serve the cookies on a doily-lined plate. Add to the tea party feel with fancy napkins.

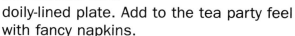 **CASE-CRACKING GAMES**

In Advance: Prepare **Clue 2** on yellow paper.

 Clue 2: "A precious metal covers it."

Include the clue in your choice of games. Let one of the children find it while playing. If no one notices it, have a leader "find" it when the game is over.

Living Room Obstacle Course Race

(G10) Supplies:

- Couch

- 2 or more ottomans or chairs

- 2 or more carpet squares

- 2 or more end tables

- 2 or more small lamp shades

Set up an obstacle course using living room items. The course can be laid out in a circle, or in a line. The couch is first, then the carpet square, the lamp shades, the end tables, and then the ottoman or chairs. This course can be run by one child at a time, or you can divide into two groups and have one child from each group go through at a time.

Here's the path: Kids jump or climb over the back of the couch to the front, run up to the carpet square and sit on it and push themselves to the lamp shade, which they put on their head while crab or duck walking to the end table. They circle the table twice, then stand up and run to the ottoman/chair, where they sit down. Then they reverse direction in the course and return the way they came, leaving the lampshade where they found it, continuing through the course until they return to the line and the next person takes off.

Be sure someone finds **Clue 2**, and have a leader read it: "A precious metal covers it."

Living Room Clean-Up

(G11) Supplies:

- A couple of garbage bags full of paper wads
- A couple of bags of cotton balls or foam packing peanuts
- Grocery bags

This game can be done with the entire group at once, or with teams, depending on the size of your play space. It works best in a non-windy area. Set up a living room scene with chairs, tables, a rug, etc, *(similar to the scene introducing the Bible story)*. Have kids work in groups of two to three, with each group receiving a grocery bag. Tell the kids their job is to clean the living room. Then create a big mess by throwing "zillions" of paper wads and foam packing pieces all over the place, on the floor and the furniture. Tell them they have a set amount of time *(one or two minutes)* to pick up the garbage in the living room. Have extra bags for those who fill theirs. At the end of the time, see who collected the most, or how clean the living room is.

Alternative: Time how long it takes the group to clean the living room. If using teams, see which one gets the job done the fastest.

PUTTING THE PIECES TOGETHER

Treasure Box

(C9) Supplies:

- Boxes *(purchase boxes or use the pattern on page R·50 of Resources)*
- Glue
- Gold spray paint
- Old newspapers
- Pasta—different shapes like elbow, bow-tie, etc.

In Advance: Spray paint the boxes and pasta pieces at least a day before to allow enough time for the paint to dry.

Directions: Have each student choose decorative pasta pieces to decorate their box. They need to glue the

pieces onto the lid. Allow the glue to dry before moving the boxes.

Hearts and Pearls

(C10) Supplies:

- Needles *(one per student)*
- Thread *(white or gold)*
- Pearl-like beads of various sizes
- 1-1/2 inch-wide wired gold ribbon
- Glue
- Spring clothespins *(one per child)*

In Advance: Thread needles with a 36" length of thread, doubling it, and knotting the ends together. Cut gold ribbon into 10-inch lengths.

Directions: Fold ribbon in half. Shape the ribbon into a heart shape. Glue ends of ribbon together with a couple of dots of glue. Clamp with clothespin until glue is dry. Choose a bead that will hang below that heart. Pass the needle through the hole of the bead, then between the threads, near the knot to secure it. Add another bead or two if you like. Then pass the needle through the bottom of the heart. Add more beads until it reaches the glued center of the heart *(at the end of the ribbon).* Stitch through the ribbon twice until the needle passes through the top of the heart. Add more beads if you like before passing the needle through the top bead twice to lock it in place. Cut the thread below the needle and knot the end. Hang the ribbon heart in a window or from a ceiling fan.

ELEMENTARY DEDUCTION

(A29) Supplies:

- Yellow or gold beads
- Lacing or cording

Yellow paper with clue 3: "These won't buy you heaven, but they remind you of heaven's streets. You'll find some in the treasure box in the Living Room."

As you sit down with the kids, have the clue lying in an obvious place. If a child doesn't discover it, be sure a leader does. After reading it and giving children a chance to figure out that the treasure is gold-wrapped candy hidden in the treasure box, let someone retrieve it. Hand out the candy; while they're enjoying it, ask children to tell you what they know about heaven. Let them take turns telling you what they've learned today.

Jesus told us the two parables about heaven so we could know that heaven is something special and beautiful. Nothing we know now compares to it. Living there will be much sweeter than the candy you're eating. And the best part is that we can be sure we're going to live in heaven if we know Jesus as our Savior. Imagine how much God loves you, that He wants you to share heaven with Him one day!

Give the children each a yellow bead to put on a lacing. Remind them that whenever they have questions about heaven, knowing Jesus, or forgiveness of their sins, leaders are available to talk to them.

DETECTIVES' DEPARTURE

(A29) Supplies:

- "The Quest Continues" take-home paper, one per child
- Craft projects from the day

Choose one early-elementary verse poster and one upper-elementary poster made during the Bible Memorization activity. Ask an early-elementary volunteer to hold the early-elementary poster and lead the rest of the younger children in reading the verse. Do the same with the upper-elementary kids and verse.

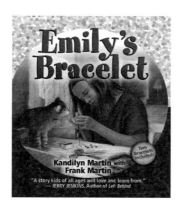

If you have sufficient time, you may want to read the book *Emily's Bracelet (©2004, available from Cook Communications Ministries, 1-800-323-7543)* and talk about the story. It will help the children understand more about the colors used in each of the sites during this week's VBS program.

Sing a favorite song, then dismiss the kids with their crafts and "The Quest Continues" take-home paper.

Today your child spent time in the formal living room at VBS and discovered that God has a wondrous treasure in store for those who know Jesus as their Savior. Jesus explained how special this treasure—heaven—is by telling two parables in Matthew 13:44-45. You may want to take time to read these two verses to have a better understanding of what your child was studying today.

Go online at **www.CookVBS.com** to learn more about what your child is experiencing at *Good News Clues*™ VBS.

TALK IT OUT

What treasures are most precious to our family?

How do our actions day to day show what we most value?

FAMILY STUFF

Treasures to Share

Point: We all have special treasures, but there is one treasure that is greater than anything we can think or imagine.

Supplies:

- Box or bag for each family member
- Treasure from each family member put inside of their own bag or box
- Sweet treat or dessert to share with the entire family

Ask each family member to search out one thing they consider a treasure, and bring it in a box or bag to share at a designated family time. Each person should keep his or her item a secret. If the item can't be brought to the family time, the person can draw a picture of the item.

At the appointed time, gather the entire family together with their bags or boxes. When everyone is seated, explain how the activity will be conducted. Have family members take turns giving clues about their item, using adjectives about its size, color, shape, function, etc. Others can try to guess. Play until everyone's treasure has been revealed. Then let individuals tell why their chosen item is special. Be sure to acknowledge each individual's treasure as special to them even if it appears common or ordinary to another family member.

After concluding the family activity, read Jesus' two parables in Matthew 13:44-45. Share with one another why heaven is a treasure greater than all the money you could ever have, or the most valuable gems. Read from the Bible the memory verse, Matthew 6:20-21. Discuss how the way we live shows where we consider our treasure to be.

Conclude your family time with a sweet treat *(ice cream, doughnuts, cookies)* as a reminder that living in heaven will be sweeter than any dessert could ever be.

BIBLE VERSE

*(Early-elementary verse in **bold** type.)*

"But lay up for yourselves treasures in heaven, *where neither moth nor rust doth corrupt, and where thieves do not break through nor steal:* **For where your treasure is, there will your heart be also."**
—**Matthew 6:20-21**

Preschool Introduction

This guide helps you adapt the *Good News Clues*™ program for preschoolers. Included are suggested schedules, descriptions of learning centers, stories, and activities suitable for three to five year olds.

Before reading, you may want to scan the Director's Guide for *Good News Clues*™ VeBS®. There you'll see that older children go to a different Discovery Site each day. Preschoolers do not; they remain in the same area. Use the suggestions in this manual to make the area a little different each day to fit with each room in the house.

Very **e**xciting **B**ible **S**chool's® learning center approach is ideal for young children because they learn best by doing, seeing, hearing, touching, smelling, and even tasting. Learning centers also help children grow socially. The activities help them think about the theme of each session. Because young children learn so much through play, we include suggestions for guided playtimes. But be sure to allow unstructured playtimes as well.

Another important aspect of VBS for preschoolers is relationships. It is important for them to connect with and trust their leaders. The learning centers and activities in VBS are designed to help those relationships develop. Children will learn best if all the leaders are familiar with each day's Bible story, Key Verse, and theme found in **Site Mission** and are looking for teachable moments during the day to reinforce what is being taught. Leaders can then focus on kids and reinforce the process of discovery.

During **Hands-on Exploration**, some Detectives may enjoy moving through all activities. However, because others will finish in your planned centers before time to move to the next activity, you might want to make available:

- Preschool books and puzzles relating to the specific Bible stories for this week. These can be placed in a Quiet Corner for Detectives to enjoy without supervision.

- An ample supply of art materials *(washable markers, glue sticks, large confetti, stickers, magazine pictures, etc.)* for Detectives to use in adding to your daily theme murals.

Remember, preschoolers are more process- than result-oriented, so enjoy each step with them without worrying too much about the final product. Your attention and approval are more important than a perfectly-made craft.

Staff needed: Two leaders *(Investigators)* and enough helpers *(called Assistant Investigators)* to provide one adult or teen for every four to six children.

Large group option: If you have a very large group of preschoolers *(more than 20 children)* you may want to use more than one area and set up a different theme or room in each area. Divide your group so that every small group gets to visit each room in the house during VBS.

The **Music Time** activities include singing. You can enhance this time by using rhythm instruments, singing song phrases antiphonally, clapping, or using motions to indicate specific words in the song. Be creative!

Daily assemblies: For the first and last 15 minutes of each day, you may want to provide separate activities for preschoolers while older children are in the large group assemblies. You might read books, listen to music, or use puppets. A review of finger plays and songs learned earlier might be fun too.

Backdrops and props: Use **Setting the Scene** sections in each of the Preschool Sites for suggestions. When setting up your room, try to create a central area for story time that is decorated to look like the living area for the day. Then arrange activity areas that fit with each day's theme around this central setting.

The storyteller may want to put on a different head covering each day to help the children imagine the characters in the stories. Simple props will spark interest and hold attention.

Preparing for children: Each day before children arrive, make sure your area is well stocked. You'll want plenty of construction paper, glue sticks, safety scissors, crayons, and washable markers. You might also want music CDs or tapes and a CD or tape player to provide background music. For outdoor play, beanbags and large, soft, playground balls provide lots of fun for preschoolers. Be sure that any "in advance" tasks in the lessons are taken care of so that you and the leaders can focus all of your attention on the children. If you know your children's names, it is very helpful to write their names on the crafts or activities in advance of the activity time. **Because snacks will be offered, be sure to check with parents on the first day of VBS regarding food allergies.** An attendance chart is provided in the Reproducible Resources section, page R·5. Name tags can be found in the Reproducible Resources section, page R·6 or on the *Good News Clues*™ CD.

Included in the *Good News Clues*™ kit is a CD containing original music and electronic clip art. Check with your VBS director concerning the use of these resources.

Colored name tags: If you have more than eight children in your group, divide into smaller teams by putting a colored dot or mark on the name tags and assigning an equal number of children to each color. If you have more than 14 children, consider using three colors on the name tags. That way, when you need to do activities in smaller groups, you can simply ask for each color group to go where you need them to go. It will also help if you assign an adult helper to each color, and give that adult a name tag with that color dot or mark.

Leader's tips: If you did not receive the Preschool Characteristics chart during staff training, ask your VBS director for this sheet. *(Reproducible Resources, pages R·17-20.)* Here are some other important points to remember when working with preschoolers:

- Try to find time during the day to talk with each child.

- Look for "teachable moments."

- Try not to rush through activities.

- Allow plenty of time for children's questions and conversation with children.

- Experience the process with them—preschoolers care more about the process than the results.

- Enjoy yourself!

Overview Chart

SITE	Garden *Site Color: Dark*	Dining Room *Site Color: Red*	Family Room *Site Color: White*	Kitchen *Site Color: Green*	Living Room *Site Color: Gold*
BIBLE STORY	Adam and Eve sin. *(Genesis 1:26-31; 2:4–3:23)*	Jesus dies and comes back to life. *(Matthew 26:17-29; 26:47–28:10)*	The Parable of the Lost Sheep. *(Luke 15:1-7)*	The Parables of Salt and Light give clues about living for Jesus. *(Matthew 5:13-16)*	The Parables of the Hidden Treasure and the Pearl give clues about our future home. *(Matthew 13:44-46)*
KEY VERSE	*"For all have sinned, and come short of the glory of God."* — Romans 3:23	*"He is not here: for he is risen."* — Matthew 28:6	*"Rejoice with me; for I have found my sheep which was lost."* — Luke 15:6	*"Let your light so shine."* — Matthew 5:16	*"The kingdom of heaven is like unto treasure hid in a field."* — Matthew 13:44
CONCEPT	We need to be forgiven.	We can be saved from our sin through Jesus.	We can be welcomed into God's family.	We can live for Jesus.	We can live with Jesus forever.
RESPONSE	Children will understand that they've sinned and turn to God.	Children will understand that through Jesus they can know God.	Children will learn that God loves and cares for us.	Children will learn that God wants others to see His love through us.	Children will understand that God wants us to live forever with Him in heaven.

Supplies

The following comprehensive supply list can be combined with the Elementary supply list *(pages D·18-26)* to make planning easier.

Each activity, craft, game, and snack in this Preschool program has a corresponding list of supplies and are referenced in the PG *(page #)*

column in the compiled list below. You may want to "✔"off the items you already have on hand, and pencil in the quantities you need of each item based on the estimated number of children attending your program.

CATEGORY & ITEM	PG	QTY	/UNIT	TOT	HAVE	NEED	✔
Common Supplies PRESCHOOL ITEMS							
Bibles							
Good News Clues™ CD *(Duplicate CDs or cassettes)*							
CD player or cassette player							
Scissors, pens or pencils, crayons, markers							
Glue, tape *(clear and masking)*, hole punch, stapler							
Serving bowls and spoons, measuring cups, measuring spoons							
Paper plates, cups, and napkins for snacks							
Preschool murals and cutout transparencies							

CATEGORY & ITEM	PG	QTY	/UNIT	TOT	HAVE	NEED	✔
THE GARDEN Preschool Supplies							
Garden Mural	R·79	1	/site				
Copy of "The Quest Continues—Preschool" student take-home paper							
(page P1·11)	P1·11	1	each/child				
(PA1) Sturdy, large cardboard boxes reinforced at the bottom with the sides cut off on the top	P1·5	1-2	each/site				
(PA1) Various plastic garden tools: e.g., shovel, rake, scoops, etc.	P1·5	1	variety/site				
(PA1) Potting soil, raw rice, or beans	P1·5	1	variety/site				
(PA1) Flowers and/or plants, either real or plastic	P1·5		quantity/boxes				
(PA2) Picture books with photos and/or drawings of bugs/insects	P1·5		several/site				
(PA3) Picture of a tree in a garden	P1·5	1	each/site				
(PS1) Healthy veggies to dip, such as carrot sticks, celery sticks, cucumber slices, and other vegetables	P1·7	2-4	each/child				
(PS1) One or two soft dips, such as ranch dip or vegetable dip (already prepared or use your own recipe)	P1·7	1-2	each/site				
(PS1) Small paper plates	P1·7	1	each/child				
(PS1) Spoons for dip	P1·7	1	each/container				
(PS2) Red crepe paper cut into 10-inch circles	P1·7	1	each/child				
(PS2) Pretzels, small crackers, or candy	P1·7	1-2	scoops/child				
(PS2) Green floral tape or green twist ties	P1·7	1	each/child				
(PS2) Bushel baskets	P1·7	1	each/site				
(PG1) Butterfly net or bag	P1·7	1	each/site				
(PG1) Picture books with photos of insects found in your location	P1·7	1	each/child				
(PG2) Garden hoses	P1·8	3-4	each/site				
(PG2) Large plastic rakes	P1·8	2	each/site				
(PG2) Small plastic shovels, spades, and small water bucket	P1·8	2	each/site				
(PG2) Rocks	P1·8	2-4	each/site				
(PG2) Flowers	P1·8	2-4	each/site				
(PG2) Wood chips	P1·8	1	bag/site				
(PC1) Brightly colored 12" x 18" construction paper	P1·8	1	each/child				
(PC1) Washable tempera paint in 3 colors	P1·8	1	each/site				
(PC1) Squeeze bottles	P1·8	3	each/site				
(PC1) Newspaper	P1·8		/site				
(PC1) Paint shirts	P1·8	1	each/child				
(PC2) Colored electrical tape	P1·9	1	roll/3-4 children				
(PC2) Waxed paper	P1·9	1	box/site				
(PC2) Yarn	P1·9	1	skein/site				
(PC2) Pressed flowers and leaves	P1·9	4-5	each/child				
(PC2) Iron	P1·9	1	each/site				
(PC2) Hole Punch	P1·9	1	each/site				
(PC2) Cardboard pieces, approximately 8-1/2" X 11"	P1·9	1	each/child				
(PA6) Treasure of the day—sunglasses	P1·9	1	each/child				
(PA6) Picture of the sun, picture of eyes	P1·9	1	each/site				

CATEGORY & ITEM	PG	QTY	/UNIT	TOT	HAVE	NEED	✔
THE DINING ROOM Preschool Supplies							
Dining Room Mural	R·80	1	each/site				
Copy of "The Quest Continues—Preschool" student take-home paper (page P2·11)	P2·11	1	each/child				
(PA7) Plastic plates, glasses/cups, and utensils	P2·5	8-10	each/site				
(PA7) Tablecloths and/or placemats	P2·5	8-10	each/site				
(PA7) Centerpieces	P2·5	1-2	each/site				
(PA7) Magazine photo or picture of set table	P2·5	1	each/site				
(PA8) Play dough (purchased or made using recipe provided)	P2·5	1	8-10/children				
(PA9) Sad/Happy puppets (see page R·47 in Resources)	P2·5	1	each/child				
(PA9) Craft sticks	P2·5	1	each/child				
(PS3) Red fruit such as cherries, watermelon balls, or strawberries	P2·7	3-4	pieces/child				
(PS3) Red candies such as red licorice, red sour balls, red hots, etc.	P2·7	3-4	each/child				
(PS3) Small paper cups	P2·7	1	each/child				
(PS3) Napkins	P2·7	1	each/child				
(PS4) Matzo crackers or other crackers	P2·8	4-5	each/child				
(PS4) Cheese slices (American, Swiss, cheddar, etc.)	P2·8	4-5	each/child				
(PS4) Napkins	P2·8	1	each/child				
(PS4) Knife for slicing cheese	P2·8	1	each/site				
(PG3) Tray	P2·8	1	each/team				
(PG3) Plastic cup, plate, knife, fork, spoon	P2·8	1	set/team				
(PG3) Napkin	P2·8	1	each/team				
(PG4) Plastic spoon	P2·8	1	each/child				
(PG4) Small foil or paper wad/ball	P2·8	1	each/child				
(PC3) Card stock, cut in strips 1" x 6"	P2·9	3-5	each/child				
(PC3) Glitter glue	P2·9	2-3	each/site				
(PC3) Silk flowers	P2·9	3-5	each/child				
(PC3) Resealable sandwich-size bags	P2·9	1	each/child				
(PC4) Plain white pot holders	P2·9	1	each/child				
(PC4) Black permanent pen	P2·9	1-2	each/site				
(PC4) Fabric paint (one color)	P2·9	1-2	bottle/site				
(PC4) Foil pie plate	P2·9	1-2	each/site				
(PC4) Paintbrush	P2·9	1-2	each site				
(PC4) Pan of soapy water if sink is not available	P2·9	1-2	each/site				
(PC4) Handwashing soap	P2·9	1	bottle/site				
(PC4) Paper towels	P2·9	1-2	roll/site				
(PC4) Paint shirts or smocks	P2·9	1	each/child				
(PA12) Treasure of the Day—red plastic cups	P2·10	1	each/child				
(PA12) Pitcher of water	P2·10	1	each/site				

CATEGORY & ITEM	PG	QTY	/UNIT	TOT	HAVE	NEED	✔
THE FAMILY ROOM Preschool Supplies							
Family Room Mural	R·81	1	each/site				
Copy of "The Quest Continues—Preschool" student take-home paper *(page P3·11)* for each child	P3·11	1	each/child				
(PA13) Variety of preschool-age games	P3·5		variety/site				
(PA14) Several hundred cotton balls	P3·5	7-8	bags/site				
(PA14) Paper sack, box, or wastebasket	P3·5	1-2	each/site				
(PA15) Robe	P3·5	1	each/site				
(PA15) Towel	P3·5	1	each/site				
(PA15) Sash	P3·5	1	each/site				
(PA15) Stuffed animal lamb	P3·5	1	each/site				
(PA15) Several classroom chairs	P3·5	8-10	each/site				
(PA16) Sheep made from pattern *(see page R·48 in Resources)*	P3·7	1	each word/verse				
(PA17) Rhythm band instruments *(optional)*	P3·7	1	each/child				
(PS5) Regular or microwave popcorn in a variety of flavors, such as kettle corn, cheese popcorn, buttered popcorn	P3·7	1-2	scoops/child				
(PS5) Large servings bowls	P3·7	1	each/flavor				
(PS5) Scoops	P3·7	1	each/bowl				
(PS5) Small paper bowls	P3·7	1	each/child				
(PS6) Napkins	P3·7	1	each/child				
(PS6) White cake mix	P3·7	1	ea/24 cupcakes				
(PS6) Eggs	P3·7		/cake mix				
(PS6) Oil	P3·7		/cake mix				
(PS6) Cupcake tin	P3·7		/cake mix				
(PS6) Cupcake liners	P3·7	1	each/cupcake				
(PS6) Canned or homemade white frosting	P3·8	1	each/cake mix				
(PS6) White sprinkles	P3·8	1	each/cake mix				
(PS6) Napkins	P3·8	1	each/child				
(PG5) Taped or chalked shapes *(circles, squares, rectangles)* on the floor	P3·8		each/site				
(PG5) Music *(CD or video)*	P3·8	1	each/site				
(PG6) Towel and sash for headdress *(optional)*	P3·8	1	each/site				
(PC5) Felt—white and light brown	P3·9	1	each/child				
(PC5) Puppet pattern *(page R·49 in Resources)*	P3·9	1	each/site				
(PC5) Fabric glue	P3·9	1-2	bottles/site				
(PC5) Mini pom-poms *(white)*	P3·9	10-15	each/sheep				
(PC5) Black permanent marker	P3·9	1	each/site				
(PC5) Resealable sandwich-size bags	P3·9	1	each/child				
(PC6) Small pink ribbon bows *(purchased or homemade)*	P3·9	4	each/child				
(PC6) Card stock	P3·9	2	pieces/child				
(PC6) Business-size envelopes	P3·9	1	each/child				

CATEGORY & ITEM	PG	QTY	/UNIT	TOT	HAVE	NEED	✔
THE FAMILY ROOM Preschool Supplies (continued)							
(PC6) Glue	P3·9	2-3	bottles/site				
(PC6) Patterns for sheep and ball caps *(page R·51 in Resources)*	P3·9	1	each/site				
(PC6) Pattern for tic-tac-toe board *(page R·52 in Resources)*	P3·9	1	each/site				
(PA18) Treasure of the Day—white sheep	P3·10	1	each/child				
(PA18) Small piece of "wool-like" fabric	P3·10	1	each/site				
(PA18) Model or picture of a farm	P3·10	1	each/site				
(PA18) Model or picture of a shepherd	P3·10	1	each/site				

CATEGORY & ITEM	PG	QTY	/UNIT	TOT	HAVE	NEED	✔
THE KITCHEN Preschool Supplies							
Kitchen Mural	R·82	1	each/site				
Copy of "The Quest Continues—Preschool" student take-home paper *(page P4·11)*	P4·11	1	each/child				
(PA19) Preschool kitchen toys, e.g., stove, refrigerator, oven, mixer measuring cups, etc.	P4·5	1	each/site				
(PA20) Sifters	P4·5	3-4	each/site				
(PA20) Measuring cups	P4·5	3-4	sets/site				
(PA20) Plastic colanders	P4·5	3-4	each/site				
(PA20) Kitchen utensils	P4·5	1	variety/site				
(PA20) Rice or beans *(used in Garden learning center)*	P4·5	1	batch/site				
(PA20) Sturdy box	P4·5	3-4	each/site				
(PA21) Unsalted popcorn	P4·5	1	bowl/site				
(PA21) Bowls	P4·5	2	each/site				
(PA21) Napkins	P4·5	1	each/child				
(PA21) Salted popcorn	P4·5	1	bowl/site				
(PA21) Plate	P4·5	1	each/site				
(PA21) Flashlight small enough to fit on the plate	P45	1	each/site				
(PA21) Bowl large enough to cover both the flashlight and plate	P4·5	1	each/site				
(PS7) Small hot dogs or sausages	P4·7	1-2	each/child				
(PS7) Refrigerated crescent rolls	P4·7	1	tube/8 hot dogs				
(PS7) Baking sheet	P4·7		/site				
(PS7) Ketchup	P47	1	bottle/site				
(PS7) Mustard	P4·7	1	bottle/site				
(PS7) Multi-colored fish crackers	P4·7	1	scoop/child				
(PS7) Serving plates or trays	P4·7		/site				
(PS7) Small bowls for ketchup and mustard	P4·7	2	each/site				
(PS7) Small plates	P4·7	1	each/child				
(PS7) Spoons for ketchup and mustard	P4·7	2	each/site				
(PS7) Napkins, cups	P4·7	1	each/child				
(PS8) Lime green gelatin	P4·7	1	pkg/4-6 children				

CATEGORY & ITEM	PG	QTY	/UNIT	TOT	HAVE	NEED	✔
THE KITCHEN Preschool Supplies (continued)							
(PS8) Clear 8-oz. cups	P4·7	1	each/child				
(PS8) Whipped topping	P4·7	2	scoops/child				
(PS8) Spoons	P4·7	1	each/child				
(PS8) Napkins, cups	P4·7	1	each/child				
(PG7) Inflated balloons *(same or greater number as there are kids)*	P4·7	1-2	each/child				
(PG8) CD or cassette player	P4·8	1	each/site				
(PG8) Music from CD or cassette	P4·8	1	each/site				
(PG8) Paper	P4·8	1	each/child				
(PG8) Picture of candle or flashlight	P4·8	1	each/site				
(PC7) White card stock	P4·8	1	each/child				
(PC7) Black construction paper, cut into 6" x 8" pieces	P4·8	1	each/child				
(PC7) Glue in bottles, not gluesticks	P4·8	1	each/child				
(PC7) Salt shakers, filled with salt	P4·8	1	each/table				
(PC7) Newspapers	P4·8		/site				
(PC7) Paint shirts or smocks *(optional)*	P4·8	1	each/child				
(PC8) Glue	P4·9		/site				
(PC8) Water in pitcher	P4·9		/site				
(PC8) Small foil or plastic pans	P4·9	3-4	each/table				
(PC8) Light switch plate covers	P4·9	1	each/child				
(PC8) Paper gum wrappers, old stamps, or tissue paper squares	P4·9		/site				
(PC8) Paintbrushes	P4·9	1	each/child				
(PC8) Utility knife	P4·9	1	each/site				
(PC9) Big preschool paintbrushes	P4·9	1	each/child				
(PC9) Watercolor sets	P4·9	3-4	each/table				
(PC9) Watercolor paper or heavy drawing paper	P4·9	1	each/child				
(PC9) Salt shakers	P4·9	2-3	each/table				
(PC9) Newspapers	P4·9		/site				
(PC9) Water containers	P4·9		/site				
(PC9) Paint shirts or smocks	P4·9	1	each/child				
(PA24) Light bulb	P4·9	1	each/site				
(PA24) Cylinder *(could be a paper towel cylinder, etc.)*	P4·9	1	each/site				

CATEGORY & ITEM	PG	QTY	/UNIT	TOT	HAVE	NEED	✔
LIVING ROOM Preschool Supplies							
Living Room Mural	R·83	1	each/site				
Copy of "The Quest Continues—Preschool" student take-home paper *(page P5·11)*	P5·11	1	each/child				
(PA25) Connecting blocks	P5·5		variety/site				
(PA26) Safety scissors	P5·5	1	each/child				
(PA26) Magazines with photos of furniture, decorated rooms in homes	P5·5		variety/site				
(PA26) Construction paper	P5·5	1	each/child				
(PA26) Glue sticks	P5·5	1	each/child				
(PA27) Shoe box decorated like a treasure chest	P5·5	1	each/site				
(PA27) Large blanket	P5·5	1	each/site				
(PA27) Bag with many balls in it *(only one ball should be white)*	P5·5	1	each/child				
(PS9) Pudding *(store bought or homemade)*	P5·7	1	cup/child				
(PS9) Clear cups—8 oz. size	P5·7	1	each/child				
(PS9) Spoons	P5·7		each/child				
(PS9) Chocolate chips, butterscotch chips, or mini marshmallows	P5·7	1	spoonful/child				
(PS10) Small decorated cookies *(store bought or homemade)*	P5·7	1-2	each/child				
(PS10) Juice, such as apple juice	P5·7	1	cup/child				
(PS10) Plates lined with doilies	P5·7	2-3	each/site				
(PS10) Fancy napkins	P5·7	1	each/child				
(PS10) Cups	P5·7	1	each/child				
(PG9) Couch	P5·7	1	each/site				
(PG9) Carpet squares	P5·7	2+	each/site				
(PG9) Lamp shades	P5·7	2+	each/site				
(PG9) End Tables *(or cardboard boxes turned upside down)*	P5·7	2+	each/site				
(PG9) Ottomans or chairs	P5·7	2+	each/site				
(PG10) Garbage bags fulls of paper wads	P5·8	2-3	each/site				
(PG10) Foam packing peanuts	P5·8	2-3	bags/site				
(PG10) Grocery bags	P5·8	1	each/team				
(PC10) Gold permanent marker	P5·8	1-2	each/site				
(PC10) Vinyl, 12" x 8" pieces *(found in fabric stores)*	P5·8	1	each/child				
(PC10) Big paper clips	P5·8	6-8	each/child				
(PC10) Cord of heavy yarn or even shoelaces, 30" lengths	P5·8	1	each/child				
(PC10) Sewing scissors	P5·8	1	each/site				
(PC10) Hole punch	P5·8	1	each/site				
(PC11) Gold foil, 6" x 8" pieces	P5·9	1	each/child				
(PC11) Magazines or newspapers	P5·9		/site				
(PC11) Adhesive backed magnet strips, 3" lengths	P5·9	2	each/child				
(PC11) Lightweight cardboard, 4" x 6" pieces	P5·9	1	each/child				
(PA30) Treasure of the Day—Fake rings	P5·9	1	each/child				
(PA30) Pictures of jewels and gems	P5·9		/site				

CREATION Adam and Eve

"For all have sinned, and come short of the glory of God."

Romans 3:23

Why Kids Need to Discover That They've Sinned and Are Separated from God

Every child who comes to VBS will know that there is a distinction between right and wrong. However, their concept of right and wrong, and what sin is, may be very skewed from God's definition. Some children have come to believe that wrong is only bad if you get caught. Others may think what's right and wrong changes depending on the situation. You might also meet children who haven't experienced forgiveness and a close relationship with their parent(s), which will influence their understanding a loving heavenly Father.

Here's one way to define sin: wanting to do things our own way and choosing to disobey God's rules. When you have the children share real-life examples of sin, they all will begin to realize they are sinners. Showing them the actual memory verse in the Bible can also help them understand their own state of sinfulness.

Once children recognize they are indeed sinful, you can illustrate the truth that they are separated from

them in Adam and Eve's shoes—sinful, separated, needy for forgiveness. But don't leave kids in the despair of their sin and separation. Be sure that within this site you also clue them in that there is a way to close the gap between them and God.

Getting More from the Bible Story

This Bible story begins as God's awesome act of creation is finished. In Genesis 2 God commissions Adam to be the caretaker and have dominion *(absolute control and authority)* over the Garden and the animals that inhabit it. Eden was a paradise that would have been like living in heaven. It was perfect, without the effect of sin, full of only good things. God gave Adam responsibility both for the garden and for his own choices while living there.

When Eve and Adam chose to eat the fruit of the tree of the knowledge of good and evil they ultimately chose to disobey God. This was sin. Eve and Adam's choice to disobey God produced the same result: death. Their sin separated them from the tree of life and thus from eternal life. The tree of life is also described in Revelation 22:2 as having 12 kinds of fruit to be enjoyed by those who spend eternity in heaven with God.

fact**oid**

Fingerprints are often useful clues for detectives. The science of fingerprinting—dermatoglyphics—was first practiced by the ancient Chinese who fingerprinted on wax seals to close important documents. Every individual's fingerprints, made of whorls, arches and loops, are unique. Today's fingerprint identification system was founded by Sir Edward Henry who created the first fingerprinting department for Scotland Yard in 1900.

The serpent that successfully tempted

God by teaching them that God is without sin. Just like oil and water separate, a sinner is separated from God by his sin.

Taking the truth of sin and salvation down to its most simple, basic bones will make it easier to teach and easier to grasp. Help each child own his own sin by being sure they have examples they can relate to. Teach the Bible story in a way that puts

Eve was Satan in disguise. Satan had been an angel who rebelled against God and was thrown out of heaven. In this first temptation, just as when he tempted Jesus in the wilderness *(Matt. 4:1-11)*, Satan used God's own words, but warped them, to lure his victim away from obedience to the Father. Like every sin, choosing one's own way leads to disobedience and death.

Adam and Eve

"For all have sinned, and come short of the glory of God."

Site Mission

Even though we sin, God wants us to be close to Him again.

Key Bible Verse

"For all have sinned, and come short of the glory of God." —**Romans 3:23**

Puppet Option

Investigator #2 or an Assistant Investigator can operate BOSWORTH to help lead the children to different areas and interact spontaneously with the teacher and children. *(See puppet pattern for BOSWORTH on pages R · 55-59.)*

Bible Passage

Genesis 1:26-31; 2:4—3:23

Procedures of the Day

20 minutes: Hands-on Exploration

10 minutes: Focus on the Bible

15 minutes: Bible Memorization

10 minutes: Music Time

15 minutes: Gumshoe Grub

Setting the Scene

This site is a garden or yard of the 316 Good News Road. Use silk trees and potted plants/flowers along a garden path at this site. You can make round stepping stones out of cardboard and paint them so that they look like rocks. Draw trees on newspaper print for the walls. Cardboard boxes can be used for planters by drawing stones on them. Garden hoses and sprinklers can weave around the "grass" and planters.

15 minutes: Case-Cracking Games

20 minutes: Putting the Pieces Together

15 minutes: Detectives' Departure

Investigator's Inventory

General

- [ ] Garden mural—Preschool version
- [ ] Good News Clues™ CD or tape copy
- [ ] CD player or cassette tape player
- [ ] Copy of "The Quest Continues—Preschool" student take-home paper (page P1 · 11) for each child

Games and Activities

- [ ] One or two sturdy, large cardboard boxes
- [ ] Various plastic garden tools, such as a shovel, rake, scoops, etc.
- [ ] Potting soil, raw rice, or beans
- [ ] Flowers and/or plants, real or plastic
- [ ] Picture books with photos or drawings of bugs and insects
- [ ] Picture of a tree in a garden
- [ ] CD player or cassette tape player
- [ ] Butterfly net or bag
- [ ] Three or four garden hoses
- [ ] Large plastic rakes
- [ ] Small plastic shovels, spades, and small water bucket
- [ ] Rocks
- [ ] Flowers
- [ ] Wood chips
- [ ] Treasure of the Day—Sunglasses, one pair per child
- [ ] Picture of Sun
- [ ] Picture of Eyes

Snacks

- [ ] Healthy veggies to dip (carrot sticks, celery sticks, cucumber slices, etc.)
- [ ] One or two soft dips, such as ranch dip or vegetable dip (already prepared or use your own recipe)
- [ ] Small paper plates
- [ ] Spoons for dip
- [ ] Red crepe paper
- [ ] Pretzels, small crackers, or candy
- [ ] Green floral tape or green twist ties
- [ ] Bushel baskets
- [ ] Paper cups and napkins

Crafts

- [ ] Construction paper, 12" x 18", bright colors
- [ ] Scissors
- [ ] Crayons or markers
- [ ] Washable tempera paint
- [ ] Squeeze bottles
- [ ] Newspaper
  - [ ] Paint shirts
    - [ ] Colored electrical tape
    - [ ] Waxed paper
    - [ ] Yarn
      - [ ] Pressed flowers and leaves
      - [ ] Iron
      - [ ] Hole punch
      - [ ] Cardboard pieces, approximately 8-1/2" x 11"

HANDS-ON EXPLORATION

Prepare your Detectives for their search by setting up two learning centers for their investigation.

Pot a Plant

(PA1) Supplies:

- One or two sturdy, large cardboard boxes reinforced at the bottom with the sides cut off on the top

- Various plastic garden tools: e.g., shovel, rake, scoops, etc.

- Potting soil, raw rice, or beans

- Flowers and/or plants either real or plastic

Fill one or two cardboard boxes with your choice of "soil," and let your preschoolers get their hands dirty. With the plastic tools, they can plant flowers into planters to help landscape the garden.

Bugs in the Garden

(PA2) Supplies:

- Picture books with photos and/or drawings of bugs/insects

Have the Detectives look through the books and find a bug they would like to pretend to be. After everyone has chosen, have them pretend to be that bug. The other Detectives can try to guess what kind of bug each child is.

FOCUS ON THE BIBLE

Bible Basis: *Genesis 1:26-31; 2:4—3:23*

(PA3) Supplies:

- Bible

- Picture of a tree in a garden

Before telling the story, open your Bible to Genesis 1. **Our story today is from the Bible. It is from the part, or book, of the Bible called Genesis.** *(Show the children Genesis 1 in your Bible. Keep your Bible open to Genesis 1 as you tell the story.)*

Our Bible story takes place in a garden. Every time I say the word "garden" and show you this picture, you should clap two times. *(Show the picture. Let the children clap two times.)*

The Bible tells us about a beautiful garden *(Show the picture. Let the children clap two times.)* **God made. It had beautiful flowers. It had wonderful trees. Rivers were in the garden.** *(Show the picture. Let the children clap two times.)* **God called it Eden.**

Two people lived in the garden. *(Show the picture. Let the children clap two times.)* **God made the man Adam and the woman Eve. God put them in the garden** *(Show the picture. Let the children clap two times.)* **to live. Adam and Eve were to take care of the animals and the garden.** *(Show the picture. Let the children clap two times.)* **God told them that they could eat the fruit from most of the trees. There was only one tree in the garden** *(Show the picture. Let the children clap two times.)* **that they could not eat from. That was the tree of the knowledge of good and evil. If Adam and Eve ate from that tree, they would die.**

Adam and Eve had a wonderful time in the garden. *(Show the picture. Let the children clap two times.)* **But one day, a snake visited Eve in the garden.** *(Show the picture. Let the children clap two times.)* **This snake was mean. He wanted Eve to break God's rule about eating from the tree of the knowledge of good and evil. The snake told Eve a lie about the tree.**

"You won't die," hissed the creature. "You will be like God."

Now Eve wanted to eat the fruit. And that is what she did! Adam ate some of the fruit, too. Then Adam and Eve knew that they had done something very, very bad.

Later, God was walking in the garden. *(Show the picture. Let the children clap two times.)* **Adam and Eve hid from God. But God asked, "Why are you hiding?"**

Adam said, "We heard you walking in the garden. *(Show the picture. Let the children clap two times.)* **We were scared."**

God said, "Why were you scared? Did you eat the fruit of the tree of the knowledge of good and evil?"

Adam and Eve told God about the snake and eating the fruit.

God told them that they had done something very, very bad. They had done something called sin. Sin keeps people away from God. Because of their sin, Adam and Eve had to leave the garden. *(Show the picture. Let the children clap two times.)* **They wouldn't be able to stay there anymore.**

Adam and Eve weren't the only ones to do wrong things. Each of us does wrong or bad things. We all sin. Our sins keep us away from God. But God had a plan to bring us back to Him.

BIBLE MEMORIZATION

(PA4) Supplies: None needed

Key Bible Verse:

"For all have sinned, and come short of the glory of God." —**Romans 3:23**

Say, **Today we have been learning about Adam and Eve living in the garden. What kinds of things do we find in a garden?** *(Let children give you their ideas, which may include: flowers, trees, bugs, birds, etc.)* **Those are good ideas. Let's pretend that we are in the garden and that we are picking flowers. Each time we pick a flower we will say one word of our Bible memory verse.** Say the verse slowly pretending to pick a flower as you say each word. Do this two or three times and have the children say the verse with you.

MUSIC TIME

It Is No Mystery

(PA5) Supplies:

- *Good News Clues*™ CD or tape copy
- CD player or cassette tape player

With the children in a group, have them listen to the song for Site 1. After listening to it, talk about the words and their meaning. Then have the children sing along with the CD. You may choose to sing other songs that they already know to get them involved in this time of singing.

GUMSHOE GRUB

Gardener's Delight

(PS1) Supplies:

- Healthy veggies to dip, such as carrot sticks, celery sticks, cucumbers slices, and other vegetables
- One or two soft dips, such as ranch dip or vegetable dip *(already prepared or use your own recipe)*
- Small paper plates
- Spoons for dip

Directions: Place small containers of the dips on tables where all the children can reach them. Explain what flavors the dips are. Have children spoon some of the dip on a small paper plate and take a few vegetables for dipping. Serve with juice or water. **NOTE: Beware of dairy allergies.**

Crepe Paper Apples

(PS2) Supplies:

- Red crepe paper cut into 10-inch circles, one per child
- Pretzels, small crackers, or candy
- Green floral tape or green twist ties
- Bushel baskets

Directions: Cut the red crepe paper into 10-inch circles. Place a handful of pretzels, small crackers, or candy in center of crepe paper circles. Gather the crepe paper to form a ball, securing with green floral tape or green twist ties. Place your "apples" in bushel baskets to serve. Also serve with juice or water.

CASE-CRACKING GAMES

Use these fun games for your preschoolers to use some energy in a meaningful way. Choose one or both options given, depending on your time and space.

Get That Bug!

(PG1) Supplies:

- Butterfly net or bag
- Picture books with photos of insects found in your location

Have Detectives spend a few minutes looking through the picture books to choose one or two bugs they will try to imitate.

Directions: One Detective will be the bug collector, looking to catch the "bugs" in the room. Each child/bug will pretend to be a certain kind of garden bug, and when the collector gets near with his net, he must guess what kind of bug the child is. If he guesses wrong, the bug can go on until the collector captures him again and guesses correctly.

The last bug caught will be the collector for the next round.

Garden Gauntlet

(PG2) Supplies:

- Three or four garden hoses
- Large plastic rakes
- Small plastic shovels, spades, and small water bucket
- Rocks
- Flowers
- Wood chips

In Advance:
Using the three or four garden hoses, create two pathways next to each other that curve and jag around your room or outside if you choose.

Directions: Divide the Detectives into two teams who will race to see who can get all the supplies for the garden to the end of their path and back first. Place the garden items along the paths and have the first child pick up the closest item, and so on.

The detectives will have to use a large plastic shovel to pick up each garden item along the path and carry it back to the start. He/she will then give the shovel to the next child to pick up the next item until all items have been carried back to the start. If the item is dropped, the child needs to go back to the start.

PUTTING THE PIECES TOGETHER

Caterpillar/Butterfly

(PC1) Supplies:

- Brightly colored 12" x 18" construction paper (one piece per student)
- Scissors
- Crayons or markers
- Washable tempera paint in 3 colors (different than the paper colors)
- Squeeze bottles
- Newspaper
- Paint shirts

In Advance: Fold the 12" x 18" construction paper so that it measures 12" x 9". Filling most of the paper, draw a simple caterpillar shape and cut out. Make one sample of the completed project to show students.

Directions: Cover the tables with newspaper. Write each child's name on his or her caterpillar. Have students color both sides of the caterpillar using markers or crayons. When finished coloring, open the caterpillar up and adorn the wings by squeezing a small amount of paint (from ketchup-type squeeze bottles) onto the paper. Limit the paint selection to about three different colors. Fold over the other wing and rub the surface of the paper to spread the paint around. Open the wings to discover the beautifully symmetrical design. Dry open.

Sun Catcher

(PC2) Supplies:

- Colored electrical tape
- Waxed paper
- Yarn
- Pressed flowers and leaves
- Iron
- Scissors
- Hole punch
- Cardboard pieces, approximately 8-1/2" x 11"

In Advance: Purchase pressed flowers or pick wildflowers or flowers from your garden and press. Place flowers and leaves in phone book *(or other large book)* to press them flat. This should be done 2 to 4 weeks prior to VBS. Cut 6" squares of waxed paper. Cut yarn into 24" lengths.

Directions: Have students choose a few pressed flowers and leaves to use on their sun catcher. Give each child a piece of cardboard. Lay one piece of waxed paper on the cardboard. Have them arrange the flowers and leaves on the waxed-paper square leaving a one-inch border. Cover the flowers with a second piece of waxed paper. Pick up the entire stack *(cardboard and waxed paper pieces with flowers in between)* and take to a designated area for ironing. *(The cardboard is to give a stiff backing to carry the project to be ironed. It will not be needed once the waxed paper has been ironed.)* Teachers press the waxed paper together with a hot iron using a cover

paper. Seal the edges with colored electrical tape. Poke a hole at the top of the sun catcher and thread with yarn.

NOTE: For safety, be sure that one particular adult uses the iron in a safe place away from the play area.

DETECTIVES' DEPARTURE

(PA6) Supplies:

- "The Quest Continues—Preschool" take-home paper
- Treasure of the Day—Sunglasses
- Picture of sun
- Picture of eyes

Review the Bible story about Adam and Eve in the garden. Talk about the fact that they had to leave the garden because of sin. But remind the children that even though we sin, God has given us a way to be forgiven. *(Most children this age are not yet ready to make a personal decision for Jesus. However, if you have a child who has questions, talk to that child separately to answer his/her questions. Be sure to follow up with the parents if this happens.)*

Then with all the children together in a group, talk about today's treasure. **We have a mystery to solve. Let's work together to find out the answer.** *(Show the picture of the sun.)* **What is this a picture of?** *(Let children answer.)* **Where is one place there is usually a lot of sunshine?** *(In a garden, yard, park, outside, etc.)* *(Show the picture of the eyes.)* **What is this a picture of?** *(Eyes.)*

What happens to your eyes when you are in bright sunshine? *(It's hard to see. I have to squint. Cover my eyes. Accept all reasonable answers.)* **Is there any way to**

make this better when you go outside? What could we use to protect our eyes? *(Let children guess. Someone may answer to cover your eyes, but another child will probably quickly say to wear sunglasses.)* **That's right! We can wear sunglasses to help protect our eyes. You were such good Detectives to figure that out that I have a special treasure for each of you to take home to help you remember about our Bible story today.** *(Let each child reach into a bag or basket and take one pair of sunglasses to keep.)*

Be sure Detectives are dismissed with their sunglasses, artwork, and "The Quest Continues" take-home page.

Today your child visited a garden/yard, and then visited the Garden of Eden where he or she learned about how sin separates us from God (Gen. 1:26-31; 2:4—3:23). For more information about *Good News Clues™*, go online to **www.CookVBS.com**.

Site Mission (Focus)

Even though we sin, God wants us to be close to Him again.

 **KEY BIBLE VERSE**

"For all have sinned, and come short of the glory of God." —**Romans 3:23**

 **ACTIVITY**

Bugs in the Garden

Supplies:

- Picture books with photos and/or drawings of bugs/insects

In your own yard, take your child to go on a bug hunt. Have your child look through the books and try to identify the bugs that they find in your yard. Talk about the creation of all creatures. Be sure to emphasize that God created Adam and Eve, the very first man and woman.

PASSION WEEK
Last Supper

"He is not here: for he is risen."
Matthew 28:6

Why Kids Need to Know
That Jesus Is the Only Way of Salvation

In contemporary socio-political society,

tolerance for everyone's view is expected and sometimes even legislated. The view that there is one way to heaven could be considered exclusionary and narrow-minded. Many children may have been exposed to such mindsets as "Many roads lead to God" or "If you're a good person God will receive you into heaven." Pray for the Holy Spirit to show each child the truth.

Especially when working with children unfamiliar with a church setting, stay away from "church language" and use more familiar, common words for biblical truths. Children will more readily understand the principles of sin and salvation if they hear words, word pictures, and examples they can relate to.

The topic of Jesus' death can be upsetting for younger children and draw questions about the

factoid

Invisible inks have been used since A.D. 600. George Washington used invisible ink to send secret military communications during the British occupation of New York in 1776. Invisible inks fall into two categories: sympathetic and organic. Sympathetic inks are visible when applied, then disappear when dry. To read these inked messages, a chemical is applied to the paper to cause the ink to show up again. Organic inks, made from substances like vinegar, milk, or fruit juice, become visible again when the writing surface is heated.

fairness of it from older kids. Many children will have experienced the death of someone they know and will connect that experience with Jesus' death. While it's a central and essential fact in our salvation, you can teach it without dwelling too long on it. Be willing to answer questions factually either during the session or afterward.

Getting More from the Bible Story

A large, hefty serving of Scripture is covered in the Dining Room—the final week of Christ's life, culminating in His death, burial, and resurrection. Many children may not have heard this story in its entirety or may know some facts and details you'll be relating.

Christ's entrance into Jerusalem at the start of the Passover is in stark contrast to the events a week later. His riding into the city on a donkey's colt was itself a clear announcement of His kingship and fulfilled Zechariah's prophecy of 500 years earlier (Zech. 9:9). This is one of the rare recorded instances when Jesus' kingship and majesty were recognized on earth.

Jerusalem was crowded with Jewish people, since all Jewish males age 12 and older had to go to Jerusalem for the Passover festival and the weeklong festival of unleavened bread which followed. Four days after entering the city on the donkey's colt, Christ shares with His closest friends His last meal before His death.

In the upstairs room, Jesus and the disciples shared both a ritual meal and a symbolic event. Jesus used two parts of the meal, passing around bread and drinking wine, to demonstrate the significance of what would soon be happening. During a typical Passover meal, wine was passed four times.

In Matthew 26:28, Jesus states that the fruit of the vine represents His blood of the covenant. Until His crucifixion, people had to approach God and have their sins forgiven through a priest and animal sacrifices. The new covenant means that individuals can approach God directly through the sacrifice of Christ.

The Last Supper

"He is not here: for he is risen."

Site Mission

Through Jesus, I can know God.

Key Bible Verse

"He is not here: for he is risen."
—**Matthew 28:6**

Puppet Option

Investigator #2 or an Assistant Investigator can operate BOSWORTH to help lead the children to different areas and interact spontaneously with the teacher and children. *(See puppet pattern for BOSWORTH on pages R · 55-59.)*

Bible Passage

Bible Basis: Matthew 26:47-75; 27:32-44, 57-61; 28:1-10

Procedures of the Day

20 minutes: Hands-on Exploration

10 minutes: Focus on the Bible

Setting the Scene

This is the dining room. Create a dining room that includes furniture just the right size for your preschoolers. Put a centerpiece with plastic flowers in the middle of each table. Have plastic plates, glasses/cups, and utensils available if you choose to set the tables for dinner. Use the mural in the Director's Guide to set the scene as a dining room.

15 minutes: Bible Memorization

10 minutes: Music Time

15 minutes: Gumshoe Grub

15 minutes: Case-Cracking Games

20 minutes: Putting the Pieces Together

15 minutes: Detectives' Departure

Investigator's Inventory

General

- ☐ Dining Room mural—Preschool version
- ☐ *Good News Clues*™ CD or tape copy
- ☐ CD player or cassette tape player
- ☐ Copy of "The Quest Continues— Preschool" student take-home paper *(page P2·11)* for each child

Games and Activities

- ☐ Plastic plates, glasses/cups, and utensils
- ☐ Tablecloths and/or placemats
- ☐ Centerpieces
- ☐ Magazine photo or picture of set table
- ☐ Play dough *(purchased or homemade)*
- ☐ Sad/Happy puppets *(One per child. See Resources page R·47.)*
- ☐ Craft sticks *(to make puppets)*
- ☐ Tray *(one per team)*
- ☐ Plastic cup, plate, knife, fork, spoon *(one set per team)*
- ☐ Napkin *(one per team)*
- ☐ Plastic spoon *(one per child)*
- ☐ Small foil or paper wad/ball *(one per child)*
- ☐ Treasure of the Day—Red plastic cups *(one per child)*
- ☐ Pitcher of water

Snacks

- ☐ A variety of pieces of red fruit, such as cherries, watermelon balls, or strawberries
- ☐ A variety of red candies such as red licorice, red sour balls, red hots, etc.
- ☐ Small paper cups
- ☐ Matzo crackers or other crackers
- ☐ Cheese slices *(American, Swiss, cheddar, etc.)*
- ☐ Knife for slicing cheese

Crafts

- ☐ Card stock
- ☐ Markers
- ☐ Glitter glue
- ☐ Silk flowers
- ☐ Glue *(not glue sticks)*
- ☐ Resealable sandwich-size bags
- ☐ Plain white pot holders *(purchased)* or plain muslin fabric to make your own pot holders *(one pot holder per child)*
- ☐ Black permanent pen
- ☐ Fabric paint *(one color)*
- ☐ Foil pie plate
- ☐ Paintbrush
- ☐ Pan of soapy water *(if sink is not available in the immediate area of the preschool room)*
- ☐ Handwashing soap
- ☐ Paper towels
- ☐ Paint shirts or smocks *(one per child)*

HANDS-ON EXPLORATION

Prepare your Detectives for their search by setting up two learning centers for their investigation.

Set the Table

(PA7) Supplies:

- Plastic plates, glasses/cups, and utensils
- Tablecloths and/or placemats
- Centerpieces
- Magazine photo or picture of set table

Have the children set the dining room table for dinner. Let them share with the others when they have their tables at home set like this, e.g., holidays, birthdays, special dinners, celebrations, etc.

Make Your Own Dining

(PA8) Supplies:

- Play dough *(use purchased play dough or use the following recipe to make your own)*

Give the detectives play dough with which to create a dining room table and chairs. They may work with other kids to make the table and chairs if desired. Have them make plates, glasses, silverware, etc., with which to set their table. Another option is for them to make the food to set on the dining room table.

Play Dough Recipe

2 cups flour

1 cup salt

4 tablespoons cream of tartar

1 pkg. unsweetened dry drink mix
for scent and color

2 cups warm water

2 tablespoons cooking oil

Stir over medium heat until mixture pulls away from sides to form a ball. Store in airtight container. *(For 8 to 10 children.)*

FOCUS ON THE BIBLE

Bible Basis: Matthew 26:47-75; 27:32-44, 57-61; 28:1-10

(PA9) Supplies:

- Bible
- Sad/Happy puppets *(see page R · 47 in Resources)*
- Craft sticks

In Advance: Create a set of Sad/Happy faces. If possible, reproduce the sad faces on red paper and the happy faces on yellow paper. Create a face "puppet" by taping a sad face to the top 1/3 of a wood craft stick. Tape a happy face to the back of the sad face,

sandwiching the craft stick between the two faces. You should have a two-sided puppet with a wood handle sticking out of the bottom of the puppet. Create enough puppets for each child to have one for the story. The storyteller will also need a puppet.

Find Matthew 26 in your Bible. **Our story today is from the Bible. It is found in the part of the Bible called Matthew.** Show the children Matthew 26 in your Bible. Keep your Bible open while you tell the Bible story.

Remember the Bible story of Adam and Eve? They had sinned, or done wrong things. Because of their sin, all people sin. We sin too. Our sin keeps us away from God. But God had a plan to bring us back to Him. The plan had to do with Jesus. That is what our Bible story is about today.

We're going to use some puppets to help us tell the story. Have a helper pass the puppets out to the children. **When I ask you how you feel about part of the story, show the sad face if you feel sad.** Show your sad face puppet to the children. **Show the happy face if you feel happy.** Show your happy face puppet to the children.

Jesus is God's Son. God sent Jesus to help bring us to God. How does that make you feel? Show the happy face puppet. **Jesus told people about God. He told them about God's love.**

Some people didn't like hearing what Jesus had to say about God. They came up with a plan to hurt Jesus. How does that make you feel? Show the sad face puppet. **Those people took Jesus away from His friends. They hurt Jesus by hitting Him. Then they wanted Jesus to die on a cross. How does that make you feel?** Show the sad face puppet. **But even their plan was part of God's plan.**

Soldiers took Jesus and put Him on a cross. It hurt Jesus to be on the cross. But while He was on the cross, He was helping us. He took all the punishment for everybody's sin: Adam and Eve's sin and each of our sins. While Jesus was on the

cross, He died. How does that make you feel? Show the sad face puppet.

Jesus' friends and family were sad too. They wrapped Jesus' body in cloths and put it in a special place.

A couple of days later, two of Jesus' friends went to visit the special place where Jesus' body was. But when they looked in the special place, Jesus' body wasn't there! Instead they saw an angel.

"Jesus isn't here. He isn't dead. He is alive again! Go tell the rest of Jesus' friends!" the angel told them. How does that make you feel? Show the happy face puppet.

As Jesus' friends were going to tell the others, they saw Jesus. The angel was right! Jesus was alive! How does that make you feel? Show the happy face puppet.

When Jesus died on the cross, He took all of our punishment for sin. But by coming alive again, Jesus brought us back to God. How does that make you feel? Show the happy face puppet.

# BIBLE MEMORIZATION

(PA10) Supplies: None needed

Key Bible Verse:

"He is not here: for he is risen."
—Matthew 28:6

Say, **Today we have been learning about Jesus' death on a cross and how He came back to life! That Jesus came back to life makes us feel happy. Sometimes when we are happy we clap our hands. Let's clap our hands.** Have everyone clap their hands together. **Good job! Now we are going to say our verse. Each time we say a word we will clap our hands.** Say the verse slowly like this. **He** *(Clap)* **is** *(Clap)* **not** *(Clap)* **here;** *(Clap)* **for** *(Clap)* **he** *(Clap)* **is** *(Clap)* **risen**

(Clap). Do this two or three times to give the children practice saying the verse with you.

# MUSIC TIME

Be Brave and Tell

(PA11) Supplies:

- *Good News Clue*™ CD or tape copy
- CD player or cassette tape player

Gather all the children together into a group to listen to the song for Site 2. After listening to the song, explain any words or their meaning that may be difficult for them to understand. Then have the children sing along with the CD. You may also choose to sing other songs that the children already know to get them involved in this time of singing.

# GUMSHOE GRUB

Red Hot Snacks

(PS3) Supplies:

- A variety of pieces of red fruit such as cherries, watermelon balls, or strawberries
- A variety of red candies such as red licorice, red sour balls, red hots, etc.
- Small paper cups
- Napkins

In Advance: If serving cherries, you may want to remove the seeds prior to serving. Wash and prepare all fruit into bite sized pieces.

Directions: Allow the children to spoon a few different pieces of fruit or candy into a small cup. Serve with water or juice. **NOTE: Be aware of allergies to strawberries or red food coloring. If serving to younger children, be sure to remove all seeds. Do not serve small, hard candies to young children.**

Passover Feast

(PS4) Supplies:

- Matzo crackers or other crackers
- Cheese slices *(American, Swiss, cheddar, etc.)*
- Napkins
- Knife for slicing cheese

In Advance: Slice cheese into small pieces. Arrange on a plate or tray by kinds so that children can select two or three pieces to eat on their crackers.

Directions: Explain to the children that Matzo crackers are used today by many Jewish people to celebrate the Passover. In Jesus' day, the bread that they used for Passover was made without leaven *(yeast).* Matzo crackers are also made without leaven. Serve this snack with water or juice.

Let children select a few crackers and pieces of cheese for their snack today. **NOTE: Be aware of dairy allergies.**

CASE-CRACKING GAMES

Use these fun games for your preschoolers to use some energy in a meaningful way. Choose one or both options given, depending on your time and space.

Dining Room Relay

(PG3) Supplies:

- Tray *(One item per team)*
- Plastic cup, plate, knife, fork, spoon *(One set per team)*
- Napkin *(One item per team)*

Divide your Detectives in two or three teams. Place all the materials at the end of your room except the trays. Each team will start with the tray and the first person will go to the dining room utensils and pick up one and put it on the tray. Then he/she will hand off the tray with the item(s), and the next child will go and pick up another item, and so on. If the tray is dropped, the child must stop and pick up all the items and place them on the tray. Continue until all the items are on the tray and returned to each team.

Simon Says Keep Your Spoon

(PG4) Supplies:

- Plastic spoon *(One per child)*
- Small foil or paper wad/ball *(One per child)*

Give each child a plastic spoon and the small foil ball. Have the child place the foil ball on the spoon and hold it in his hand. Now comes the

fun part, a friendly game of "Simon Says." The Detectives must literally do two things at once. Listen for when Simon says to do something and do it without dropping the foil ball on the ground. Whenever a child drops his ball or does something without it being prefaced by "Simon Says," the child must sit out until the next game. Play as many times as you have time for.

PUTTING THE PIECES TOGETHER

Napkin Rings

(PC3) Supplies:

- Card Stock
- Markers
- Glitter glue
- Silk flowers
- Glue
- Resealable sandwich-size bags

In Advance: Cut strips of card stock, 1" x 6"

Directions: Have students decorate strips of paper with markers and glitter glue. Have students glue one silk flower to the center of the paper strip. Teachers help the students glue the ends of the strips together to form a ring. Allow the students to make a napkin ring for each family member. Put each child's name on a resealable bag and insert the napkins rings into it.

Pot Holders

(PC4) Supplies:

- Plain white pot holders *(one per child)*
- Black permanent pen
- Fabric paint *(one color)*
- Foil pie plate
- Paintbrush
- Pan of soapy water if sink is not available
- Handwashing soap
- Paper towels
- Paint shirts or smocks

In Advance: Purchase plain white pot holders or sew them out of muslin fabric.

Directions: Pour fabric paint in a foil pie plate. *(If available, you can "paint" the student's hand using the paint brush rather than having them place their hand into the paint. Be sure to have enough paint on the hand to leave a good print on the fabric.)* Have students wear paint smocks to protect their clothing. One at a time, have each student put his/her hand in the paint plate. Let students make their hand print on the pot holder. Helpers should be available to help students immediately wash their hands to prevent accidents. Teachers then print student's name and date under hand print. Be sure to let the pot holders dry before sending them home. *(You may want to do this project earlier in the day's activities to allow sufficient drying time.)*

DETECTIVES' DEPARTURE

(PA12) Supplies:

- "The Quest Continues—Preschool" take-home paper
- Treasure of the Day—Red plastic cups
- Pitcher of water

Review the Bible story about Jesus and the last supper. Talk about the fact that Jesus took the punishment for our sin when He died on the cross. But today we can be happy that Jesus is alive in heaven. *(Be sensitive to the spiritual readiness of the children in your class as you discuss this subject. If you have a child who has questions about salvation and making a personal decision for Jesus, talk to that child separately to answer his/her questions. Be sure to follow up with the parents if this happens.)*

Then with all the children together in a group, talk about today's treasure. **We have another mystery to solve today! Let's all think about the clues we have to see if we can figure out this mystery.**

Today's treasure is something you use when you eat dinner. *(Children may immediately want to start guessing. If you have sufficient time, that's fine. However, don't give them an affirmative answer to any particular item.)* **Let's use more clues to guess what our treasure is.** Show the children a pitcher of water. **What do you think is in this pitcher?** *(Let children guess. They may say milk, fruit juice, drink mix, etc. When someone says "water" immediately respond.)* **How do you drink the water from this pitcher?** *(Children should respond by saying that it must be poured into a glass.)* **That's right! And you have now figured out today's treasure.** Show them the red plastic cups. *(The color red correlates with today's story. If you can't find red cups, another color will work just as well.)* **We will write your name on one of these cups that you can take home today. When you use this cup at home, it can help you remember our story about Jesus having the last supper with His disciples.**

Be sure Detectives are dismissed with their cups, artwork, and "The Quest Continues—Preschool" take-home page.

Today, your child spent his time in a dining room, just as Jesus did in His last days. By learning about Jesus' last days, your child has looked at how Jesus' death provides the way to God (Matt. 26:47-75; 27:32-44, 57-61; 28:1-10). For more information about *Good News Clues™*, go online to **www.CookVBS.com**.

Site Mission (Focus)

Through Jesus, I can know God.

KEY BIBLE VERSE

"He is not here: for he is risen."
—**Matthew 28:6**

ACTIVITY

Set the Table

Supplies:

- Plastic plates, glasses/cups, and utensils
- Tablecloths and/or placemats
- Centerpieces
- Magazine photo or picture of set table

Have your child set the table for dinner. Talk about special times of sharing meals together with family and friends, e.g., holidays, birthdays, special dinners, celebrations, etc.

Lost Sheep

"Rejoice with me; for I have found my sheep which was lost."

Luke 15:6

Why Kids Need to Discover That Jesus Wants Them to Know Him as Their Savior

Even with the range of ages in your VBS, every child can relate to their need and desire for unconditional love. Each child knows they have done wrong and that it causes problems in their family relationships. Many younger children may not be able to verbalize or even consciously understand how sin affects their relationships at home. But each one will certainly be able to identify with the lost sheep in some way, if only in wistfulness for the way the father lovingly and unconditionally welcomed the one sheep into his arms. This act of love and care will help every child envision the picture of how the heavenly Father has open arms, inviting each child to come to Him.

Some children may not have experienced forgiveness from their parents like the unconditional love that God offers. It might seem impossible or unrealistic to them. If you sense this is true, you can point out to the kids that God is able to love them no matter what they may have done wrong, what their sin is, and His love for them is greater than their wrongs. Be prepared and expect the Holy Spirit to move children to acknowledge their need for Christ during this site, and have workers ready to talk one-on-one with children who express the need or have questions and concerns.

Getting More from the Bible Story

The lost sheep parable is an illustration of a lost sinner's relationship with God. Even though 99 out of 100 are still with the shepherd, the shepherd cares and loves each one as if it were the only one. In this care, he leaves the 99 to find the one. And after finding the one, he rejoices and tells his friends and neighbors. "Rejoice with me; for I have found my sheep which was lost" *(Luke 15:6)*.

As we think of Jesus as the Good Shepherd, there are several qualities that can give us a clear picture of His relationship with us, the sheep. A good shepherd makes sure the sheep know him and always puts the flock's well-being before his own. In John 10:3, 11-13 we see how God demonstrates these characteristics in His relationship with us.

The Good Shepherd is also a loving disciplinarian. A shepherd uses his crook to take hold of a sheep and change its direction. Proverbs 3:11-12 and Revelation 3:19 reveal God's motive behind His discipline in our lives.

Tending a flock has a direct, personal impact on the shepherd, who owns the sheep. A shepherd's mentality is not one of "nine-to-five and then forget it." He is constantly committed to every aspect of caring for the sheep. John 10 is very clear in presenting this fact.

Finally, a good shepherd knows how to soothe his sheep and bind up their wounds. As you read Luke 12:32 and Ezekiel 34:15-16, think of the comfort you have received from God's Word!

What a clear picture, we have of the unconditional love that Jesus has for each of us, that we are as important as the 99.

factoid

Magnifying glass was invented by the Romans. While experimenting with different glass shapes, they discovered that glass that's thicker in the middle and thinner on the edges magnified objects they saw through the glass. The name "magnifier" or "burning glasses" stuck after someone discovered that the glass's shape could focus, or magnify, the sun's rays so intensely as to start a fire. Magnifying lenses weren't used commonly until the 13th century, when they became used for eyeglasses. Eventually magnifying lenses led to the discovery and use of microscopes.

Lost Sheep

"Rejoice with me; for I have found my sheep which was lost."

setting the scene

A casual family room setting: recliners or beanbag chairs, VHS player and tapes, TV, stereo, casual decor, a lamp, etc. Add reality with a throw rug, afghan, a coffee table, whatever gives the flavor of a lived-in, relaxed room. A wall hanging or poster could be hung on a wall. If you can, find and use "preschooler" size furniture, that would add to the comfort of the room for the children.

Site Mission

God loves and cares for us.

Key Bible Verse

"Rejoice with me; for I have found my sheep which was lost." —**Luke 15:6**

Puppet Option

Investigator #2 or an Assistant Investigator can operate BOSWORTH to help lead the children to different areas and interact spontaneously with the teacher and children. *(See puppet pattern for BOSWORTH on pages R · 55-59.)*

Bible Passage

Luke 15:1-7

Procedures of the Day

15 minutes: Case-Cracking Games

20 minutes: Putting the Pieces Together

15 minutes: Detectives' Departure

20 minutes: Hands-on Exploration

10 minutes: Focus on the Bible

15 minutes: Bible Memorization

10 minutes: Music Time

15 minutes: Gumshoe Grub

Investigator's Inventory

General

- ☐ Family Room mural—Preschool version
- ☐ *Good News Clues*™ CD or tape copy
- ☐ CD player or cassette tape player
- ☐ Copy of "The Quest Continues—Preschool" student take-home paper *(page P3 · 11)* for each child

Games and Activities

- ☐ Variety of preschool-age games *(can be borrowed from church members)*
- ☐ Several hundred cotton balls
- ☐ Paper sack, box, or wastebasket
- ☐ Robe
- ☐ Towel
- ☐ Sash
- ☐ Stuffed animal lamb
- ☐ Several classroom chairs
- ☐ Sheep made from pattern found on page R · 48 in Resources
- ☐ Rhythm band instruments
- ☐ Taped or chalked shapes *(circles, squares, rectangles)* on the floor
- ☐ Music *(CD or video)*
- ☐ Towel and sash for headdress for child *(optional)*
- ☐ Treasure of the Day—White sheep
- ☐ Small piece of "wool-like" fabric
- ☐ Model or picture of a farm
- ☐ Model or picture of a shepherd

Snacks

- ☐ Regular or microwave popcorn in a variety of flavors, such as kettle corn, cheese popcorn, buttered popcorn
- ☐ Large serving bowls
- ☐ Scoops
- ☐ Small paper bowls
- ☐ Napkins
- ☐ White cake mix, eggs, and oil
- ☐ Cupcake tin and cupcake liners
- ☐ Canned or homemade white frosting
- ☐ White sprinkles

Crafts

- ☐ Felt—white and light brown
- ☐ Puppet pattern *(see page R · 49 in Resources)*
- ☐ Fabric glue
- ☐ Mini pom-poms *(white)*
- ☐ Black permanent marker
- ☐ Resealable sandwich-size bags
- ☐ Small pink ribbon bows
- ☐ Card stock
- ☐ Business-size envelopes
- ☐ Patterns for sheep and ball caps *(see page R · 51 in Resources)*
- ☐ Pattern for tic-tac-toe board *(page R · 52 in Resources)*

HANDS-ON EXPLORATION

Prepare your Detectives for their search by setting up two learning centers for their investigation.

Game Room

(PA13) Supplies:

- Variety of preschool-age games *(You may be able to borrow several from families in your church.)*

Since the Detectives are in the family room, give them a chance to play games with one another. Have two or three games available for the children to play and provide whatever guidance for them to get going. Have Assistant Investigators available to help each separate group as they play the games.

'Wool' Toss

(PA14) Supplies:

- Several hundred cotton balls
- Paper sack, box, or wastebasket

Set the bag/box a reasonable distance for the detectives to throw the cotton balls into it. Have the children take turns, each time throwing a different way into the bag, for example, overhand, underhand, hook shot, left hand, further away, etc.

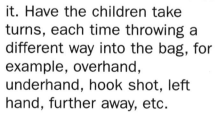

FOCUS ON THE BIBLE

Bible Basis: Luke 15:1-7

(PA15) Supplies:

- Bible
- Robe
- Towel
- Sash
- Stuffed animal lamb
- Several classroom chairs

The Bible story can be told with the storyteller dressed as a Bible-time shepherd. The storyteller should be dressed in the robe. The towel can be a headpiece. The stuffed animal lamb should be hidden somewhere in the storytelling area. Put the classroom chairs in a tight circle.

Today's story is found in the Bible. It is found in the book of the Bible called Luke. Show the children where Luke is in the Bible. Keep the Bible open to Luke 15 as the story is told.

The Bible tells us many things about Jesus. It has many of the stories that Jesus told. We have a special visitor today who wants to tell us about one of Jesus' stories.

The shepherd should sit down among the children and continue telling the story. If at all possible, the shepherd should have the story memorized or be able to present it without using notes.

One day Jesus told a story to some people who had come to listen to Him. He told them a story about

a shepherd. That's what I am. A shepherd takes care of sheep. He makes sure they have food to eat and water to drink. A shepherd keeps his sheep safe. Let me tell you Jesus' story.

The shepherd had one hundred sheep. That is a lot of sheep! Every day the shepherd kept his sheep safe. He helped them find food and water. Every night the shepherd counted the one hundred sheep as he put them in a safe place where they could sleep. Every day and every night the shepherd counted his one hundred sheep.

One night the shepherd counted his sheep as he put them in the safe place. Move over to the circle of chairs. Let's count together. 1-2-3-4-5-6-7-8-9-10. Have the children count with you. The shepherd kept counting. But he only counted ninety-nine sheep. He counted again just in case he had missed a sheep. Again the shepherd only counted ninety-nine sheep. One of his sheep was missing! The shepherd knew he had to look for the lost sheep right away. Let's look with him.

The shepherd looked near where he had taken the sheep to get a drink of water. The shepherd and the children should walk to one end of the room. The shepherd looked by the stream, but the lost sheep wasn't there. So the shepherd kept looking.

He looked behind a large rock. The shepherd should encourage the children to look behind a chair or beanbag. But the lost sheep wasn't behind the rock. What should the shepherd do? He should keep looking for the lost sheep.

Then the shepherd saw a bush. Maybe the sheep was behind the bush. So the shepherd looked behind the bush. The shepherd and the children should walk over to the TV/stereo area. The sheep was there! Let the children find the stuffed animal sheep hidden in the area. The shepherd had found the lost sheep!

The shepherd was very happy! He picked up the lost sheep and gently carried it back to the safe place and the other ninety-nine sheep. The shepherd should pick up the stuffed animal sheep and carry it back to the area where the group started. The children should sit down in that area. After the lost sheep was back in the safe place, the shepherd called his friends and neighbors. "Come be happy with me! I found my lost sheep."

Then Jesus told the people that God loved them just like the shepherd loved his sheep. God loves you and me just like He loved the people in the Bible.

BIBLE MEMORIZATION

(PA16) Supplies:

- Sheep made from pattern *(page R · 48 in Resources)*

Key Bible Verse:

"Rejoice with me; for I have found my sheep which was lost." —**Luke 15:6**

In Advance: Prepare one sheep for each word in the verse. You can photocopy the pattern that is included in the Resources section *(page R · 48)* and cut them out. If possible, glue cotton balls on each sheep to make them feel woolly.

Directions: Have the sheep lying on a table in the center of a large area. Ask the children to line up. Say, **Today we are going to pretend we are the shepherd in the story. We are going to say one word of the verse each time the shepherd touches the sheep. We will take turns letting each of you pretend to be the shepherd and touch the sheep.** As the designated "shepherd" touches the first sheep say "Rejoice." When he/she touches the second sheep, say "with," and so on. If you have a very large group of children, divide into two groups and have twice as many sheep so that each child gets a chance to be the shepherd while saying the verse.

MUSIC TIME

Coming Back to You

(PA17) Supplies:

- *Good News Clues*™ CD or tape copy
- CD player or cassette tape player
- Rhythm band instruments *(optional)*

With the children in a group, have them listen to the song for Site 3. After listening to it, talk about the words and their meaning. Then have the children sing along with the CD. If you have rhythm band instruments available, this would be a good time to use them. Talk about the different instruments as you pass them out. Then let the children play along with the CD. If no instruments are available, have the children march and clap while you play the song.

GUMSHOE GRUB

Popcorn Day Treats

(PS5) Supplies:

- Regular or microwave popcorn in a variety of flavors, such as kettle corn, cheese popcorn, buttered popcorn
- Large serving bowls
- Scoops
- Small paper bowls
- Napkins

Directions: Prepare the popcorn and put into large serving bowls. Allow the children to scoop the popcorn they would like to eat into their bowls. *(If you feel your children will understand, you can tell them that the color white of the popcorn reminds us that Jesus washes our sin away when He forgives us.)* **NOTE: Be aware of any allergies when choosing and serving the different popcorn flavors.**

White-as-Snow Cupcakes

(PS6) Supplies:

- White cake mix
- Eggs
- Oil
- Cupcake tin
- Cupcake liners

- Canned or homemade white frosting
- White sprinkles
- Napkins

Directions: Prepare and bake cupcakes according to the cake mix directions. Frost with white icing and top with white sprinkles. Remind the children that when God forgives us, it is as if our sins become white as snow (Ps. 51:7). Allow each child to select a cupcake to eat for their snack.

CASE-CRACKING GAMES

Use these fun games for your preschoolers to use some energy in a meaningful way. Choose one or both options given, depending on your time and space.

Chair Share

(PG5) Supplies:

- Taped or chalked shapes (circles, squares, rectangles) on the floor
- Music (CD or video)

Just like many people race to get into their favorite chair in the family room before someone else grabs it, this game is about squeezing as many people as possible into a small space. Mark out two or more shapes on the floor, small enough so that the expected number of players will have to really squeeze to fit in the spaces.

Explain that you'll play

music while kids hop, jump, or move around the area (outside the shapes). When you turn off the music, everyone must try to crowd into one of the shapes. This will take cooperation so that the kids can get all their body parts inside the boundaries.

Follow the Shepherd

(PG6) Supplies:

- Towel and sash for headdress (optional)

Sheep are known for following anyone, but today the children will need to follow one leader, the shepherd. Line your children up, and choose one child to be the shepherd. He/she will walk around the room, and the other children need to do whatever the shepherd does (raise their arms, skip, run, etc.). When a child doesn't follow, he is out until only one child is left. This child will be the shepherd for the next time.

PUTTING THE PIECES TOGETHER

Sheep Finger Puppets

(PC5) Supplies:

- Felt—white and light brown
- Puppet pattern *(page R·49 in Resources)*
- Fabric glue
- Mini pom-poms *(white)*
- Black permanent marker
- Resealable sandwich-size bags

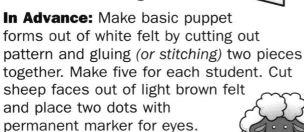

In Advance: Make basic puppet forms out of white felt by cutting out pattern and gluing *(or stitching)* two pieces together. Make five for each student. Cut sheep faces out of light brown felt and place two dots with permanent marker for eyes.

Directions: Have students glue white pom-poms to the prepared puppet form. Students then glue sheep faces to each puppet. When the glue is dry, let the children place the puppets on their fingers and practice retelling the Bible story.

Sheep Tic-Tac-Toe

(PC6) Supplies:

- Small pink ribbon bows *(purchase pre-made ribbons or make your own)*
- Card stock
- Business size envelopes
- Glue

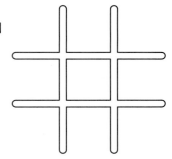

- Patterns for sheep and ball caps *(Page R·51 in Resources)*
- Pattern for tic-tac-toe board *(page R·52 in Resources)*

In Advance: Copy tic-tac-toe board *(page R·52 in Resources)* with Key Verse onto card stock. Glue business size envelope to the back of the card stock game board. Copy sheep pieces on the card stock and cut out. Copy ball caps on different colored paper and cut out. If not using pre-made ribbons, cut pink ribbon into 8" lengths and tie.

Directions: Give each student four sheep pieces. Have them glue small pink ribbon bows on each sheep piece. Let dry. Give each student four more sheep pieces. Have students glue ball caps to sheep pieces. Let dry. Teach kids how to play tic-tac-toe. O = girl sheep with pink ribbon, X = boy sheep with ball cap. When finished the children should put the sheep into the envelope that is attached to the back of the game board.

DETECTIVES' DEPARTURE

(PA18) Supplies:

- "The Quest Continues—Preschool" take-home paper
- Treasure of the Day—White sheep
- Small piece of "wool-like" fabric
- Model or picture of a farm
- Model or picture of a shepherd

Review today's Bible story of the lost sheep. You may want to have the children use the finger puppets they made during craft time to act out the story as you retell it. Follow up by asking the children to say the Site Mission with you as a reminder— **God loves and cares for us.**

Now let's see what kind of mystery we have to solve today! First, show the children the piece of "woolly" fabric. **What do you think this is?** *(Let the children guess.)* **Do you know where it comes from?** *(Again, let the children guess.)* Show the model or picture of a farm. **What kinds of animals would you find on a farm?** *(Let the children name all the animals they can think of.)* Show the picture or model of the shepherd. **What kind of job does this person do?** *(Let the children respond. They will probably guess easily with all the previous clues.)* **Now, let's try to guess what our treasure might be. It has something to do with this piece of fabric, lives on a farm, and is watched over by a shepherd. What is it?** *(Most of the children should guess sheep.)* Let each child reach into a bag or a basket and take one of the sheep you have for them. *(Be sure that the sheep is not too small. You could give sheep stickers, pictures, etc., instead of a small toy.)*

Today, your child discovered the story of the shepherd who left his 99 sheep to find the one lost *(Luke 15:1-7)*. Like the shepherd, Jesus has unconditional love for each of us, wanting to bring us home to Him and the Father. For more information about *Good News Clues*™, go online to **www.CookVBS.com.**

Site Mission (Focus)

God loves and cares for us.

KEY BIBLE VERSE

"Rejoice with me; for I have found my sheep which was lost." —**Luke 15:6**

ACTIVITY

Follow the Shepherd

Supplies:

■ None needed

Sheep are known for following anyone, but today play a game with your child so that he/she will follow one leader, the shepherd. You be the leader and walk around the room while your child does whatever you do *(raise your arms, skip, run, etc.)*. When your child doesn't follow, change places and let him be the leader.

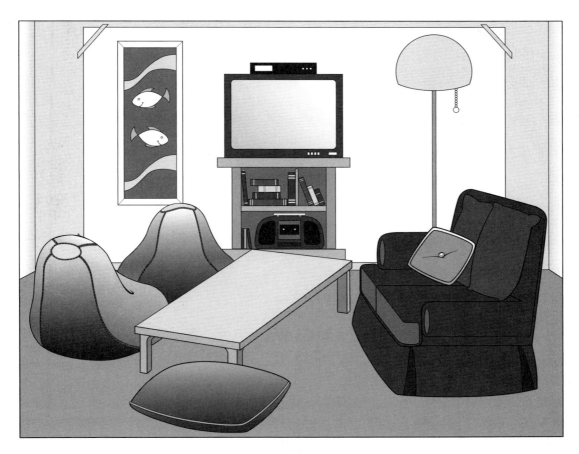

site**4**

Parables Salt and Light

"Let your light so shine."

Matthew 5:16

Why Kids Need to Know That Once They Trust in Jesus, They Should Seek to Grow as Believers

Many of the children who attend VBS will be in the concrete stage of thinking and learning. Grasping the realities of a spiritual life and what follows a decision to trust in Jesus are abstract concepts for many of these youngsters. Because kids can't see the God they're learning to love, it takes a gigantic leap of understanding to figure out how to grow in their relationship with Him.

As you teach them the practical, day-by-day ways they can learn, understand, and mature in their faith in Christ, you'll be helping them connect spiritual growth with physical growth, which they more readily comprehend. Remember that these youngsters may have little familiarity with church-speak and few or no experiences in worship, Bible reading, and prayer. Tangible examples of how to manage these things are best accomplished by showing them how to do it. Come alongside kids to help them learn a Bible verse, let them listen to

Getting More from the Bible Story

The parable of the salt and light found in Matthew 5:13-16 uses examples that are very familiar in the Middle Eastern culture. Salt was obtained from the shores of the Dead Sea and the Hill of Salt at the southwest corner of the Sea. The salt we use today is purified, unlike the salt from the Dead Sea which was contaminated with other minerals. When the salt was dissolved out, only a tasteless substance was left behind.

The salt was used to preserve food and to bring out its flavor. Eating it could prevent dehydration. It was also used as a fertilizer, a weedkiller, and to slow the decay of meat.

Jesus compared believers to salt. He noted that when salt becomes contaminated with foreign substances, it can lose its distinctive flavor and preservative qualities. This was a figurative way of referring to spiritual qualities that should be present in our lives. We need to have a wholesomeness about us to help be a blessing and moral preservative in today's world.

Cities in Jesus' day were often built of white limestone. They gleamed in the sunlight and couldn't be hidden. Furthermore, at night the inhabitants burned oil lamps which could be seen glowing over the area. Likewise, believers who are fully devoted to Jesus could not remain hidden, for the spiritual light of their lives would be visible to everyone.

We are also to be salt and light in today's world. Jesus wants us to be a blessing and moral preservative as we are lights shining for all to see.

factoid

Codes: The science of writing in code is called cryptography. Secret codes were created thousands of years ago. Ancient Jewish writers sometimes hid sacred texts by reversing the alphabet. This type of code, called a cipher, appears in the Bible. One instance is Jeremiah 25:26, in which "Sheshach" is written for "Babel" (Babylon), using the second and twelfth letters from the end of the Hebrew alphabet instead of from the beginning. Greek and Spartan military men communicated by sending messages written across the edges of parchment strips wrapped around a staff. The message was read by unrolling the strip and wrapping it onto an identical size staff.

simple prayers they can imitate or model their own prayers after, or invite them to church and see that they get there. These practical, realistic actions will give children handholds on the journey to spiritual growth.

Salt & Light

"Let your light so shine."

Site Mission

God wants others to see His love through us.

Key Bible Verse

"Let your light so shine." —**Matthew 5:16**

Puppet Option

Investigator #2 or an Assistant Investigator can operate BOSWORTH to help lead the children to different areas and interact spontaneously with the teacher and children. *(See puppet pattern for BOSWORTH on pages R • 55-59.)*

Bible Passage

Matthew 5:13-16

Procedures of the Day

20 minutes: Hands-on Exploration

10 minutes: Focus on the Bible

15 minutes: Bible Memorization

10 minutes: Music Time

15 minutes: Gumshoe Grub

15 minutes: Case-Cracking Games

20 minutes: Putting the Pieces Together

Setting the Scene

Create a working kitchen as much as possible, using preschool size counters and appliances. Have a large table at center stage, with a mixer, mixing bowls, spatula, wooden spoon, recipe book, some baking ingredients *(sugar, baking powder, etc.)*. The background could be an actual baker's shelf or some cabinets and a counter with other kitchen items such as a crock of utensils, coffee maker, more recipe books, boxes of cereal, a fruit bowl, a knife block, some pans, a tea kettle, etc. A real or pretend window can be mounted above the counter in the background with a red and white checked curtain. Have some kitchen towels on hand too.

15 minutes: Detectives' Departure

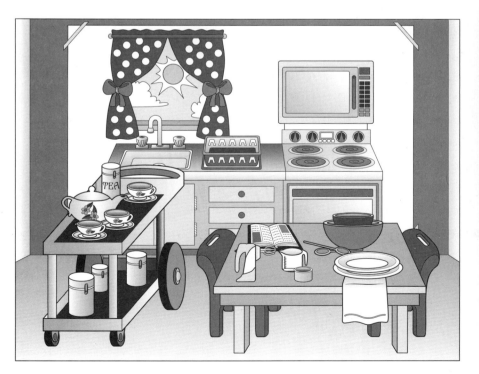

Investigator's Inventory

General

☐ Kitchen mural—Preschool version

☐ *Good News Clues*™ CD or tape copy

☐ CD player or cassette tape player

☐ Copy of "The Quest Continues—Preschool" student take-home paper (*page P4·11*) for each child

Games and Activities

☐ Preschool kitchen toys (*e.g., stove, refrigerator, oven, mixer, measuring cups, etc.*)

☐ Sifters

☐ Measuring cups

☐ Plastic colanders

☐ Kitchen utensils

☐ Rice or beans

☐ Sturdy box

☐ Unsalted popcorn

☐ Bowls

☐ Napkins

☐ Salted popcorn

☐ Plate

☐ Flashlight small enough to fit on the plate

☐ Bowl large enough to cover both the flashlight and plate

☐ Inflated balloons (*same or greater number as there are kids*)

☐ Large pieces of construction paper to tape on floor

☐ Picture of candle or flashlight

☐ Treasure of the Day—Small flashlights, one per child

☐ Light bulb

☐ Cylinder (*such as a paper towel cylinder, etc.*)

Snacks

☐ Small hot dogs (*one per child*)

☐ Refrigerated crescent roll dough

☐ Ketchup

☐ Mustard

☐ Multi-colored fish crackers

☐ Baking sheets

☐ Small plates

☐ Lime green gelatin (*prepared in advance*)

☐ clear cups, 8-oz. size (*one per child*)

☐ Whipped topping

☐ Plastic spoons

☐ Paper cups and napkins

Crafts

☐ White card stock

☐ Black construction paper, 6" x 8"

☐ Glue in bottles, not glue sticks

☐ Salt shakers, filled with salt

☐ Newspapers

☐ Paint shirts or smocks (*optional*)

☐ Water in pitchers (*if sink is not close by*)

☐ Small foil or plastic pans

☐ Light switch plate covers

☐ Paper gum wrappers, old stamps, and/or tissue paper squares

☐ Paintbrushes

☐ Utility knife

☐ Large preschool paintbrushes

☐ Watercolor paint sets

☐ Watercolor paper or heavy drawing paper

☐ Salt shakers

☐ Water containers

HANDS-ON EXPLORATION

Prepare your Detectives for their search by setting up two learning centers for their investigation.

What's Cooking in the Kitchen

(PA19) Supplies:

- Preschool kitchen toys, e.g., stove, refrigerator, oven, mixer, measuring cups, etc.

Have the children work in the kitchen by preparing a pretend meal. If you still have your tables close by, let them pretend to serve the meal to one another.

How Much Does It Take?

(PA20) Supplies:

- Sifters
- Measuring cups
- Plastic colanders
- Kitchen utensil
- Rice or beans
- Sturdy box

Use the rice or beans that you used with the garden learning center, and have the children pour, measure, etc., with the rice or beans. This is a fun way for them to experiment and explore using the kitchen utensils.

FOCUS ON THE BIBLE

Bible Basis: Matthew 5:13-16

(PA21) Supplies:

- Bible
- Unsalted popcorn
- Bowls
- Napkins
- Salted popcorn
- Plate
- Flashlight small enough to fit on the plate
- Bowl large enough to cover both the flashlight and plate

Have the children sit around the tables of the kitchen. The Bible storyteller could wear a chef's hat and apron. Have the Bible open to Matthew 5.

Our story today comes from the Bible. It is found in the book of the Bible called Matthew. Show the children Matthew 5 in the Bible. Keep the Bible open to Matthew 5 throughout the Bible story.

The Bible tells us about Jesus. Jesus told people stories to help them know about God. Jesus told stories to help people know how to show that they loved God.

One of Jesus' stories used salt. Salt is used in the kitchen to help food taste better. Let's learn a little about salt. Pass around the bowl of salted popcorn. Let the children take a taste of the popcorn. **This popcorn has salt. The salt added flavor to the popcorn. Let's try some other popcorn.** Pass around the bowl of unsalted popcorn. Let the children take a taste of the popcorn. **This popcorn has no salt. It doesn't have much flavor.**

Sometimes salt loses its flavor. Then it has to be thrown out. It isn't any good anymore.

Jesus' story calls some people the "salt of the earth." These people are the people who love God. They show His love to others. They give the "flavor" of God's love to the people around them by what they do and say.

Jesus told another story about the people who love God.

In Bible times, cities were built on the top of hills. Sometimes white rocks were used. It was impossible for those cities to hide. Jesus called the people who love God the "light of the world." Just as a city couldn't be hidden, their love for God couldn't be hidden.

Let's try Jesus' story. Put the flashlight on the plate and turn it on. You may need to have someone turn off any lights in the room to make the light from the flashlight shine more prominently. **Here is our light. The light helps us see in the room. What happens if I cover the light with a bowl.** Put the bowl over the light. **It's hard to see in our room with the light covered. But if I take the bowl off of the light and put the light up high, the light helps us see.** Take the bowl off the flashlight and stand the flashlight up on the plate.

People who love God show His love to others just like the light shines without being covered.

Do you love God? Then you are the salt and light that Jesus talked about in His stories. What we say and how we act toward others shows our love for God. Because we love God, we want to say nice things to others. Because we love God, we want to do things that are nice to others. That helps others see God's love in us.

BIBLE MEMORIZATION

(PA22) Supplies:

■ Flashlight used in the Bible story

Key Bible Verse:

"Let your light so shine." —Matthew 5:16

Take time to show the children how to use a flashlight and turn it on and off. Then ask them to pretend they are flashlights. They can stand straight and tall but when they are flashlights they hold their arms up and out. Tell the children to listen carefully when you say to turn their flashlight "on." When you say "on" they are to "turn their lights on." Practice a few times so they get the idea.

Say, **Now we are going to learn to say our verse and pretend we are flashlights too! When we say the word shine, turn on your "light."** Do this several times as follows: **Let your light so shine** *(turn flashlight on).*

MUSIC TIME

Grow in Grace and Wisdom

(PA23) Supplies:

■ *Good News Clues*™ CD or tape copy

■ CD player or cassette tape player

With the children seated on the floor in a group, play the song for Site 4. After listening to the song, talk about the meaning of the words. Then have the children sing along with the CD. You may also want to sing other songs that the children know.

GUMSHOE GRUB

Hot Dogs in a Blanket

(PS7) Supplies:

- Small hot dogs *(one or two per child)*
- Refrigerated crescent roll dough
- Ketchup
- Mustard
- Multi-colored fish crackers *(if desired)*
- Baking sheet(s)

In advance: Prepare the hot dogs in a blanket following the recipe below. Provide one or two small hot dogs per child.

Directions: Place hot dogs on small plates. All children take a small amount of ketchup or mustard to dip their hot dogs into. Allow the children to take a scoop of fish crackers to put on their plates. Serve with juice or water.

Hot Dogs in a Blanket

(serves 4–6 children)

1 8-oz. tube refrigerated crescent rolls

8 hot dogs

Preheat oven to 400 degrees. Separate the crescent dough into eight triangles. Place one hot dog on the wide end of each triangle and roll up. Place, with the dough tip down, on an ungreased baking sheet. Bake at 400 degrees for 10–15 minutes or until golden brown. Hot dogs can be cut into two pieces to make smaller pieces if desired.

Gelatin Parfaits

(PS8) Supplies:

- Lime green gelatin
- Clear cups, 8-ounce size
- Whipped topping
- Spoons

In Advance: Make lime green gelatin in a shallow pan the day before serving. Cut gelatin into cubes.

Directions: Allow children to spoon the gelatin into a clear 8-oz. cup so that it is about one-fourth full. Add a spoonful of whipped topping. Add another layer of gelatin, then one more layer of whipped topping. Be sure to have spoons for the children to eat the parfaits.

CASE-CRACKING GAMES

Use these fun games for your preschoolers to use some energy in a meaningful way. Choose one or both options given, depending on your time and space.

Popcorn

(PG7) Supplies:

- Inflated balloons *(same or greater number as there are kids)*

Let the children imitate being a gigantic popcorn maker. Everyone lies on his/her back on the ground within a designated area, an arm's distance from each other. Leaders and helpers should stand around the edges of the group.

At the "go" signal, leaders toss in all the balloons *(popcorn kernels)*, which the kids have to keep in the air using their feet and hands. Try not to let any hit the ground. Leaders and helpers around the perimeter punch the balloons back to the center when they float away from the group.

Light Walk

(PG8) Supplies:

- CD or cassette player
- Music from CD or cassette
- Paper
- Picture of candle or flashlight

Think of an old-fashioned cake walk. Put the picture of the candle or flashlight on one of the plain pieces of paper. Then spread out the same number of papers as you have children in a large circle. Only one paper will have the candle or flashlight (place it face down).

Have each child stand on one of the papers. When the music begins, tell kids to move around the circle, stepping on the papers. They need to stop on the paper they are on when the music stops. Then they should look under their paper to see if they have the picture of the candle or flashlight. That person will be out, and you should take one piece of paper out with them. Continue until only one child is left.

PUTTING THE PIECES TOGETHER

Salt Pictures

(PC7) Supplies:

- White card stock
- Black construction paper, cut 6" x 8", one per child
- Glue in bottles, not gluesticks
- Salt shakers, filled with salt
- Newspapers
- Paint shirts or smocks (optional)

In Advance: Cut black construction paper into 6" x 8" pieces, one per child. On 8-1/2" x 11" white card stock, copy today's Key Bible Verse. The verse should be written at the bottom edge.

Directions: Cover work surface with newspaper. Let children "draw" with glue. While glue is still wet, have children shake salt over entire surface, so all glue is covered. Gently tilt paper so excess salt falls off non-glued areas. Teachers help students mount the black construction paper to card stock. Let dry.

Switch Plate Cover

(PC8) Supplies:

- Glue
- Water in pitcher
- Small foil or plastic pans
- Light switch plate covers, one per child
- Paper gum wrappers, old stamps, or tissue paper squares
- Paintbrushes
- Utility Knife

In Advance: Prepare glue solutions: 3 parts glue to 1 part water. If using tissue paper, cut into 1-inch squares.

Directions: Have children cover light switch plate covers using paper gum wrappers, stamps, or tissue paper. First, brush glue solution onto switch plate. Then have children place stamps, wrappers, or tissue paper overlapping to cover switch plate cover. Brush glue solution over paper. Using a utility knife, teachers will need to cut through paper to open holes for switch and screws.

Watercolors

(PC9) Supplies:

- Big preschool paintbrushes
- Watercolor sets
- Watercolor paper or heavy drawing paper
- Salt shakers
- Newspapers
- Water containers
- Paint shirts or smocks

Directions: Cover work surface with newspapers. Instruct students to "paint" their whole paper with clean water. Then have students paint with watercolors on the wet surface of the paper. This wet-on-wet technique of watercolor allows the colors to bleed and run. Don't overwork the paint surface. To finish, let kids shake the salt over certain areas of their painting. The salt will draw up the water and color creating a neat effect.

DETECTIVES' DEPARTURE

(PA24) Supplies:

- "The Quest Continues" take-home paper
- Popcorn *(from Focus on the Bible)*
- Flashlight *(from Focus on the Bible)*
- Bowl *(from Focus on the Bible)*
- Light bulb
- Cylinder *(could be a paper towel cylinder, etc.)*

Treasure of the Day—Small, inexpensive flashlights, one per child *(available from discount stores or mail order catalogs)*

Review today's Bible story about the salt and light. You will want to use the bowl and flashlight used during Focus on the Bible as you review. Briefly talk about the Bible stories while looking at the popcorn and using the flashlight and bowl.

Now it's time to solve another mystery! Show the cardboard cylinder *(or other object this shape)* to the children. **This is our first clue. What does this shape remind you of?** *(Let the children guess. They may immediately say paper towels or other objects.)* Show the light bulb. **Do you know what this is?** *(Let children respond.)* **What is it used for?** *(Again, let the children explain their ideas.)* **What could these two objects have to do with each other?** *(Let the children discuss their ideas. Some may easily guess that it reminds them of a flashlight.)* If they still need another clue, use this next statement. **The object is something that can give us light in a dark room. Now can you guess what it is?** *(The children should guess that it is a flashlight.)* Bring out a bag or basket of small, inexpensive flashlights. Each child can choose one to take home to help them remember today's lesson.

Today your child studied Christ's parables of salt and light. By studying the properties of light and salt, we can see how God wants to share Himself through us. *(Matt. 5:13-16)* For more information about *Good News Clues™*, go online to **www.CookVBS.com**.

Site Mission (Focus)

God wants others to see His love through us.

KEY BIBLE VERSE

"Let your light so shine." —**Matthew 5:16**

ACTIVITY

What's Cooking in the Kitchen

Supplies:

- Preschool kitchen toys, e.g., stove, refrigerator, oven, mixer, measuring cups, etc., if available

Have your child work in the kitchen by preparing a pretend meal. Let them pretend to serve the meal to you. Talk about the Bible story as you "eat" what they have prepared.

site 5

Parables Hidden Treasure and Pearl

"The kingdom of heaven is like unto treasure hid in a field."

Matthew 13:44

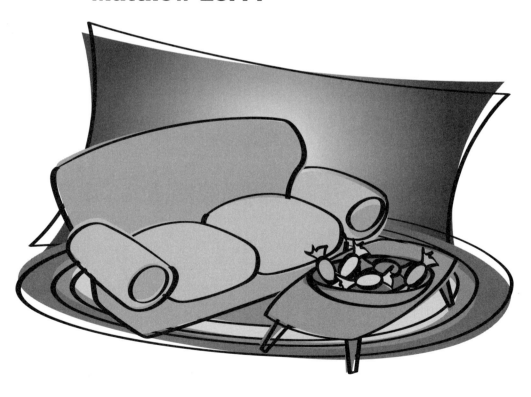

Why Kids Need to Know
That Heaven Can Be Their Eternal Home

Current society is more transient than just 10 years ago.

Families move more often, neighborhoods aren't the safe haven they once were, and a sense of community is harder to find in most places. Children can't count on knowing they'll finish their education in the same location, or that life as they know it will be the same a year from now.

That absence of certainty often creates insecurity and anxiety, especially for younger children. That's one reason heaven is so important for children to know and understand.

The concept of heaven is vague, intangible, and often webbed with misconceptions and myths. Kids develop all types of imaginative images of heaven, from the false belief that everyone there becomes an angel, to what heaven is like, and what God requires to enter heaven. This lesson offers children a solid foundation of truth about heaven, the God who inhabits it, and the promise of the future it holds for each of us. Let this lesson be a wellspring of hope and a firm handhold for kids who are often coping with fearful images about the future.

Getting More from the Bible Story

The setting for these two parables would have seemed very common to listeners in Jesus' day. Banks and safety deposit boxes didn't exist in those times, so people typically hid their most valuable possessions by burying them. *(See Matt. 25 for another parable where someone buries a valuable item.)*

In Jesus' time, Jewish Rabbinic law stated that if someone found money, it belonged to him. Those hearing Jesus' parable would have known that the man who found the treasure had the right to keep it under this Jewish law. The main point of this parable and the following one is that both individuals received such joy from their discoveries that they were willing to give up all else to possess them. Jesus used these word pictures to teach that the person who realizes the invaluable worth of heaven will go to any length to attain that goal. It's worth anything one owns or can give to reach heaven.

The parable of the found pearl also relates closely to Jesus' listeners. Back then, people considered pearls desirable for the monetary value and beauty. A gem merchant continually searched for the most valuable pearl. In this story, a merchant finds such a pearl and is willing to do whatever it takes to acquire and keep it.

Both these parables illustrate how significant it is for a person to gain knowledge of Christ and the surety of heaven, and that it's worth any sacrifice to securely anticipate eternity with God.

factoid

Sherlock Holmes—Author Sir Arthur Conan Doyle's introduction of his character Sherlock Holmes greatly influenced detective fiction. Sherlock Holmes first appeared in *Beeton's Christmas Annual* in Doyle's story, "A Study in Scarlet" in 1887. Most of the Holmes tales were short stories printed in magazines. Over 40 years, Sir Arthur Conan Doyle wrote 56 short stories and four novels about the fictional detective. The character expanded in the public's imagination when first Sidney Paget and then Frederic Dorr Steele drew illustrations of Holmes. Eventually Sherlock Holmes became a literary character, a folk hero, and a cultural icon.

Treasure & Pearl

"The kingdom of heaven is like unto treasure hid . . ."

Site Mission

God wants us to live forever with Him in heaven.

Key Bible Verse

"The kingdom of heaven is like unto treasure hid in a field." —**Matthew 13:44**

Puppet Option

Investigator #2 or an Assistant Investigator can operate BOSWORTH to help lead the children to different areas and interact spontaneously with the teacher and children. *(See puppet pattern for BOSWORTH on pages R · 55-59.)*

Bible Passage

Matthew 13:44-46

Procedures of the Day

20 minutes: Hands-on Exploration

10 minutes: Focus on the Bible

15 minutes: Bible Memorization

10 minutes: Music Time

15 minutes: Gumshoe Grub

15 minutes: Case-Cracking Games

Setting the Scene

The room would be set up as a formal living room with fancy upholstered furniture, elegant rugs, a vase of arranged flowers, coffee or end table, and posed photos of a family in fancy frames *(some of which should be gold toned)*. There should be gold toned accents in the room, such as a lamp, pillows, candlesticks, etc. Draperies can be mounted on a *wall (closed as if there is a window underneath)*. Feel free to use preschool size furniture if you have it for the same effect.

20 minutes: Putting the Pieces Together

15 minutes: Detectives' Departure

Investigator's Inventory

General

- ☐ Living Room mural—Preschool version
- ☐ *Good News Clues*™ CD or tape copy
- ☐ CD player or cassette tape player
- ☐ Copy of "The Quest Continues—Preschool" student take-home paper *(page P5·11)* for each child

Games and Activities

- ☐ Connecting blocks
- ☐ Safety scissors *(one pair per child)*
- ☐ Magazines with photos of furniture, decorated rooms in homes
- ☐ Construction paper
- ☐ Glue sticks
- ☐ Shoe box decorated like a treasure chest
- ☐ Large blanket
- ☐ Bag with many balls in it *(only one of the balls should be white)*
- ☐ Couch *(if available)*
- ☐ Two or more carpet squares
- ☐ Two or more lamp shades
- ☐ Two or more end tables *(or cardboard boxes turned upside down)*
- ☐ Two or more ottomans or chairs
- ☐ Two or three garbage bags full of paper wads
- ☐ Two or three bags of foam packing peanuts
- ☐ Grocery bags
- ☐ Treasure of the Day—Fake rings
- ☐ Pictures of jewels and gems

Snacks

- ☐ Pudding *(store bought or homemade)*
- ☐ Clear 8-oz. cups
- ☐ Spoons
- ☐ Chocolate chips, butterscotch chips, or mini marshmallows
- ☐ Small decorated cookies *(store bought or homemade)*
- ☐ Juice
- ☐ Doilies
- ☐ Fancy napkins
- ☐ Paper cups

Crafts

- ☐ Gold permanent marker
- ☐ Vinyl *(found in fabric stores)*
- ☐ Big paper clips
- ☐ Cord of heavy yarn or shoelaces
- ☐ Hole punch
- ☐ Sewing scissors
- ☐ Gold foil
- ☐ Magazines or newspapers
- ☐ Adhesive backed magnet strips
- ☐ Lightweight cardboard

HANDS-ON EXPLORATION

Prepare your Detectives for their search by setting up two learning centers for their investigation.

Have a Seat!

(PA25) Supplies:

- Connecting blocks

Encourage the children to build a living room with furniture. They can work together to build sofas, chairs, tables, etc. Have them arrange the furniture like they have theirs at home or what they've seen in other living rooms.

Design a Room

(PA26) Supplies:

- Safety Scissors *(one for each child)*
- Magazines with photos of furniture, decorated rooms in homes
- Construction paper
- Glue sticks

Hand out the magazines, and have the children look for pictures of furniture, decorations, etc. Give each child a pair of scissors, one piece of construction paper, and a glue stick. They will cut out the pictures to create their own "living room" collage, gluing them to the construction paper.

FOCUS ON THE BIBLE

Bible Basis: Matthew 13:44-46

(PA27) Supplies:

- Bible
- Shoe box decorated like a treasure chest
- Large blanket
- Bag with many balls in it *(only one of the balls should be white)*

Before telling the story, put the box in the middle of the area where you will tell the story. Cover the box with the blanket. Have the children sit around the edge of the blanket. Open your Bible to Matthew 13.

Our story today comes from the Bible. It is found in the book of the Bible called Matthew. Show the children Matthew 13 in your Bible. Keep the Bible open while you tell the story to the children.

The last two days you've heard stories that Jesus told. These stories told people how much God loves them. Other stories told us how to show people that we love God. Our Bible story tells us about two other stories that Jesus told. These stories tell us about heaven.

In the first story, Jesus talked about a worker. This worker worked for another man. He worked in his field. Let's pretend that this blanket is the field. The worker dug in the field. Encourage the children to pretend to dig on the top of the blanket. **One day the worker found a treasure hidden in the field.** Have the children lift up the blanket until they find the box. Don't let the children move the box. **What do you think the worker did?** Listen to the children's responses. **The worker hid the treasure again. He really wanted the treasure. But he couldn't just take it. It belonged to the man who owned the field. So the worker went home.** Pat your knees. **Then the worker gathered together everything he owned: all his clothes, all his furniture, maybe even his food. He sold it all! Then the worker took the money he got for selling his things and bought the man's field. The worker owned the field. He also owned the treasure that was hidden.** Remove the blanket. Leave the treasure box in the middle of the circle.

Jesus said that heaven is like that hidden treasure. The treasure was worth more than what the worker paid for it. Heaven is worth more than any treasure we might ever find.

Put the bag in front of you. **Jesus told another story about heaven. In this story, there was a man who bought pearls. Pearls are usually white. They are used to make necklaces and rings. They are very expensive. Let's look in this bag for a pearl.** Give each child a turn taking a ball out of the bag. Ask them to hold them very still. **You each have a pearl. But the most special pearl is the white one. Which pearl is it?** Have all the children put their balls back in the bag. Put the white ball next to the treasure box.

When the man found the most special pearl, he knew he had to have it. He went back home. Pat your knees. **The man gathered together everything he owned: all his clothes, all his furniture, maybe even his food. He sold it all! Then the man took the money he got for selling his things and bought the most special pearl.**

Look at our treasure and our pearl. Jesus' stories about a treasure and a pearl can help us know about heaven. Heaven is more special than anything we have on earth.

BIBLE MEMORIZATION

(PA28) Supplies:

- None needed

Key Bible Verse:

"The kingdom of heaven is like unto treasure hid in a field." —**Matthew 13:44**

Have the children pretend to be digging in the ground to find a treasure like the man in the story did. Explain that today's Bible verse talks about a treasure that is hidden. Ask, **Does every treasure have to be hidden in the ground?** (*Let the children have time to think of their answers and then respond.*) **Not every treasure is hidden in the ground. But this is how the people in Jesus' day hid their important treasures. Let's learn our Bible verse and pretend to be looking for treasure.**

Say the verse for the children. Then have the children say the verse with you. The next time you say the verse together have them pretend to be digging in the ground looking for treasure when you get to the second part of the verse.

MUSIC TIME

Treasures in Heaven

(PA29) Supplies:

- *Good News Clues*™ CD or tape copy
- CD player or cassette tape player

With the children seated on the floor in a group, play the song for Site 5. After listening to the song, talk about the meaning of the words. Then have the children sing along with the CD. You may also want to sing other songs that the children know.

GUMSHOE GRUB

Treasure in a Cup

(PS9) Supplies:

- Pudding—can be store bought in large containers or make your own
- Clear cups—8-ounce size
- Spoons
- Chocolate chips, butterscotch chips, or mini marshmallows

In Advance: Prepare the pudding according to the directions if you are making your own.

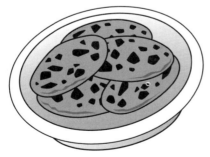

Directions: Spoon pudding into a clear cup about one-half full. Spread the pudding up the sides of the cup, leaving a space in the middle of the pudding. Add about a tablespoon of the chips or mini marshmallows in the space. Top with a

spoonful of pudding to hide the surprise!
NOTE: Be aware of any allergies to chocolate or dairy products.

Tea Party

(PS10) Supplies:

- Small decorated cookies, store-bought or homemade
- Juice, such as apple juice
- Doilies
- Fancy Napkins
- Cups

In Advance: If you are preparing homemade cookies, plan ahead to have time to make and decorate them. Children enjoy simple cookies like sugar cookies or chocolate chip cookies which can still be decorated.

Directions: Have a "tea" party with apple juice *(or water)* and fancy cookies. Serve the cookies on a doily-lined plate. Add to the tea party feel with fancy napkins.

CASE-CRACKING GAMES

Use these fun games for your preschoolers to use some energy in a meaningful way. Choose one or both options given, depending on your time and space.

Living Room Obstacle Course Race

(PG9) Supplies:

- Couch
- Two or more carpet squares
- Two or more lamp shades
- Two or more end tables *(or cardboard boxes turned upside down)*
- Two or more ottomans or chairs

Set up one or two obstacle courses using living room items. Set up the course either in a line or circle. The couch is first, then the carpet squares, the lamp shades, the end tables, and then the ottoman or chairs. This course can be run by one child at a time, or you can divide into two groups and one child from each group goes through at a time.

Here's the path: Kids jump or climb over the back of the couch to the front, run up to the carpet square and sit on it and push themselves to the lamp shade, which they put on their head while crab or duck walking to the end table. *(After each child is finished, return the lamp shade to its original place.)* They circle the table once, then stand up and run to the ottoman/ chair, where they sit down and count to five. Then they need to run back to the front of the line and the next child will follow the same route.

Clean Up

(PG10) Supplies:

- Two or three garbage bags full of paper wads
- Two or three bags of foam packing peanuts
- Grocery bags

This game can be done with the entire group at once or with teams, depending on your play space size. It works best in a non-windy area. Use the living room scene from Setting the Scene. Have kids work in groups of two or three, and give each group a grocery bag. Tell the kids their job is to clean the living room. Then create a big mess by throwing the paper wads and Styrofoam peanuts all over the place, on the floor, and on the furniture. Tell them they have a set amount of time *(one to two minutes)* to pick up the garbage in the living room. Have extra bags for those who fill theirs. At the end of the time, see who collected the most or how clean the living room is.

Alternative: Time how long it takes the group to clean the living room. If using teams, see which one gets the job done the fastest.

PUTTING THE PIECES TOGETHER

Treasure Bag

(PC10) Supplies:

- Gold permanent marker
- Vinyl *(found in fabric stores)*
- Big paper clips
- Cord of heavy yarn or even shoelaces
- Sewing scissors
- Hole punch

In Advance: Cut vinyl into 12" x 8" lengths, fold in half to 6" x 8", paper clip to keep in place. Hole punch through the two open sides, 1/2" from the sides, 1" apart. Cut cording into 30" lengths *(2 per child).* You can dip the end of each cord into glue and let it dry so it will be easier to lace. Tie a cord to the last hole near the fold in the vinyl on the back of each side. Draw the student's initial with gold marker on side of bag. The letter should be about 2" to 3" tall. Write the Key Bible Verse or the reference below the initial.

Directions: Like a sewing card, have students lace each side of the bag with the cords attached to each side. Knot the two cords together to form a handle. Remove paper clips.

Foil Embossing

(PC11) Supplies:

- Gold foil
- Magazines or newspapers
- Tape
- Adhesive backed magnet strips
- Lightweight cardboard

In Advance: Cut foil into 6" x 8" pieces, one per child. Cut light-weight cardboard into 4" x 6" pieces, one per child. Cut magnets into 3" lengths, two per child.

Directions: Place foil on a soft surface like a magazine or section of newspaper. Have students draw a design with ballpoint pen. Teacher wraps foil, embossed side up, around cardboard and tapes down. Add magnet to back top and bottom.

DETECTIVES' DEPARTURE

(PA30) Supplies:

- "The Quest Continues" take-home paper
- Treasure of the Day—Fake rings
- Pictures of jewels and gems

Review today's Bible story about the hidden treasure. Take a few minutes to talk about different kinds of treasures. Let the children give you their ideas of treasures, which may vary greatly from an adult view of treasures. Then emphasize that this Bible story is talking about heaven being the treasure.

We have one last mystery to solve today. By now the children will realize that they are guessing to find out the special Treasure of the Day. Show the pictures of jewels and gems. *(You should be able to find some pictures on the internet that can be printed if you don't have pictures in any books.)* Do you know what these are pictures of? *(Some children may be familiar with various gems, such as diamonds, pearls, etc. Give them an opportunity to give you their ideas.)* **Have you ever seen any of these gems before?** *(Once again, let the children respond. Some may say their mother has a ring or necklace made of gems. Other children may*

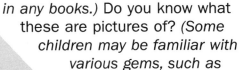

tell you they have a gem that came in a special box of treats, etc.) Ask the children to guess what kind of special treasure might be waiting for them today. You may want to hold up the bag or basket holding the rings. **Today's treasure has something to do with fingers. What kind of treasure do you think is in our basket (bag) today?** (Let the children guess. Someone will probably guess rings, but if not, give them one last clue.) **This treasure is in the shape of a circle.** (Let children make a final guess, then help them if necessary.) Allow each child to select one ring from the basket and put it on his/her finger.

Before dismissing the children, be sure they have their artwork, take-home papers, and rings.

Today's lesson offers children a **solid foundation of truth about heaven,** the God who inhabits it, and the promise of the future it holds for each of us *(Matt. 13:44-45)*. For more information about *Good News Clues™*, go online to **www.CookVBS.com**.

Site Mission (Focus)

God wants us to live forever with Him in heaven.

KEY BIBLE VERSE

"The kingdom of heaven is like unto treasure hid in a field." —**Matthew 13:44**

ACTIVITY

Design a Room

Supplies:

- Scissors
- Magazines with photos of furniture, decorated rooms in homes
- Construction paper
- Glue sticks

Give your child magazines to look for pictures of furniture, decorations, etc. Give them a pair of scissors, one piece of construction paper, and a glue stick. They will cut out the pictures to create their own "living room" collage, gluing them to the construction paper. The living room may look like yours or it may be one of their own creation. Talk about how someday we will be living in heaven with God.

Reproducible Resources

PLAN

TRAIN

SHEET MUSIC

PROMOTE

FOLLOW UP

ACTIVITIES

TRANSPARENCIES

OTHER RESOURCES

VeBS® Budget Chart

CRAFT & GAME SUPPLIES

Item(s) Purchased	Cost $	Item(s) Purchased	Cost $
Item(s) Purchased _____	Cost $_____	Item(s) Purchased _____	Cost $_____
Item(s) Purchased _____	Cost $_____	Item(s) Purchased _____	Cost $_____
Item(s) Purchased _____	Cost $_____	Item(s) Purchased _____	Cost $_____
Item(s) Purchased _____	Cost $_____	Item(s) Purchased _____	Cost $_____
Item(s) Purchased _____	Cost $_____	Item(s) Purchased _____	Cost $_____
Item(s) Purchased _____	Cost $_____	Item(s) Purchased _____	Cost $_____
Item(s) Purchased _____	Cost $_____	**SUBTOTAL ITEM(S) PURCHASED $**_____	

CURRICULUM

Item(s) Purchased _____	Cost $_____	Item(s) Purchased _____	Cost $_____

PROMOTION

Item(s) Purchased _____	Cost $_____	Item(s) Purchased _____	Cost $_____
Item(s) Purchased _____	Cost $_____	Item(s) Purchased _____	Cost $_____
Item(s) Purchased _____	Cost $_____	**SUBTOTAL ITEM(S) PURCHASED $**_____	

PERSONNEL

Item(s) Purchased _____	Cost $_____	Item(s) Purchased _____	Cost $_____
Item(s) Purchased _____	Cost $_____	Item(s) Purchased _____	Cost $_____
Item(s) Purchased _____	Cost $_____	Item(s) Purchased _____	Cost $_____
Item(s) Purchased _____	Cost $_____	**SUBTOTAL ITEM(S) PURCHASED $**_____	

SNACKS

Item(s) Purchased _____	Cost $_____	Item(s) Purchased _____	Cost $_____
Item(s) Purchased _____	Cost $_____	Item(s) Purchased _____	Cost $_____
Item(s) Purchased _____	Cost $_____	Item(s) Purchased _____	Cost $_____
Item(s) Purchased _____	Cost $_____	Item(s) Purchased _____	Cost $_____
Item(s) Purchased _____	Cost $_____	Item(s) Purchased _____	Cost $_____
Item(s) Purchased _____	Cost $_____	Item(s) Purchased _____	Cost $_____
Item(s) Purchased _____	Cost $_____	**SUBTOTAL ITEM(S) PURCHASED $**_____	

DECORATIONS

Item(s) Purchased _____	Cost $_____	Item(s) Purchased _____	Cost $_____
Item(s) Purchased _____	Cost $_____	Item(s) Purchased _____	Cost $_____
Item(s) Purchased _____	Cost $_____	Item(s) Purchased _____	Cost $_____
Item(s) Purchased _____	Cost $_____	Item(s) Purchased _____	Cost $_____
Item(s) Purchased _____	Cost $_____	**SUBTOTAL ITEM(S) PURCHASED $**_____	

FOLLOW-UP

Item(s) Purchased _____	Cost $_____	Item(s) Purchased _____	Cost $_____

TOTAL $_____

GOOD NEWS CLUES™

REIMBURSEMENT FORM

GOOD NEWS CLUES!
SEARCHING FOR NEW LIFE IN JESUS

Name _____

Date _____ $ _____

Amount spent *(Include a copy of the receipt.)*

What the money was spent on _____

_____

Reimbursement given _____ Approved by _____

REIMBURSEMENT FORM

GOOD NEWS CLUES!
SEARCHING FOR NEW LIFE IN JESUS

Name _____

Date _____ $ _____

Amount spent *(Include a copy of the receipt.)*

What the money was spent on _____

_____

Reimbursement given _____ Approved by _____

REIMBURSEMENT FORM

GOOD NEWS CLUES!
SEARCHING FOR NEW LIFE IN JESUS

Name _____

Date _____ $ _____

Amount spent *(Include a copy of the receipt.)*

What the money was spent on _____

_____

Reimbursement given _____ Approved by _____

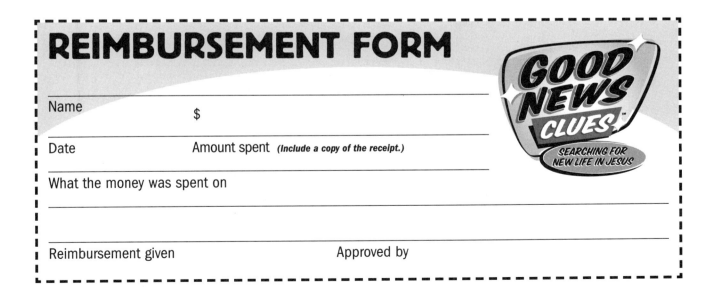

VeBS® REGISTRATION

Child's Name _____ Color Group Assignment _____

Birth Date _____ Age _____ Grade _____

Names of Siblings Attending VeBS® _____

Parents' Names _____

Address _____

City/State/Zip _____

Home Phone _____ Work Phone _____

Pager or Cell Phone _____ Church Home _____

★Emergency Contact _____ ★Relationship _____

★Phone _____

★Allergy/Health Conditions _____

My child has my permission to attend and participate in Good News Clues™ VeBS® program.

Parent Signature _____

Date _____

VeBS® REGISTRATION

Child's Name _____ Color Group Assignment _____

Birth Date _____ Age _____ Grade _____

Names of Siblings Attending VeBS® _____

Parents' Names _____

Address _____

City/State/Zip _____

Home Phone _____ Work Phone _____

Pager or Cell Phone _____ Church Home _____

★Emergency Contact _____ ★Relationship _____

★Phone _____

★Allergy/Health Conditions _____

My child has my permission to attend and participate in Good News Clues™ VeBS® program.

Parent Signature _____

Date _____

Group Color:

SITE NO.   **SITE NO.**   **SITE NO.**   **SITE NO.**   **SITE NO.**

Name	Dates Attended					Allergies/Notes
1						
2						
3						
4						
5						
6						
7						
8						
9						
10						
11						
13						

NAMETAG STICKERS (AVERY® LABEL 15395; SCALE SHOWN: 100%)

HI! MY NAME IS:

_____

HI! MY NAME IS:

_____

HI! MY NAME IS:

_____

HI! MY NAME IS:

_____

HI! MY NAME IS:

_____

HI! MY NAME IS:

_____

HI! MY NAME IS:

_____

HI! MY NAME IS:

_____

Door Hangers (Scale shown: 80%)

cut along lines
to create door hanger

VeBS!
JOIN THE FUN!

_____
PLACE

_____
CONTACT

_____
DATE

_____
TIME

GOOD NEWS CLUES
SEARCHING FOR NEW LIFE IN JESUS

cut along lines
to create door hanger

VeBS!
JOIN THE FUN!

_____
PLACE

_____
CONTACT

_____
DATE

_____
TIME

GOOD NEWS CLUES
SEARCHING FOR NEW LIFE IN JESUS

Announcing…

VeBS!®
JOIN THE FUN!

PLACE

CONTACT

DATE

TIME

SPECIAL

GOOD NEWS CLUES™

SEARCHING FOR NEW LIFE IN JESUS

Certificate (Scale shown: 95%)

CERTIFICATE of COMPLETION

This certificate is hereby awarded to

_____

for the successful completion of *Good News Clues™* Program!

_____
VeBS® Director

_____
Date

PLACE

DATE / TIME

CONTACT

PLACE

DATE / TIME

CONTACT

PLACE

DATE / TIME

CONTACT

PLACE

DATE / TIME

CONTACT

Prayer Reminder | Volunteer Flyer

VeBS! PRAYER REMINDER!

Please pray for the Detectives, the Investigators (leaders), and all of the support personnel that help put together this Very exciting Bible School® program!

PLEASE PRAY DURING THESE DATES:

_____

VeBS! PRAYER REMINDER!

Please pray for the Detectives, the Investigators (leaders), and all of the support personnel that help put together this Very exciting Bible School® program!

PLEASE PRAY DURING THESE DATES:

_____

WANTED!

Adventurous youths, adults, and seniors with a heart for kids, who are willing to share your gifts to be part of

GOOD NEWS CLUES™
SEARCHING FOR NEW LIFE IN JESUS

Don't miss this opportunity to be a part of this year's VBS!

Name _____

Address _____

Daytime phone_____

Evening phone _____

I am interested in:

❏ Teaching ❏ Assistant Investigator

❏ Crafts ❏ Snacks ❏ Sewing puppets

❏ Building sets ❏ Organizing volunteers

❏ Building relationships with kids

❏ Other: _____

_____

Leader Hints

How to lead children to Jesus and into God's family

It's amazing how often adult Christians say that they first came to understand the unfolding of God's story when they were six to twelve years old. These years are a key time for children to make personal decisions for Christ and to begin their faith journeys. This decision is important, and we need to be very sensitive to children who are considering it.

When you have opportunities during VBS to talk with children about God's saving grace, keep in mind that no two children are at the same point of spiritual preparedness. Many children are not ready to trust in Christ—other children are. They are sensitive to their need for forgiveness and acceptance into God's family. Be open to the Holy Spirit's leading. Be available to answer questions, but let children decide themselves when the time is right to receive Christ. Here are a few tips:

- It's good to be eager for children to trust Christ for salvation. Just be careful not to let your eagerness spur children to make that decision. A commitment to trust Christ for eternal life should not be made just to please an adult.

- Usually it's best not to offer group invitations in which kids are asked to raise their hands. Kids are great conformists; they may respond to such an invitation just because everyone else is doing it.

- Encourage children to talk privately with you about questions regarding salvation and what Jesus wants to do in their lives.

- Have the child tell you in his or her own words what he or she wants.

- If you feel the child understands the concept of salvation and is ready to receive Christ by faith, take a few minutes to pray with him or her. You and the child will want to talk with his

or her parents about this decision to accept Christ. Unchurched parents may have questions about salvation, which opens the door for you to witness to them and invite them to your church.

- Don't forget your important ministry of follow-up. Pray for the child and encourage discipleship and Christian growth.

The following suggestions may be helpful as you explain the message of salvation.

Help the child know the truths that are fundamental for all Christians. The child needs to know that:

1. God loves each of us, but we all have done things that displease Him.

2. Jesus, God's Son who never sinned, is the only one able to take away the wrong things we have done. He is able to do this because He died on the cross for our sins.

3. We must believe that Jesus died to forgive us for these wrong things so we can become a part of God's family—become a Christian—by asking Him into our lives.

4. We become Christians when we have Christ living in us. We become children of God and new people who want to follow Jesus when we receive Him by faith.

Let the Word of God prompt a child to come to Christ. Here are some verses relating to salvation:

- John 1:12–"But as many as received him, to them gave he power to become the sons of God, even to them that believe on his name."

- John 3:16–"For God so loved the world, that he gave his only begotten Son, that whosoever believeth in him should not perish, but have everlasting life."

- Romans 3:23–"For all have sinned, and come short of the glory of God."

- Romans 5:8–"But God commendeth his love toward us, in that, while we were yet sinners, Christ died for us."

- Romans 6:23–"For the wages of sin is death; but the gift of God is eternal life through Jesus Christ our Lord."
- Romans 10:9-10–"That if thou shalt confess with thy mouth the Lord Jesus, and shalt believe in thine heart that God hath raised him from the dead, thou shalt be saved. For with the heart man believeth unto righteousness; and with the mouth confession is made unto salvation."
- 2 Corinthians 5:17–"Therefore if any man be in Christ, he is a new creature: old things are passed away; behold, all things are become new."
- 1 John 5:11-12–"And this is the record, that God hath given to us eternal life, and this life is in his Son. He that hath the Son hath life; and he that hath not the Son of God hath not life."

Because many children still think concretely—they don't understand abstract concepts or symbolism—have the child explain to you the decision he or she has made. Then you can clear up any confusion.

How to help children understand the Bible

Some adults think they can't teach because they don't know the Bible well enough. No one can prepare to answer all the questions children have! So how do we handle those questions?

With humility: There's nothing wrong with saying, "I honestly don't know, but I'll do some studying and find out" *(as long as you keep your promise)*. Don't avoid the challenge by saying something like, "Well, I guess you'll have to ask the pastor about that one."

With skill: Don't forget that, even though a child's question may throw you off guard, you're more prepared for the lesson than he or she is! Collect your thoughts and use your resources. Remember that one of those resources is the class as a whole. Why not repeat the question for the whole class to think about? Even though they're "just kids," the

Holy Spirit can bring clarity and understanding to the group through the group.

With knowledge: Remember to use your knowledge of all Scripture when considering questions about interpreting a particular passage.

With love: Love of the Bible is a natural outgrowth of serious and sustained contact with it. Let love for kids and for God's Word interplay with each other. The more kids see that the Bible is part of what makes you who you are, the more they'll want to get into it on their own.

How to get children involved in discussions

Here are some suggestions on how to get children to discuss:

- Respond to children in a warm, accepting, and non-threatening way so they can speak without fear.
- Be open about yourself. You don't have to share intimate details, of course, but tell kids about your life to help them know you as a whole *(albeit imperfect)* person.
- Ask questions of varying depth. The first level is the literal or "comprehension" question: What did the characters do? A little deeper is the interpretative question: Why did the characters act as they did? At the deepest level is the opinion question: Why do you think that happened? Try to balance all three levels. For interpretative and opinion questions, avoid giving the impression that there is only one "right" answer.
- Instead of asking a question that might be awkward or too personal, present a hypothetical situation and let children comment on that. Ask, "What should the girl in the story do?" rather than, "What would you do?"
- Don't be afraid of silence. If you want children to face a tough issue, give them plenty of time to think about it in silence or during silent prayer.

- Don't force "openness." Just as children should feel free to share, they should also feel free not to.

How to get children involved in more difficult activities.

The Site Settings in this Very exciting Bible School® have children involved in a variety of learning activities. How do you get children involved in them?

Carefully: Children like challenges and will rise to the occasion more often than not. But even more than challenges, they like success. They'll play along with you if they have confidence in you and feel they'll succeed at the challenge. For children, the "payoff" shouldn't be too far away.

Positively: Introduce your project or activity with enthusiasm and a spirit of adventure. Make it clear that you're in this together, and you'll be there to give help when it's needed. When describing a project, explain the steps clearly and get feedback from kids as you go along to make sure they understand.

Respectfully: Try to involve as many children as possible, especially the shy or more introverted ones. But don't force involvement; encourage, but never demand participation. One quiet child may be resisting what you're trying to do, but another may be thinking deeply about what you've said.

How to help children understand abstract concepts and symbols.

Children, especially younger ones, can't understand abstract concepts and expressions easily. Take care when this kind of language comes up.

- Don't assume anything. A Bible expression such as "born again" is widely used today, but that doesn't mean children understand it.

- When explaining a poetic term or abstract concept, use the simplest, most concrete language that you can.

- After you explain a concept, encourage children to put it into their own words. Listen carefully to see whether they really understand it.

- Watch children's facial expressions. You can usually tell when they're puzzled and need to have something presented in a different way.

- Avoid explaining one symbol by using another. For example, when Scripture refers to God's Word as "a lamp unto my feet," don't say it's like a flashlight that you'd use to find your way on a dark trail.

- Try explaining what a symbolic term does not mean. For example, when Jesus says, "I am the Bread of Life," He is not really saying that He is a loaf of bread. After you've cleared the ground in this way, go on to explain what the term does mean.

- Always try to relate biblical teaching to the children's everyday lives. For example, if you're talking about "being born again," or if you're describing Jesus as the Good Shepherd, stop to ask yourself what that means for the children. What does rebirth into God's family mean when children feel lonely or sad? What kind of shepherd-like things does Jesus do for kids when they go through scary times or places?

- Don't be afraid to tell children that something may be difficult to understand. This can encourage them to really think. It makes them feel good about themselves when they struggle through to understanding.

How to play games with children

Children enjoy playing games. Here are suggestions for making games work with children:

- Keep rules as simple as possible and think through your explanation in advance so you can present it quickly.

- Be sensitive to children's ability levels. If you think that the skills necessary for a certain game might leave some children out, adapt it so everyone is included.

- Allow enough time for a game so kids don't feel rushed, but be sure they don't get bored. Tell them when the last round begins so the end doesn't take them by surprise.

- Think through how and where the game will be played. You don't want to start something, discover it won't work, and have to end it. Figure out how much noise will be made and how much room will be needed, in case you'll have to move.

How to help children feel needed and important

Children need to know how special and important they are. We need to show and tell them that they matter. How can we do this?

Nonverbally: Never underestimate the power of a smile, a wink, a touch on the shoulder, or a look that says, "I'm glad you're here."

Verbally: Children love it when you know and use their names. They also love it when you ask for their opinions and suggestions, especially if you listen well and take them seriously. Encourage them sincerely and frequently. Don't use or allow cutting remarks.

Physically: Children love it when you display their work at every opportunity. Sit down and make a list of every job you could delegate to them. Children love to do even menial tasks, and having them do these with a partner makes it extra special.

How to discipline

A well-prepared, organized classroom encourages positive behavior. Discipline means training and helping children with self-control; it doesn't only mean punishment.

- Praise and affirm children for good behavior and things they do well. Don't wait for undesirable behavior before noticing a child.

- Correct a child's behavior, not his or her person. Avoid statements like, "You never listen."

- Children will misbehave if rules conflict. Be careful not to state a rule that cannot be enforced. Children know which rules are real.

- Children may misbehave to vent frustration with some aspect of the learning experience or activity. Search for the cause rather than just punishing the misbehavior.

- Children may misbehave because of boredom. Keep learning active and relevant. Be prepared and excited about what you are teaching.

- Children may misbehave because of home situations. Be sensitive to the effect that family life can have on behavior in the classroom.

- Decide in advance what your "or else" circumstances are going to be. Remember that the disruptive child is setting himself or herself against the group, not just against you. Deal with disruption the first time it happens by giving the child a warning.

- Never give more than two warnings. If misbehavior persists, send the child to a "time-out" spot at the back of the room. By doing this, you're teaching that being allowed to sit with your friends is a privilege—a privilege you have to show you can handle.

- Never use physical punishment, ridicule, or empty threats. Don't wait until something becomes a problem to do something about it; think through trouble spots in advance. An ounce of prevention . . .

- Assume leadership. You're the teacher; let children know what you expect. Follow through consistently and fairly.

- Move freely about the classroom so that you can be close to all the children.

How to work with children of differing ages

Sometimes it's necessary to work with a group of children who range in age from 5 to 12 years old. If this is your situation, the following tips may help:

- Use older children in more responsible positions. These children feel good about themselves when they are able to help. Allow older kids to help younger ones with craft projects and activities. Older children also may be able to help give instructions and present or dramatize Bible stories.

- Incorporate a lot of visuals for the benefit of younger children!

- Sometimes if a difficult activity or one that takes a long time to complete is suggested, it may be appropriate to have a separate activity for younger children.

- Provide more challenging activities for older children who may complete work ahead of time.

- Recognize developmental differences in ages and provide for those differences in the equipment you use. If possible, have different sizes of chairs, crayons, tables, etc. *(See the charts of developmental characteristics on pages R·17–20.)*

- Incorporate various levels of questions for the levels of understanding children have.

- Have additional adults available.

- Provide opportunities for the younger children to "succeed." Often in mixed age groups, older kids dominate.

How to tell a story

Stories provide an exciting way for children to learn important truths. Special preparation by the storyteller helps children imagine that they are experiencing the story's events. Use the following guidelines:

1. Carefully and thoroughly read the entire story in advance.

2. Review the aims of the site so these can be emphasized throughout the telling.

3. Reread the story two or three more times. The more time you spend becoming familiar with it, the more naturally and effectively you will be able to present it.

4. Outline the main points of the story on note cards.

5. Practice telling the story using simple words and phrases with which you and the children will be comfortable.

6. Add hand gestures and actions that are natural for you to help the story come to life. Use of action words, good eye contact, and frequent pauses emphasize the meaning of the story.

7. Try to involve yourself emotionally with the events you're talking about.

8. Be sure to stay in character as long as you are dressed for the part.

Preschool Characteristics

Ages 2–4 Years

Physical	Mental	Emotional	Social	Spiritual
· Small, but growing. · Active—needs frequent opportunity to use large muscles. · Learning to cut, color, sort, and string. · Boisterous and noisy. · Restless. · Loves repetition. · Susceptible to disease. · Sensitive eyes, ears, and voice. · Still needs lots of sleep.	· Single aspect thinker—focuses on one thing at a time. · Doesn't differentiate between fantasy and reality. · Learns through senses. · Learns by asking questions (usually "why" or "how"). · Learns by imitation. · Displays increased verbal ability. · Has wide scope of interests. · Engages in much imaginary play. · Curious. · Doesn't think symbolically, but in concrete terms.	· Has ups—joy, warmth, sympathy, love. · Has downs—fear, anger, anxiety. · Insecure. · Is a show-off. · Developing sense of humor. · Physically aggressive, sometimes rough and careless with toys.	· Egocentric. · Struggles with authority. · Home-centered. · Beginning to be interested in friends. · Still has imaginary playmates.	· Ideas about God are extensions of ideas about people (usually parents and teachers.) · Enjoys attending Sunday school. · Learning to pray. · Enjoys stories about Jesus. · Interested in God. · Gets Jesus and God confused.

Early Elementary Characteristics

Kindergarten and 1st Grade

Physical	Mental	Emotional	Social	Spiritual
· Restless. · Loves strenuous activity. · Works hard; often overdoes. · Tires easily. · Is attempting to master a variety of new motor skills. · Willing to try anything without regard for danger. · Often stumbles and falls; awkward in movements. · Small-muscle and eye-hand coordination developing; enjoys coloring, cutting, pasting, painting, building, and creating with hands. · Seems to look everywhere at once; easily distracted. · Eyes easily strained from overuse. · Touches, handles, explores all materials within reach. · Expresses himself/ herself through movement.	· Attention span increasing, up to 20 minutes, but varying according to interest. · Differentiates some between fantasy and reality. · Thinks in concrete terms. · Just beginning to develop reasoning ability. · Sphere of interest is widening. · Eager to learn. · Becomes excited about new learning tasks but may get discouraged in the middle and quit. · Can shift from one activity to another. · Recognizes sequence. · Has good memory when facts are presented in a meaningful context. · Likes to listen to stories. · Learns best by active participation, self-activation, and dramatic assimilation.	· Shifts between emotional extremes. · Needs routine, familiar surroundings. · Many new feelings are emerging. · Easily becomes angry at himself/ herself, situations, others; younger early elementary may cry, have tantrums, become violent; kids on the older end of this age group may sulk. · May set goals that are too high. · Ashamed of mistakes; irritated by failure. · May be defiant and rude, asserting independence from adult domination. · Responds negatively to direct demands, but benefits from reminders and verbal guidance. · Often inconsistent, indecisive when making difficult choices; when a choice is made, may be uncompromising.	· Shows loyalty, pride, and interest in family. · Attitudes vary toward brothers and sisters; may be bossy, jealous, proud, protective, or brutal. · Desires friends but does not get along well. · Has two or three best friends. · Wants to win. · Tries to dominate in social situations by showing off, acting silly, bullying others. · Critical of other children's behavior; tattles. · Desires attention; thrives on praise and approval. · Dislikes criticism. · Still quite self-centered. · Enjoys frequent and complex pretend play.	· Can grasp concept of God as Creator. · May ask questions— Who made God? Where is He? · May fear God because God sees everything he does. · Developing a concept of God as a real person. · Sees Jesus as a real person. · Limited awareness of who Jesus is. · Can grasp simple explanation that Jesus is the Savior who died, came alive again, and someday will return to earth. · Understands that Jesus took the blame for our wrong-doings. · Limited understanding of sin; realizes one can choose right or wrong. · Recognizes Bible characters as real. · Considers prayer important.

GOOD NEWS CLUES™

Middle Elementary Characteristics

2nd and 3rd Grades

Physical	Mental	Emotional	Social	Spiritual
· High activity level; interested in games and organized activities such as baseball. · Fondness for rough, boisterous games. · Expresses himself/ herself in variety of postures, gestures, and stunts; more self-conscious in expression than earlier. · Increasingly fluid and graceful in bodily movements. · Courage and daring in physical activity; frequent accidents. · Less easily fatigued than earlier. · Increased speed and smoothness in fine motor performance; improved manipulative ability; works very quickly and with increasing control. · Becoming better observer. · Interested in skill building; persistent in practicing complex motor skills. · Frequent repetition of enjoyed activities. · Drawing shows increasing awareness of body proportions; starting to draw in perspective; likes to draw figures in action. · Girls ahead of boys in physical development. · Able to take responsibility for personal hygiene.	· Capable of prolonged interest and concentration. · Expresses amazement and curiosity. · Beginning to see patterns, contexts, and implications; universe becoming less disconnected. · Sees similarities because two things share observable features or abstract attributes. · Likes to plan ahead. · Good at memorizing short sentences; remembers better if something is written. · Enjoys reading. · Likes stories of fantasy, adventure, travel, faraway places, humor; comic books are favorites. · Increasing independence. · Does not like to fail, but likes to be challenged; does not become upset when tasks are difficult; persistent in completing tasks. · Older pupils make up mind rapidly, definitely. · Starting to apply logical thought to practical situations; mostly unsystematic, trial-and-error approach. · Understands concept of money.	· Shows definite signs of empathy. · Widely variable emotional be-havior—shyness to boldness, morbid to cheerful, lethargic to excitable. · Likely to overextend oneself in thought and activities; when these become too much, retreats, leaving "a mess." · Often delays responses. · Anticipates with great eagerness; interest often short-lived; shifts rapidly. · Ready to tackle anything; likes challenges. · Feelings easily hurt; not given to pro-longed depression; seeks reconciliation after being hurt. · Sensitive to criticism from adults. · Likes orderliness and neatness. · Frequently complains, sulks, mutters, "lets off steam" as outlet for tension. · May fear dark, fights and physical injury, failing, not being liked; often will not admit fears, even to oneself. · Worries frequently, often in midst of pleasant experiences. · Seeks friendly relationships with adults.	· Prefers peer play to family outings. · May complain about assigned chores. · Hates playing alone; wants to have a best friend. · Learning to subordinate personal interests to group. · Developing self-discipline through responsibilities assigned by peer group and peer criticism; needs less constant adult supervision during play. · Enters group projects on extended basis; forms short-lived, loosely organized clubs; older children form more elaborate, purposeful, and last-ing clubs. · Learning to give and take peer criticism constructively. · Admires and seeks friendships with older children. · Acquiring "company manners." · May show antagon-ism toward opposite sex; marked separation of sexes in play. · Growing conscious-ness of own racial, ethnic status. · Image of ideal self forming. · Feels tensions of pulling away from parental domination and achieving inde-pendence.	· Open to instruction about right and wrong; has ability to make deliberate choices regarding his/her actions. · Wants to be good; aware of urges to do good and bad. · Wants his/her goodness to be appreciated. · Older child is more concerned about what he/she has not done than about what he/she has done wrong. · Starting to feel the influence of conscience; feels wrongness of own sins; strives to be honest. · Capable of feeling shame; can admit wrongdoing; frequent excuses. · Has active interest in God. · Likes stories about Jesus; beginning to develop an understanding of history & Jesus' part in it. · Recognizes Jesus as God's Son. · Concepts of sin and salvation are more clearly understood. · Able to do Bible study because of growing reading skill and critical judgment. · Enjoys doing simple Bible map work.

Upper Elementary Characteristics

4th and 5th Grades

Physical	Mental	Emotional	Social	Spiritual
· High energy level. · Greater self-control and calmness in performing motor activities. · Improved ability to budget time and athletic ability greatly influence status with peers and self-concept. · Early physical maturing in boys and girls is related to more positive self-concept. · Girls begin pre-adolescent growth spurt; they are taller, heavier, often stronger than boys; often surpass boys in athletic prowess. · Girls start developing secondary sexual characteristics. · Quiescent growth period for boys.	· Alert, eager to learn; younger child may have short attention span. · Transitioning from concrete to abstract thinking. · Likes to identify facts, put items in order. · Likes to memorize. · Likes to read; enjoys stories. · Avid interest in history, people, current events, science, nature, and geography. · Beginning to do independent, critical thinking; can consider why Bible characters acted as they did and why God dealt with them as He did. · Can apply logic to solving problems; starting to form hypotheses and test things.	· Younger upper elementary kids are generally cheerful, content, carefree, relaxed. · Older kids in this range experience more emotional peaks, more variable moods. · Younger ones are oriented toward action rather than reflection, not self-conscious about feelings. · Older ones are aware of feelings but do not usually understand their causes. · Strong feeling related to likes and dislikes. · Older ones are sensitive to hurt feelings and criticism; subject to jealousy. · Occasional short-lived bursts of anger and violence. · Relieves tension through bodily movement. · Frequently bursts into laughter, especially when unsure of self.	· Wants many friends, but wants one best friend of same sex. · Girls prefer smaller, more intimate peer groups; boys want larger, less close-knit groups. · Shares "secrets" and personal information with friends. · Frequently fights and argues with peers. · Enjoys participating in gangs and clubs; spontaneous clubs are fluid in their organization. · Enthusiastically participates in teams and games. · Respects teachers, taking their word over parents'. · Thrives on certain amount of routine. · Exhibits best behavior away from home. · Loves teasing, chasing, pushing, hitting, nudging, poking, etc.	· Responsive to teaching about God's character. · Starting to realize he/she must follow his/her own convictions about Jesus. · Capable of understanding salvation and Jesus' part in it; able to confess belief in Jesus and accept Him as Savior. · Understands the purpose of prayer; makes up own prayers. · Draws heroes from the Bible. · Primarily concerned with Bible facts. · Values belong to group; anxious to join church and be part of group. · Basic understanding of ethical concepts. · Has strict moral code. · Capable of making value judgments about one's own actions. · Often puzzled about right and wrong.

GOOD NEWS CLUES

Words and Music by John H. Morton

Theme Song

We're goin' lookin' for clues, for good
  news clues.
We're goin' lookin' for clues right now.
It's a mystery; what will we see?
Who, what, where, when, why, and how?
(Repeat)

We're searching for new life in Jesus.
We're gonna give it all we've got.
Jesus is standing at your heart's door;
Now, open when you hear Him knock!

We're goin' lookin' for clues, for good
  news clues.
We're goin' lookin' for clues right now.
It's a mystery; what will we see?
Who, what, where, when, why, and how?
(Repeat)

We're searching for new life in Jesus.
We're gonna give it all we've got.
Jesus is standing at your heart's door;
Now, open when you hear Him knock!

We're goin' lookin' for clues, for good
  news clues.
We're goin' lookin' for clues right now.
It's a mystery; what will we see?
Who, what, where, when, why, and how?
(Repeat)

Lyrics available in Word· documents on the included CD-ROM.

IT IS NO MYSTERY

Words and Music by Christy Long

Site 1: The Garden

It is no mystery. The clues are there to see.

It's elementary that Jesus loves me.

It is no mystery. The clues are there to see.

It's elementary that Jesus loves me.

Start at the beginning, the scene of the crime.

Go back to the garden, way back in time.

Closely examine all evidence, and I think you will find

It is no mystery. The clues are there to see.

It's elementary that Jesus loves me.

It is no mystery. The clues are there to see.

It's elementary that Jesus loves me.

Start at the beginning, the scene of the crime.

Go back to the garden, way back in time.

Closely examine all evidence, and I think you will find

It is no mystery. The clues are there to see.

It's elementary that Jesus loves me.

It is no mystery. The clues are there to see.

It's elementary that Jesus loves me.

It is no mystery.

Lyrics available in Word® documents on the included CD-ROM.

BE BRAVE AND TELL

Words and Music by John H. Morton

Site 2: The Dining Room

A B C   B-R-A-V-E

Be brave and willing to tell the Good
News.

A B C   B-R-A-V-E

Be brave and willing to tell.

"A" — Admit that you have sinned.

"B" — Believe that Jesus forgives you.

"C" — Confess Him as your Lord and
you'll be saved!

A B C   B-R-A-V-E

Be brave and willing to tell the Good
News.

A B C   B-R-A-V-E

Be brave and willing to tell.

"A" — Admit that you have sinned.

"B" — Believe that Jesus forgives you.

"C" — Confess Him as your Lord and
you'll be saved!

A B C   B-R-A-V-E

Be brave and willing to tell the Good
News.

A B C   B-R-A-V-E

Be brave and willing to tell.

A B C   B-R-A-V-E

Be brave and willing to tell the Good
News.

A B C   B-R-A-V-E

Be brave and willing to tell.

Be brave and willing to tell.

Be brave and willing to tell.

Lyrics available in Word° documents on the included CD-ROM.

COMING BACK TO YOU

Words and Music by John H. Morton

Site 3: The Family Room

O Lord, You see that I have sinned again.

I walked away from all the good that You have given.

It seems that I just try to please myself.

You know my heart, and I am sorry again.

I'm coming back to You.

I see Your arms are open to welcome me home.

I'm giving You my heart.

Now, wrap Your arms around me.

Forgive me, Lord, I pray;

I am here to stay.

O Lord, You see that I have sinned again.

I walked away from all the good that You have given.

It seems that I just try to please myself.

You know my heart, and I am sorry again.

I'm coming back to You.

I see Your arms are open to welcome me home.

I'm giving You my heart.

Now, wrap Your arms around me.

Forgive me, Lord, I pray;

I am here to stay.

Thank You for Your grace, for covering my sin,

Your mercy in my life displayed.

I'm coming back to You.

I see Your arms are open to welcome me home.

I'm giving You my heart.

Now, wrap Your arms around me.

Forgive me, Lord, I pray;

I am here to stay.

I am here to stay.

_____

Lyrics available in Word* documents on the included CD-ROM.

GROW IN GRACE AND WISDOM

Words and Music by John H. Morton

Site 4: The Kitchen

When you follow God He will help you
   grow in Him.

He gives His Word, that's the best place
   to begin.

Like a little seed that grows into a tree,

Lord, I want my life to be strong in faith
   and power,

Rooted deep, you see.

I'm gonna grow in grace and wisdom.

I'm gonna do what He asks me to do.

I'm gonna learn all He has to teach me.

Shape me, Lord, make me just like You.

When you follow God He will help you
   grow in Him.

He gives His Word, that's the best place
   to begin.

Like a little seed that grows into a tree,

Lord, I want my life to be strong in faith
   and power,

Rooted deep, you see.

I'm gonna grow in grace and wisdom.

I'm gonna do what He asks me to do.

I'm gonna learn all He has to teach me.

Shape me, Lord, make me just like You.

I'm gonna grow in grace and wisdom.

I'm gonna do what He asks me to do.

I'm gonna learn all He has to teach me.

Shape me, Lord, make me just like You.

Shape me, Lord, make me just like You.

Lyrics available in Word® documents on the included CD-ROM.

TREASURES IN HEAVEN

Words and Music by Phil Reynolds

Site 5: The Living Room

Treasures in heaven no one can take away.

Treasures in heaven that last for always.

Treasures in heaven no one can take away.

Treasures in heaven that last for always.

I will give my life to You;

You're my only prayer.

All the world can offer me is nothing compared to

Treasures in heaven no one can take away.

Treasures in heaven that last for always.

Treasures in heaven no one can take away.

Treasures in heaven that last for always.

I will give my life to You;

You're my only prayer.

All the world can offer me is nothing compared to

Treasures in heaven no one can take away.

Treasures in heaven that last for always.

Treasures in heaven no one can take away.

Treasures in heaven that last for always.

Treasures in heaven that last for always.

Lyrics available in Word* documents on the included CD-ROM.

GOOD NEWS CLUES™

Good News Clues

Words & Music by
John H. Morton

It Is No Mystery

Words & Music by
Christy Long

Lyrics:

It is no mys-ter-y. The clues are there to see. It's el-e-men-ta-ry that Je-sus loves me. It is no mys-ter-y. The clues are there to see. It's el-e-men-ta-ry that Je-sus loves me. Start at the be-gin-ning, the scene of the crime. Go back to the gar-den,

GOOD NEWS CLUES™

Be Brave and Tell

Words & Music by
John H. Morton

GOOD NEWS CLUES™

Coming Back to You

Words & Music by
John H. Morton

O Lord, You see that I ___ have sinned a-gain. ___ I walked a-way ___ with all the good that You ___ have given. It seems that I just try to please ___ my - self. ___ You know my heart, ___ and I am sor - ry ___ a - gain. I'm com-ing back to You. ___ I see Your arms ___ are o - pen ___ to wel - come me home. ___

GOOD NEWS CLUES™

Grow in Grace and Wisdom

Words & Music by
John H. Morton

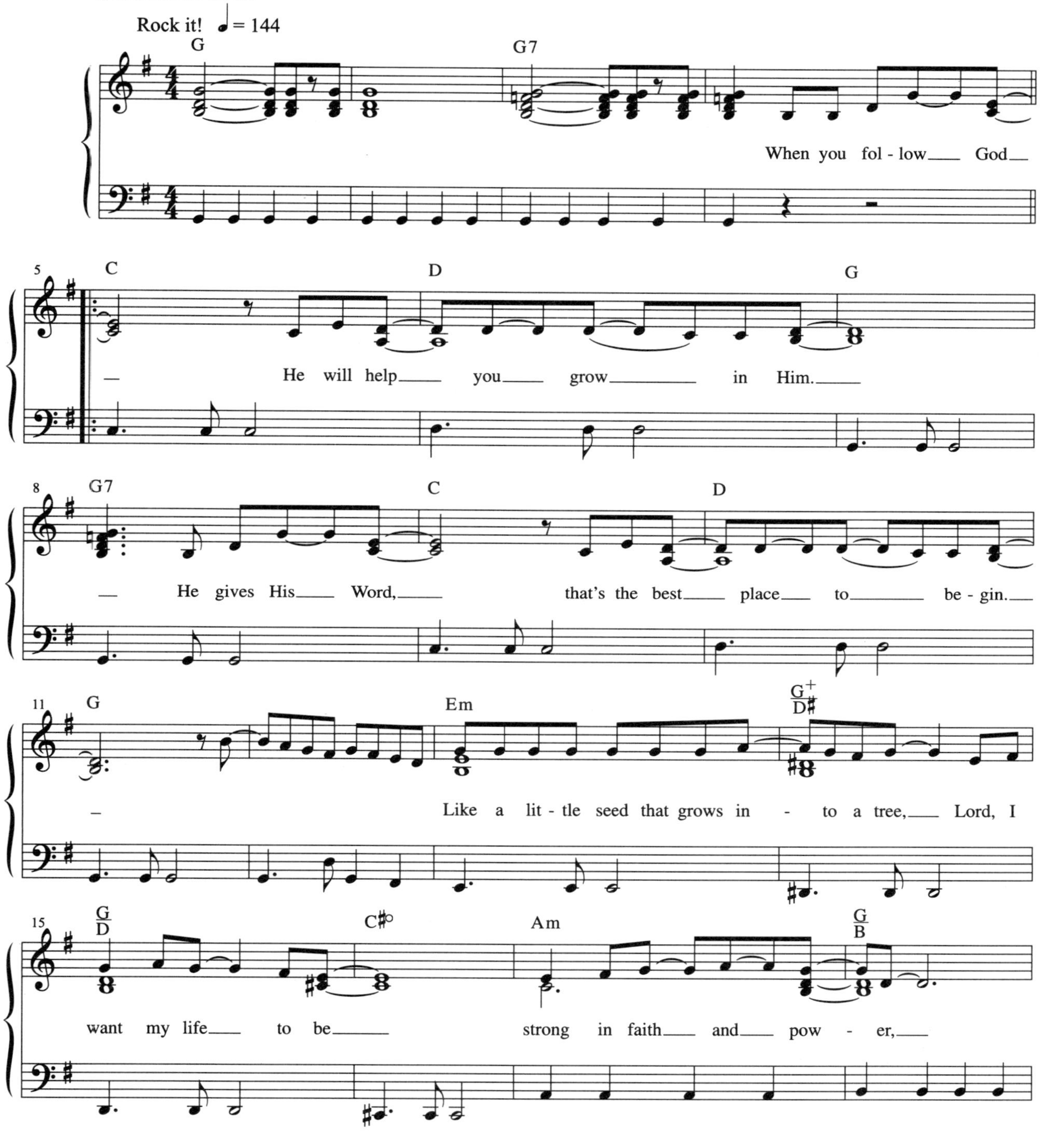
Rock it! ♩= 144
G
G7
When you fol - low God
5
C
D
G
He will help you grow in Him.
8
G7
C
D
He gives His Word, that's the best place to be - gin.
11
G
Em
G+/D♯
Like a lit - tle seed that grows in - to a tree, Lord, I
15
G/D
C♯°
Am
G/B
want my life to be strong in faith and pow - er,

GOOD NEWS CLUES™

Treasures in Heaven

Words & Music by
Phil Reynolds

project SHARE GOD'S TREASURE

Children sharing the treasure of Jesus with children of the world

The New Testament Picture BIBLE

"For where your TREASURE is, there will your heart be also."

Matt. 6:21

We know that God's Word is full of truth leading to Salvation. But what about the children who are growing up without the truth in distant villages and cities of the world?

Many have never heard the Gospel or held a Bible. How will they find the treasure of Jesus?

Project Share God's Treasure gives colorfully illustrated Bibles to children all over the world—from the vastness of South America and Africa to the Middle East, Asia, and India.

With a few coins you can share God's treasure and provide Bibles to lost ones around the globe. $5.00 will give 4 children a *New Testament Picture Bible* of their very own.

Will you reach out and touch a life for Christ?

An agency of Cook Communications Ministries International

Bulletin (Scale shown: 85%)

Announcing…

VeBS! JOIN THE FUN!

Come join in the fun and mystery as we investigate new life in Jesus. You'll love searching for clues as we visit different rooms in a house that will help you learn to live your life for Jesus.

Searching for clues in the garden, the dining room, the family room, the kitchen, and the living room, children will become detectives engaged in fun games, meaningful activities, Bible memory, cool crafts, and creative snacks—all with one purpose—to learn about living each day for Jesus.

Children (and adults) ages _____ to _____ are invited to join the excitement for this Very exciting Bible School® program!

Keep your eyes and ears open for how to get involved and be part of the excitement!

CONTACT

PLACE

DATE / TIME

GOOD NEWS CLUES SEARCHING FOR NEW LIFE IN JESUS

For Immediate Release

Church _____

Address _____

City, State, Zip _____

Contact Person _____ Phone # _____

is sponsoring a **V**ery **e**xciting **B**ible **S**chool® program for the kids of_____.
(community)

Being held _____, from _____.
(dates) *(times)*

Good News Clues™ is an interactive learning experience for children
ages _____ to _____. Kids will learn about living for Jesus in five very
different Discovery Sites.

For more information or to register for *Good News Clues*™,

call _____ at _____.
(phone number) *(church name and/or director's name and best time to call)*

GOOD NEWS CLUES™
SEARCHING FOR NEW LIFE IN JESUS

For Immediate Release

Church _____

Address _____

City, State, Zip _____

Contact Person _____ Phone # _____

is sponsoring a **V**ery **e**xciting **B**ible **S**chool® program for the kids of_____.
(community)

Being held _____, from _____.
(dates) *(times)*

Good News Clues™ is an interactive learning experience for children
ages _____ to _____. Kids will learn about living for Jesus in five very
different Discovery Sites.

For more information or to register for *Good News Clues*™,

call _____ at _____.
(phone number) *(church name and/or director's name and best time to call)*

GOOD NEWS CLUES™
SEARCHING FOR NEW LIFE IN JESUS

Family Evaluation

Thank you for allowing your child to participate in

Good News Clues™

To help us provide the best VBS possible, please take a moment to fill out this survey and return it to the church office.

Age(s) of child(ren) who participated: _____

Were you also part of the VBS staff? ❑ Y ❑ N

Indicate how you feel each of these areas was handled:

	Excellent	Good	Fair	Poor
Registration	❑	❑	❑	❑
Record Keeping	❑	❑	❑	❑
Leaders & Helpers	❑	❑	❑	❑
Publicity	❑	❑	❑	❑
Daily Schedule	❑	❑	❑	❑
Assemblies	❑	❑	❑	❑
Discipline	❑	❑	❑	❑
Props/Sets	❑	❑	❑	❑
Crafts	❑	❑	❑	❑
Snacks	❑	❑	❑	❑
Lessons	❑	❑	❑	❑
Support from Church	❑	❑	❑	❑
Safety	❑	❑	❑	❑
Closing Program	❑	❑	❑	❑

How did you see God at work in the lives of your children?

What did you enjoy most about this VBS experience?

What could have been done to make this VBS experience easier?

What would you like to see changed for future VBS programs?

Do you regularly attend church services at this church?
❑ Y ❑ N

Another local church? ❑ Y ❑ N

Are you willing to help with follow-up of other families who participated in VBS? ❑ Y ❑ N

If Yes, how?
❑ **To pray: Day/Time:**_____
❑ **To visit in their homes**
❑ **To invite a family to my home for a meal**
❑ **Other:** _____
_____
_____

Staff Evaluation

An evaluation is the last important step of a successful VBS program. Complete this form as soon as possible and hand it in to the church office.

Name: _____   Phone **Work:** _____   **Home:** _____

Address: _____

Age range of participating kids:_____

Were you also part of the VBS staff? ❑ Y ❑ N

What was your role?_____

Indicate how you feel each of these areas was handled:

	Excellent	Good	Fair	Poor
Registration	❑	❑	❑	❑
Record Keeping	❑	❑	❑	❑
Administration	❑	❑	❑	❑
Publicity	❑	❑	❑	❑
Daily Schedule	❑	❑	❑	❑
Assemblies	❑	❑	❑	❑
Discipline	❑	❑	❑	❑
Props/Sets	❑	❑	❑	❑
Crafts	❑	❑	❑	❑
Snacks	❑	❑	❑	❑
Goals Communication	❑	❑	❑	❑
Support from Church	❑	❑	❑	❑
Safety	❑	❑	❑	❑
Closing Program	❑	❑	❑	❑

How did you see God at work in the lives of your learners?

What did you enjoy most about this VBS experience?

What could have been done to make your part in this VBS easier?

What would you like to see changed for future VBS programs?

Do you regularly attend church services at this church? ❑ Y ❑ N
Another local church? ❑ Y ❑ N

Are you willing to help with follow-up of families who participated in VBS? ❑ Y ❑ N   If Yes, how?
❑ To pray: Day/Time:_____
❑ To visit in their homes
❑ To invite a family to my home for a meal
❑ Other:_____

Director's Evaluation

Please take a moment to fill out this questionnaire and send it back to us. This will help us to continue to meet your VeBS® needs and to create the best products to help you in your VeBS® ministry. **Thank you!**

Your Name _____

Church Name _____

Church Address _____

_____

Church E-mail Address _____

Denomination _____

What is the average attendance of your Sunday school?

❏ 0-50   ❏ 51-100   ❏ 101-150   ❏ 151-200   ❏ 201+

Please check the Children's Ministry programs your church provides.

❏ Children's Church/Worship
❏ Midweek Programs
❏ Children's Choir/Music Program
❏ Children's Drama Program
❏ Puppet Ministry to Children
❏ After-School Outreach Programs
❏ Other _____

What is your position with the church?

_____

Who is responsible for choosing and purchasing your VBS curriculum?

❏ Director of Children's Ministry
❏ VBS Committee
❏ The Senior Pastor
❏ Other _____

How many children . . .

attended your VBS? _____

were first time visitors of your church? _____

accepted Jesus as Savior during VBS? _____

Did you . . . *(check all that apply)*

❏ reproduce the CD onto cassette?
   If so, how many copies did you make? _____
❏ use the bonus materials from the CD?
❏ use the editable PDF files from the CD?
❏ use the puppet pattern to make puppets; if so, how many puppets did you make? _____

What version of the VBS program did you use?

❏ NIV ❏ KJV

Please rate the following components of:

Good News Clues™
Training to Win God's Way!

1 = Dissatisfied, 5 = Completely Satisfied

Up-front materials of the Director's Guide
Didn't Use   1   2   3   4   5

Comprehensive Supply List
Didn't Use   1   2   3   4   5

Reproducible Resources
Didn't Use   1   2   3   4   5

***Good News Clues*™ CD**
Didn't Use   1   2   3   4   5

Promotional Materials
Didn't Use   1   2   3   4   5

Preschool Program
Didn't Use   1   2   3   4   5

Opening Skits
Didn't Use   1   2   3   4   5

Closing Program
Didn't Use   1   2   3   4   5

Project Share God's Treasure Missions Project
Didn't Use   1   2   3   4   5

Cook's VBS web site www.CookVBS.com:
Never Visited   1   2   3   4   5

How we can improve the web site?

_____

_____

_____

_____

(TAPE HERE)

(FOLD HERE SECOND)

l''llll'''l''l'l'l'l'l'l''lll''l'l''llll'l..ll..l

COLORADO SPRINGS, CO 80918-9951
4050 LEE VANCE VIEW
COOK COMMUNICATIONS MINISTRIES
ATTN: VBS EDITOR

POSTAGE WILL BE PAID BY ADDRESSEE

FIRST-CLASS MAIL PERMIT NO.720 COLORADO SPRINGS, CO

BUSINESS REPLY MAIL

NO POSTAGE
NECESSARY
IF MAILED
IN THE
UNITED STATES

STATE _____
ZIP _____
CITY _____
STREET _____
NAME _____

(FOLD HERE FIRST)

What was your favorite part of the program?

_____
_____
_____
_____
_____
_____
_____
_____
_____

What would you change (if anything) about VeBS® curriculum for the future? _____

_____
_____
_____
_____
_____
_____
_____
_____

GOOD NEWS CLUES™   **KJV Version**

Preschool Site 4: Happy/Sad Face Patterns

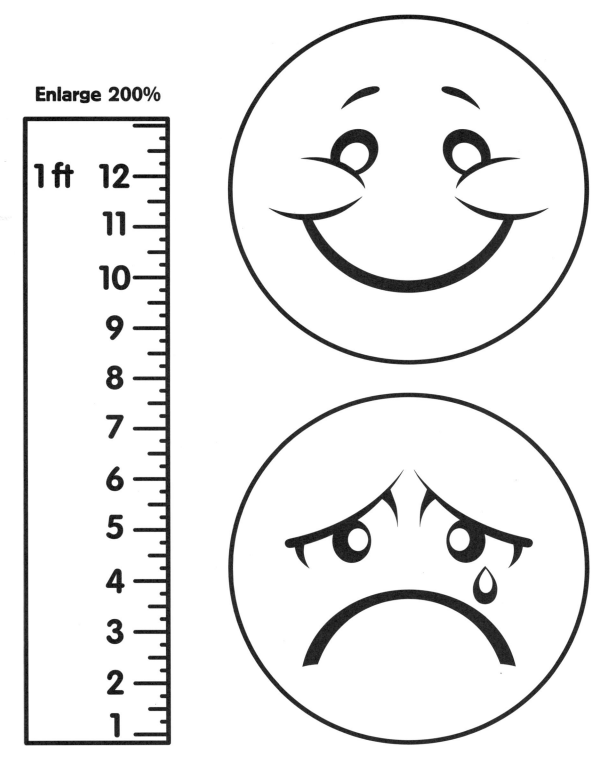

Enlarge 200%

1 ft

12
11
10
9
8
7
6
5
4
3
2
1

**Elementary Site 4:
Growth Chart Craft Tape Measure Pattern**

CRAFT PATTERNS

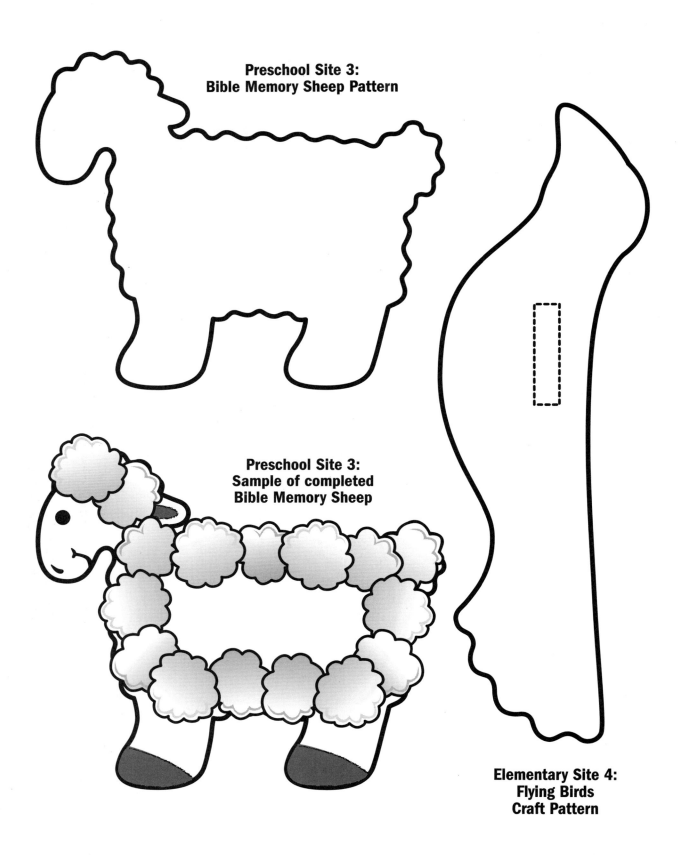

**Preschool Site 3:
Bible Memory Sheep Pattern**

**Preschool Site 3:
Sample of completed
Bible Memory Sheep**

**Elementary Site 4:
Flying Birds
Craft Pattern**

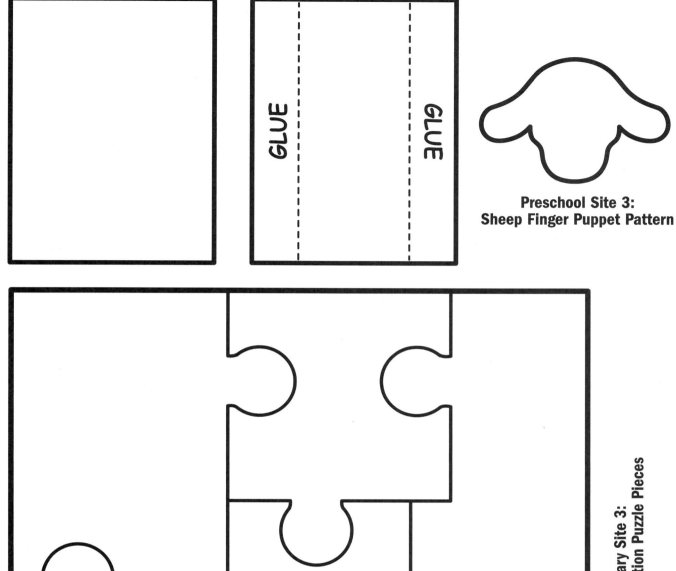

GLUE

GLUE

**Preschool Site 3:
Sheep Finger Puppet Pattern**

**Elementary Site 3:
Bible Memorization Puzzle Pieces**

CRAFT PATTERNS

**Elementary Site 5:
Treasure Box Pattern**

Preschool Sheep Tic-Tac-Toe Patterns

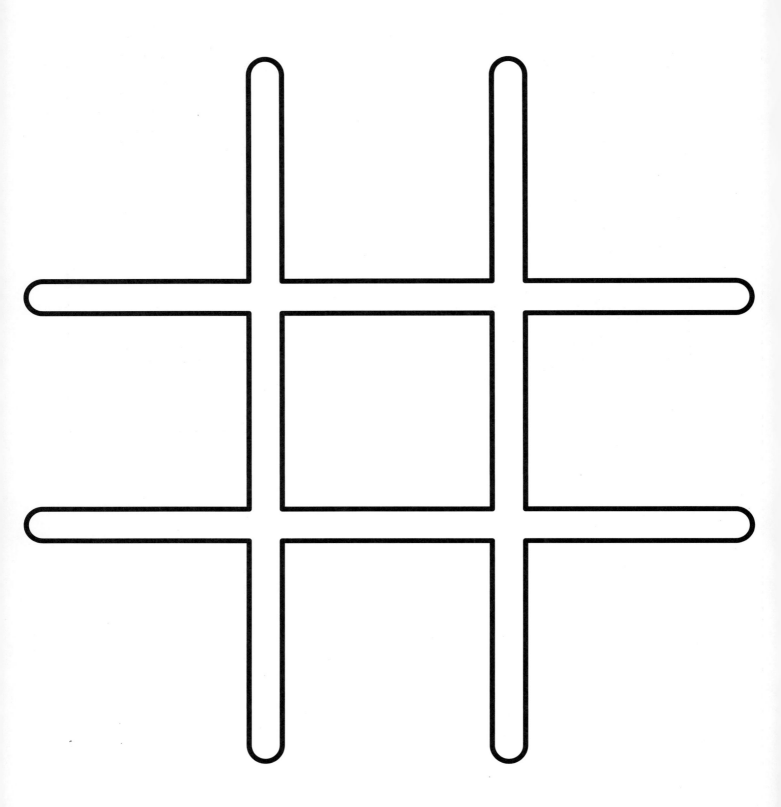

Dear _____

This photo frame was
made especially for you.

Love _____

Tape to back of frame

Elementary Site 4:
Ladybug Pattern for Growth Chart
(For use at 100%)

Kitchen Utensils Patterns

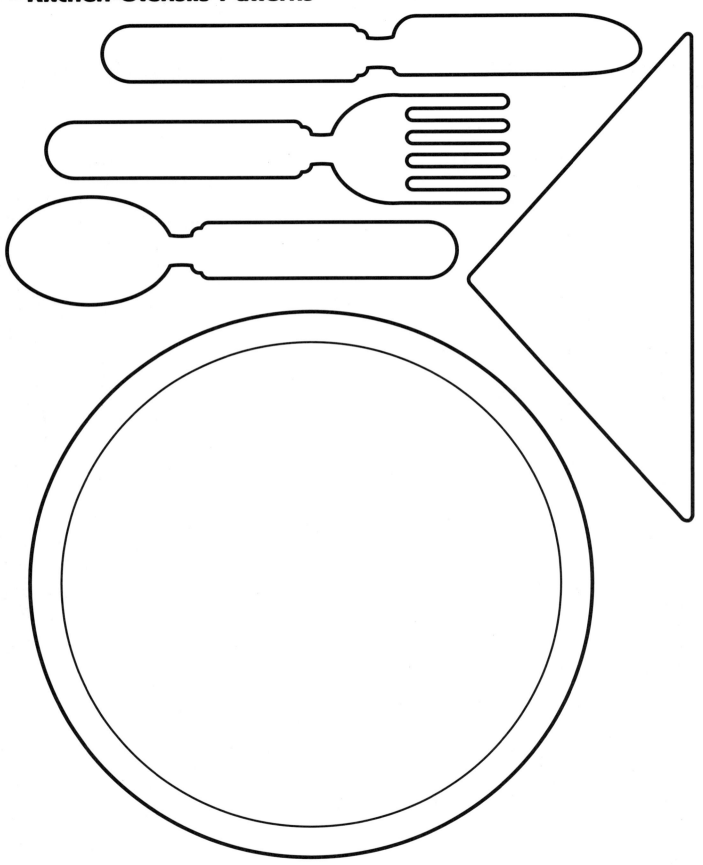

***GOOD NEWS CLUES*™**

Bosworth Reproducible Puppet

MATERIALS:

- 1/2 yard brown fake fur
- One 12" x 8" rectangle of black craft felt for ear lining, inner mouth, and eyes
- Scrap of off-white for eyes
- 1/4 yard fine to medium weight wool plaid and scraps of fusible interlining for hat (option: Two 12" x 8" rectangles of felt instead of the wool plaid)
- One half-inch button
- Brown thread
- White thread (optional to use for hat)

INSTRUCTIONS:

Enlarge pattern pieces as directed. Arrange **Back (1)**, **Front (2)**, **Center Front (3)**, **Forehead (4)**, **Snout (5)**, **Snout Lining (6)**, and **Ear (7)** on wrong side of fur, and outline all pieces with ballpoint pen or colored pencil. Transfer all pattern markings to fabric. Cut out pieces 1 through 7.

Arrange **Ear Linings (8)**, **Inner Mouth (9)**, **Nose (10)**, and **Inner Eye (12)** on black felt and outline with white tailor's chalk. Transfer pattern markings to fabric. Cut out pieces 8 through 11. Trace outline of **Eye (11)** on off-white felt. Cut out.

Arrange **Hat Crown (13)**, **Strap (14)**, **Front Brim (15)**, and **Back Brim (16)** on wool plaid. Transfer pattern markings to fabric. Cut out pieces 13 through 16. Arrange Front Brim (15) and Back Brim (16) on interlining. Cut out.

ASSEMBLE AS FOLLOWS:

BLOODHOUND: Pin Ears 7 to Ear Linings 8, right sides together, easing ear to match notches on lining. Sew together. Clip curves. Turn right side out. Finger press seam flat. Line up top edges of ear and ear lining; baste together. Slash along ear lines to large dots marked on Back 1 and Front 2.

Pin Front 2 to Back 1 at side seam, lining up slash. Sew together with one seam above ear slash lines and with a separate seam below ear slash lines. Clip curves at neck, paw, and under-arm shaping. Finger press side seams open at slash lines and fold back along slash lines, right sides together, lining up edges. Insert ears, placing right sides of ears to right side of forehead edge of slash lines. Sew all thicknesses together with a scant 1/4 inch seam.

Pin, right sides together, Snout 5 to Front 2, matching notches and dots. Sew from top edge to mouth corner, stopping at dot.

Pin then sew darts on Forehead 4. Pin Forehead 4 to assembled back, snout and front sections, matching notches and dots, right sides together. Sew.

Pin Snout Lining 6 to Snout 5, right sides together, matching notches and dots and easing to fit. Sew from dot to dot. Clip curves and turn. Finger press seam flat.

Pin long edges of Inner Mouth 9 to Snout Lining 6, right sides together, matching notches and dots. Sew both long edges between dots.

Pin Center Front 3 to Fronts 2, right sides together, matching notches. Sew together. Pin remaining curved edge of Inner Mouth 9 to lower edge of snout formed by Front 2 and Center Front 3, right sides together, matching notches and dots. Sew together.

Fold up bottom hem 1/2 inch and sew with topstitch. Glue Inner Eyes 12 to Eyes 11. Glue completed eyes to corner of forehead and snout seam. Glue nose on snout at triangle seam.

HAT: Pin Hat Crown 13 sections, right sides together, matching notches and large dot. Sew from bottom edge to large dot. Turn right side out. Press seams open.

With right sides together, pin two Hat Strap 14 sections to two remaining sections. Sew together, leaving double-notched edge open. Clip curves. Turn right side out. Press straps flat.

Pin straps, right sides together, to two opposite crown-bottom edges, matching notches. Sew.

Fuse Front Brim 15 interlining to wrong side of one Front Brim 15 section. Pin remaining Front Brim 15 section, right sides together, to interlined section. Sew, leaving double-notched edge open. Clip curves. Turn right side out and press. Repeat procedure for Back Brim 16.

Pin Front Brim 15 to a crown-bottom edge and Back Brim 16 to remaining edge. Sew. Press seam allowances toward wrong side of crown and strap toward right side of crown. Pin in place. Sew through all thicknesses around crown opening with 1/4 inch topstitch. Bring straps together at top of hat and secure with button.

Puppet Pattern page 1

Scale: 1 square = 1" (Enlarge 168%)

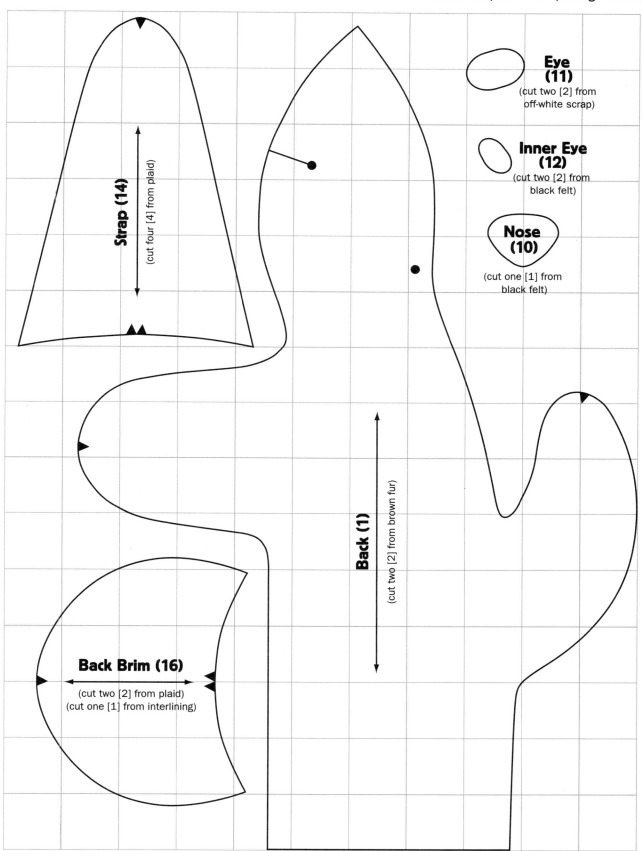

Strap (14)
(cut four [4] from plaid)

Eye (11)
(cut two [2] from off-white scrap)

Inner Eye (12)
(cut two [2] from black felt)

Nose (10)
(cut one [1] from black felt)

Back (1)
(cut two [2] from brown fur)

Back Brim (16)
(cut two [2] from plaid)
(cut one [1] from interlining)

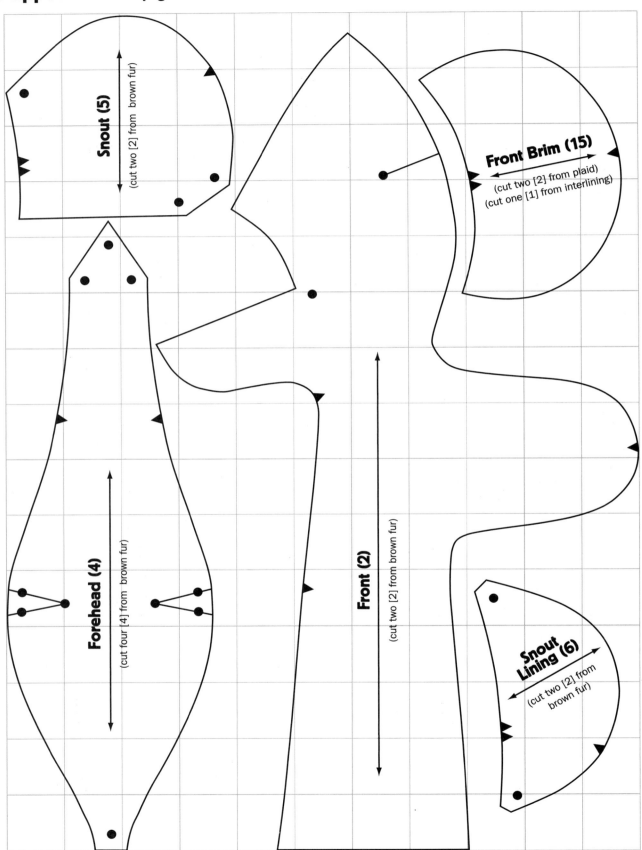

Snout (5)

(cut two [2] from brown fur)

Front Brim (15)

(cut two [2] from plaid)
(cut one [1] from interlining)

Forehead (4)

(cut four [4] from brown fur)

Front (2)

(cut two [2] from brown fur)

Snout Lining (6)

(cut two [2] from brown fur)

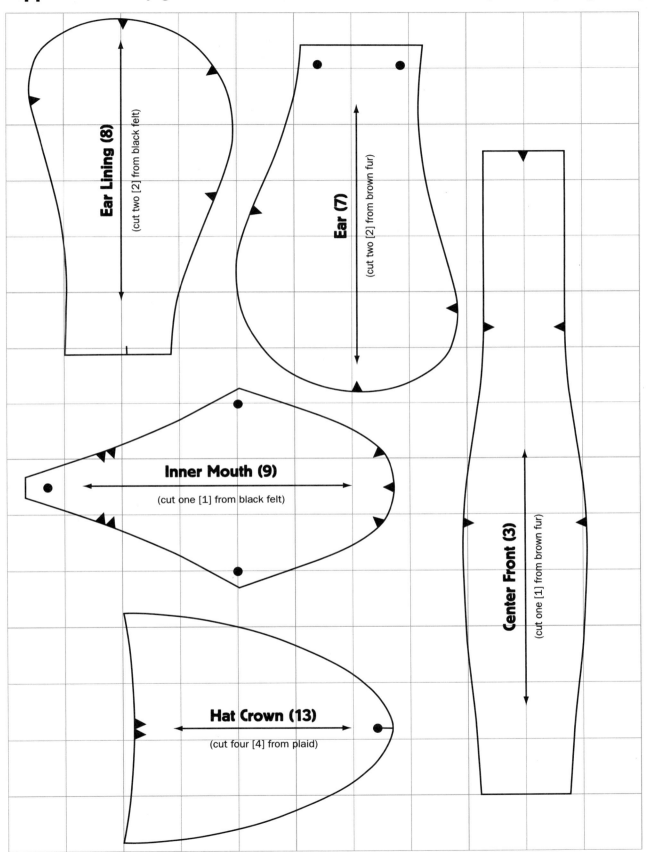

Ear Lining (8)
(cut two [2] from black felt)

Ear (7)
(cut two [2] from brown fur)

Inner Mouth (9)
(cut one [1] from black felt)

Center Front (3)
(cut one [1] from brown fur)

Hat Crown (13)
(cut four [4] from plaid)

Key Verse Cards

Photocopy and cut out cards. Place a "hinge" of tape at the top of the card, and adhere it to page 7 of each Detective's Diary. Starting at the bottom of the page, layer each card so that the Discovery Site shows. *Early-elementary verse in **bold** type.*

"For all have sinned, and come short of the glory of God."

Romans 3:23

Site 1
Garden

"But God commendeth his love toward us, in that, **while we were yet sinners, Christ died for us.**"

Romans 5:8

Site 2
Dining Room

"For God so loved the world, that he gave his only begotten Son, that whosoever believeth in him should not perish, but have everlasting life."

John 3:16

Site 3
Family Room

"*But lay up for yourselves treasures in heaven, where neither moth nor rust doth corrupt, and where thieves do not break through nor steal: **For where your treasure is, there will your heart be also.**" Matthew 6:20-21*

Site 5
Living Room

"*Grow in grace, and in the knowledge of our **Lord and Saviour Jesus Christ.**"

2 Peter 3:18*

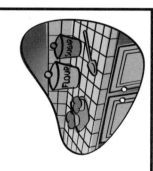

Site 4
Kitchen

GOOD NEWS CLUES™

VeBS!
OLDER ELEMENTARY

GOOD NEWS CLUES™

SEARCHING FOR NEW LIFE IN JESUS

detective's Diary

DETECTIVE:

_____
(NAME)

OFFICIAL DETECTIVE CERTIFICATE

This is to certify that

_____
(NAME)

has completed the Detective Coursework and is now an official **Good News Clues**™ Detective.

SIGNED: _____
(INVESTIGATOR OR ASSISTANT INVESTIGATOR)

DATE: _____

CHURCH NAME: _____

Site 1
The Garden

Directions:

Use the list of words to help you find and circle behaviors (ways we act). Some will be good behaviors and some will not be good behaviors.

On the list of words, put a star by the behaviors that are good and draw a line through the behaviors that are sinful.

```
V B H H V Q G S C A S A
A K M E I P Z U R R S E
C H E E R F U L I G E W
E I L U T M Q M T U N S
U H Z S O T F K I E D H
M U R T N A T Y C B N A
L U F K N A H T I R I R
O B E Y V Q F G Z A K E
S U N D T R N Q E G H G
E N C O U R A G E A E R
E L B M U R G T L B L V
V Y V N E D P R V K P C
```

Obey
Lie
Tantrum
Grumble
Brag
Criticize
Help
Cheerful
Argue
Share
Encourage
Envy
Kindness
Thankful

Detective's Question:

What was the result of Adam and Eve's disobedience?

_____.

Key Verses

Directions:

Using a "hinge" of tape, attach each of the key verse cards below. Start at the bottom of the page and layer the cards as you go up the page.

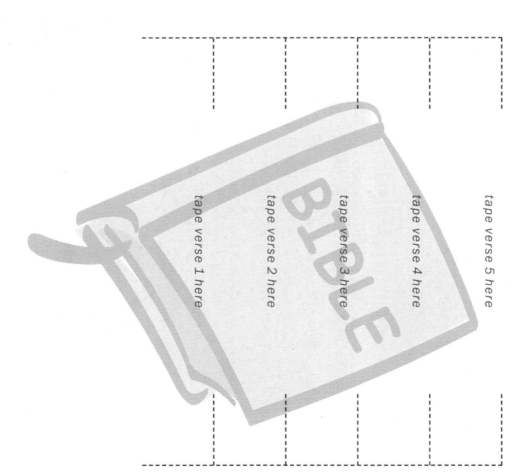

tape verse 5 here

tape verse 4 here

tape verse 3 here

tape verse 2 here

tape verse 1 here

Site 3
The Family Room

Secret Writing Directions: Use your invisible ink and a paintbrush or toothpick to write what God gives you (on the present) and what you give God (on the heap of rags). Be sure to write your name on the tag of the present and on the basket of rags.

Let the writing dry for 30 minutes. Then you or someone else can make the message appear by shading the writing area with a pencil held horizontal to the paper.

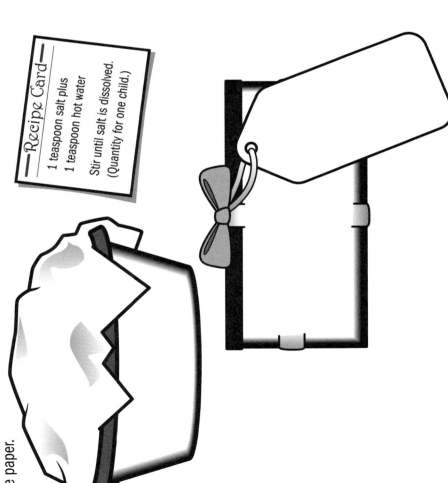

— Recipe Card —

1 teaspoon salt plus
1 teaspoon hot water

Stir until salt is dissolved.
(Quantity for one child.)

"For God so loved the world, that he gave his only begotten Son, that whosoever believeth in him should not perish, but have everlasting life." **John 3:16**

Site 4
The Kitchen

Mystery Message Directions: Write a mysterious message that tells how you will grow as God's child. Here's an activity to do before you write your mystery message on this page.

1. Write your idea on a plain piece of paper.

2. Tape two sheets of paper together with two short pieces of tape. See diagram A.

3. Write your message on the bottom sheet. See diagram B.

4. Fold the blank, top sheet down to the back of the page with your writing.

5. Hold your two papers together up to a window with the blank page on top. Your writing should be backward.

6. Trace the letters onto the blank paper. See diagram C.

7. When it's all copied, take off your original message and the tape. When you look at the new message, the letters look like mixed-up words. To read the message, stand facing a mirror and hold the paper in front of you. You can read the words in the mirror! Now see who can decode your secret message. See diagram D.

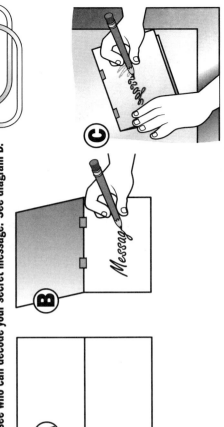

"Grow in grace, and in the knowledge of our Lord and Saviour Jesus Christ." **2 Peter 3:18**

Site 5
The Living Room
Hidden Treasure Directions:

Use your Detective's manual (the Bible) to complete this puzzle. When you finish it, you'll be an advanced Detective.

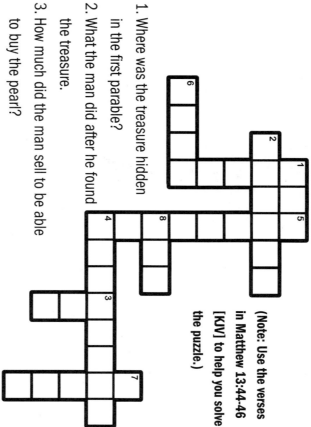

(Note: Use the verses in Matthew 13:44-46 [KJV] to help you solve the puzzle.)

1. Where was the treasure hidden in the first parable?
2. What the man did after he found the treasure.
3. How much did the man sell to be able to buy the pearl?
4. What is the kingdom of heaven like?
5. Who looked for fine pearls?
6. What the man felt when he found the special pearl.
7. What value did the special pearl have?
8. How much did the first man sell to get money to buy the field?

"But lay up for yourselves treasures in heaven, where neither moth nor rust doth corrupt, and where thieves do not break through nor steal: For where your treasure is, there will your heart be also." **Matthew 6:20-21**

Site 2
The Dining Room
Secret Message Directions:

There is a coded message in these letters. To decode the message, start at the circled letter "C." Circle every fifth letter until you reach the end of the list. (CLUE: The next letter you should have circled is "H.") When you have finished, write the letters you have circled on the spaces below. (Hint: Be sure to go from left to right as you transfer the letters to the spaces.)

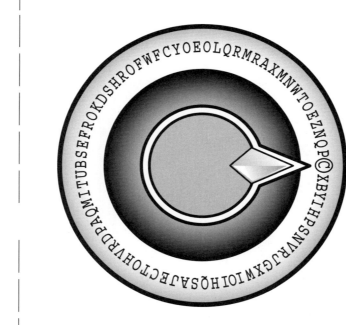

___ ___ ___ ___ ___

"But God commendeth his love toward us, in that, while we were yet sinners, Christ died for us." **Romans 5:8**

VeBS!
YOUNGER ELEMENTARY

GOOD NEWS CLUES™

SEARCHING FOR NEW LIFE IN JESUS

detective's Diary

DETECTIVE: _____
(NAME)

OFFICAL DETECTIVE CERTIFICATE

This is to certify that

_____
(NAME)

has completed the Detective Coursework and is now an official **Good News Clues**™

Detective.

SIGNED: _____
(INVESTIGATOR OR ASSISTANT INVESTIGATOR)

DATE: _____

CHURCH NAME: _____

GOOD NEWS • DETECTIVE • #1

Site 1
The Garden

Instructions: 8 apples are hidden in this garden.

Find them and color them with a red crayon or pencil.

Detective Question: How did Adam and Eve sin?

Tell a friend or your Investigator two ways you are tempted to disobey. When you are tempted this week, remember that sin separates you from God.

"For all have sinned, and come short of the glory of God." **Romans 3:23**

Key Verses

Directions:

Using a "hinge" of tape, attach each of the key verse cards below. Start at the bottom of the page and layer the cards as you go up the page.

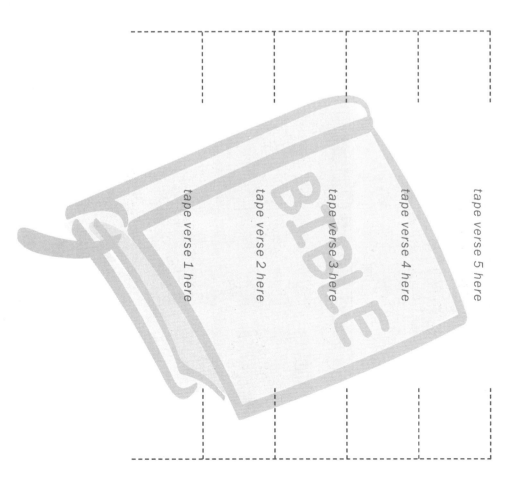

BIBLE

tape verse 1 here

tape verse 2 here

tape verse 3 here

tape verse 4 here

tape verse 5 here

Site 4
The Kitchen

Directions: Use your pencil or a crayon to follow each pathway to the square at the bottom. When you get there, write the letter from the beginning of the pathway in the square you have found. When you have filled in all the squares, you will have the answer to the question below.

What should you be doing as a follower of Jesus?

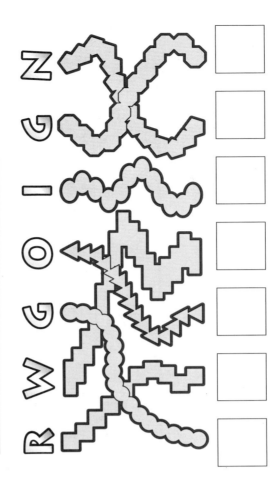

Write the mystery word here.

Site 3
The Family Room

What happened to the son when he came back to his father and asked forgiveness?

To find out the answer, connect the dots using a white crayon. Press hard with the crayons and draw lines between shapes that match (●—●, ★—★).

Do not connect shapes if you have to draw over a line. After writing the message, paint with water color markers to see the message.

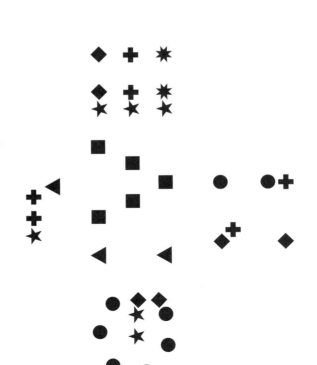

"For God so loved the world, that he gave his only begotten Son, that whosoever believeth in him should not perish, but have everlasting life." **John 3:16**

YOUNGER ELEMENTARY

"Grow in . . . the knowledge of our Lord and Saviour Jesus Christ." **2 Peter 3:18**

YOUNGER ELEMENTARY

Site 5
The Living Room
Hidden Letters Directions:

Using a yellow crayon or marker, color in all the spaces with the ♥ symbol. Leave all the other spaces uncolored. When you finish, you'll know what is waiting for you because God loves you.

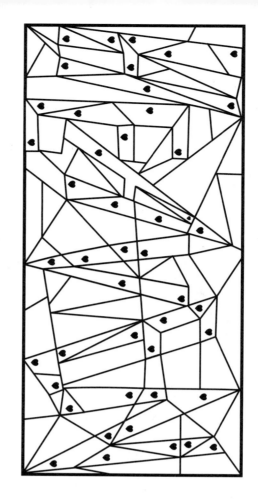

Write the word here that tells what is waiting for you.

_____

"But lay up for yourselves treasures in heaven. . . . For where your treasure is, there will your heart be also."
Matthew 6:20-21

Site 2
The Dining Room
Secret Message Directions:

To read the secret message in the dining room, use the Detective's code below. In the blank space, write the letter that matches the first letter of the picture.

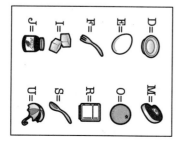

D=   M=
E=   O=
F=   R=
I=   S=
J=   U=

"While we were yet sinners, Christ died for us."
Romans 5:8

Salvation Choker or Bracelet

Supplies:

• Lacing cut to bracelet or choker length (see below)

• Colored beads—dark, red, white, green, gold (one of each color for each child)

To help the children understand the various topics during this week of Very exciting Bible School® , have them each make a bracelet or choker that they will take home at the end of the week. This offers each child the opportunity to explain what they have learned about salvation during the VeBS® program.

The colors will represent the different sites (rooms) we are in each day. The dark color represents sin, as we learn in The Garden. Red represents the blood of Jesus, which cleanses us from sin (The Dining Room). The white bead represents our heart after it is cleansed by Jesus' blood and we are forgiven (The Family Room). The green bead represents growing in Jesus as we live for Him (The Kitchen). Finally, the gold bead represents heaven, which will one day be our eternal home (The Living Room).

In Advance:

Cut lacing or cording the appropriate length depending on whether you are making bracelets or chokers. The bracelet cord should be approximately 20" long. The choker cord should be cut approximately 30" to 32" in length.

Directions:

Each day the children should add the color bead for the site they are visiting. You can write names on resealable plastic sandwich size bags to keep each child's bracelet or choker. The Assistant Investigator for each group should take the bracelets to the next site along with the children. After the last bead has been added, tie a slip knot around the cord on each side (see diagram). The cord can now be adjusted to fit each child's wrist or neck so they can easily remove it.

Creating Discovery Sites

Creating your VBS Discovery Sites is easy when you use these Mural Transparencies. You can simply trace and color a backdrop or create an elaborate environment—all using the traceable art figures and suggestions in this section. Use your imagination and have fun!

You will find the following inside this section:

- Five background murals *(one for each site)*
- Two pages of site-related art to create additional props

How to use the art in this section

Create an environment where your kids can learn and have fun! Simply follow these three easy steps and make each site as elaborate or as simple as you desire. For ideas on how to set up your room for each site, see the "Site/Introduction" section for sites 1-5. The Director's Guide section also contains tips for recruiting people to help create decorations.

Step 1: Choose images for each site.

There is a mural and many related objects to be used at each of the sites. First you will need to choose which art scenes and objects you will use based on the space you have and your room setup. You will probably want to begin with the mural as your most basic decoration and then build from there. Other objects can be used as add-ons to the mural to create a 3-D effect, such as stand-up figures and room decorations. *(See subsequent pages for more ideas.)* Once you have chosen your transparencies, remove them from the book.

Step 2: Set up your work area.

The use of transparencies allows you to make your murals as large as your space allows.
To simply trace and color your mural, hang newsprint, table covering paper, white bed sheets, craft paper, poster board, tag board, or lightweight cardboard on a wall. Set up an overhead projector so that the image you want is projected onto the

mural material on the wall. If you have a number of people working on this project, you may want to duplicate the transparencies and use more than one projector. You can adjust the size of the images by moving the projector closer to or farther away from the wall.

Step 3: Trace the images.

Once you are satisfied with the shape and size of

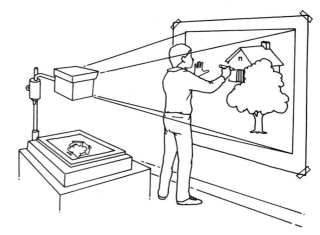

the image, trace the figure with pencil or marker. Next, color the murals and/or figures as much or as little as you wish. For coloring figures and adding background details, consider using crayon, marker, colored pencils, chalk, or paint. Larger, less detailed images can be traced onto and cut out of colored paper or poster board.

Creating stand-up figures

Add some fun to your site by creating stand-up figures! To do this, follow the previous steps for tracing the images but be sure to use cardboard, foam core, or other sturdy material. Carefully cut out the figure using sharp scissors, a razor blade, or a utility knife. Then brace the figure by attaching a rectangular piece of cardboard to the back.

Constructing flats, or frames

If you have the budget and the labor, you can easily create "flats" or frames for the backdrops of your set. Each flat will be a little over four feet wide by eight feet tall. Depending on your space, you may choose to use two or more of these flats to create an interesting corner—a focal point for your activities. Besides a hammer, drill, nails or screws, here is what you will need to build each flat:

- Three 8' x 1" x 2" boards *(1 x 2's).* Have one of the boards cut down to two 4-foot pieces.

- One 4' x 9' sheet of 1/2" thick styrofoam insulation.

- Four 8" 90-degree triangle corner braces cut from plywood *(Fig. B)* OR four steel corner braces. You'll need two extra braces when forming a corner with two flats.

1. Lay two 8-foot 1 x 2's parallel to each other, about 4 feet apart, broad side down. These will be the sides of your frame. *(Fig. A)*

2. Place the two 4-foot boards broad side down, between the side boards, at the top and bottom of the frame. (**NOTE:** *Four optional steel "L" brackets on the inside corners will help add stability, and make joining each of the corner pieces easier. See Fig. C.)*

3. Position a triangle corner brace at each corner and secure with nails or screws. *(Fig. B)*

4. Flip the frame over *(triangles on the floor)* and glue or nail the sheet of styrofoam insulation to the frame.

5. Repeat the process for the second flat. After allowing enough time for the glue to dry, stand the flats up and position them next to each other, forming a corner at a 90-degree angle. To secure the corner shape, nail or screw triangle corner braces in place on top and bottom of the flats.

If a larger set is desired, attach more flats using 1 x 2's for braces. Position a 1 x 2 across the top of two frames, connecting them. Nail or screw in place. Repeat at the bottom.

Now the fun begins! Cover the styrofoam insulation using rolls of brightly-colored art paper or paint with

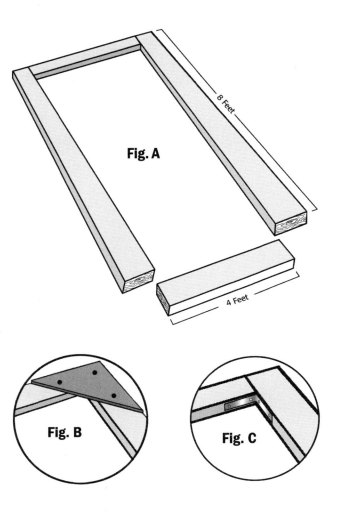

Fig. A

8 Feet

4 Feet

Fig. B

Fig. C

a non-gloss paint *(gloss paint will reflect glare).* If you choose to paint the flats, you should first cover the seams neatly with wide tape, such as packing or drywall tape.

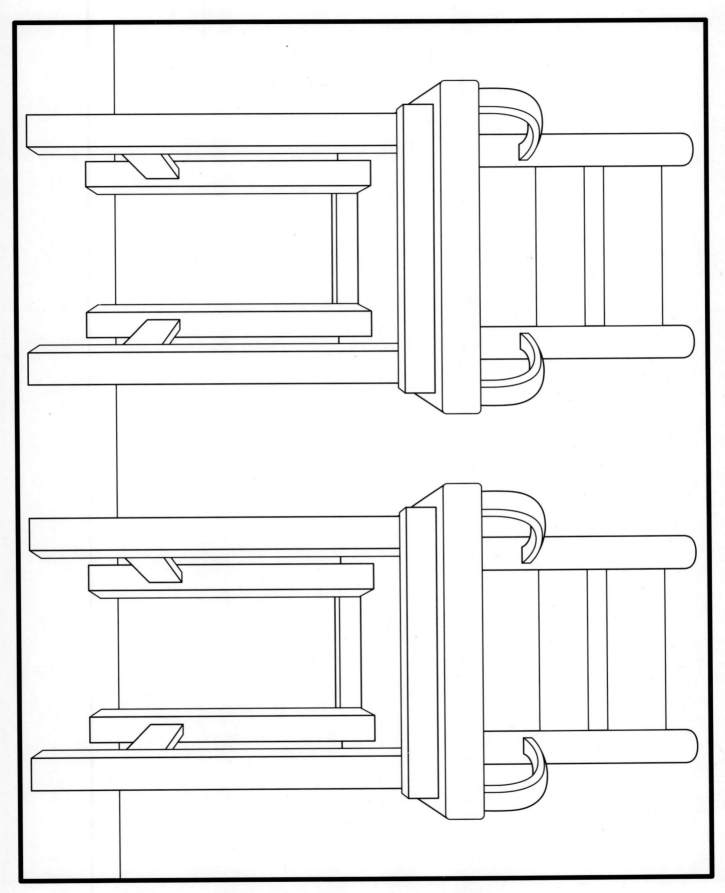

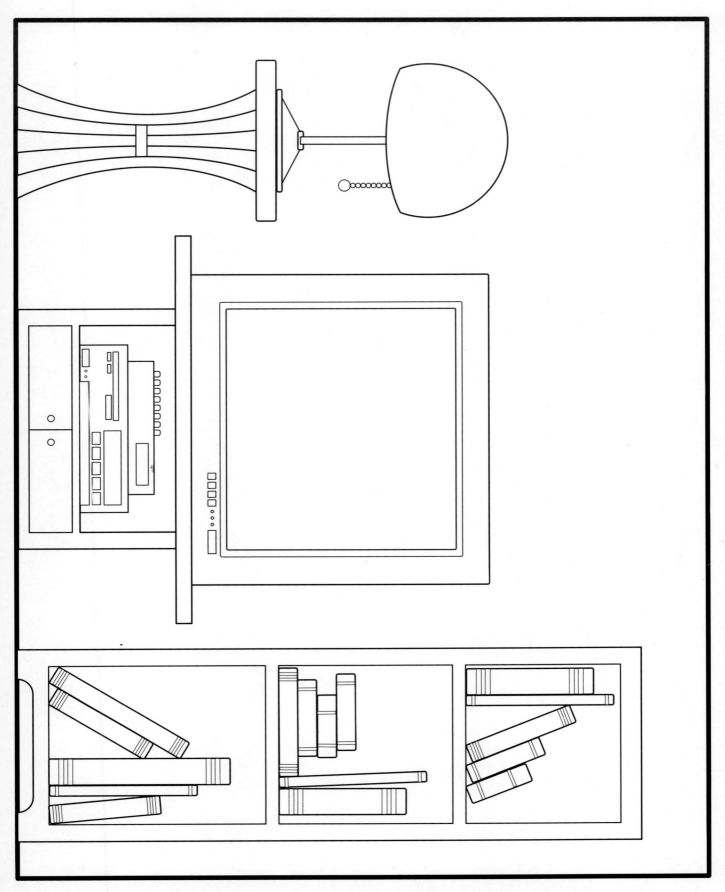

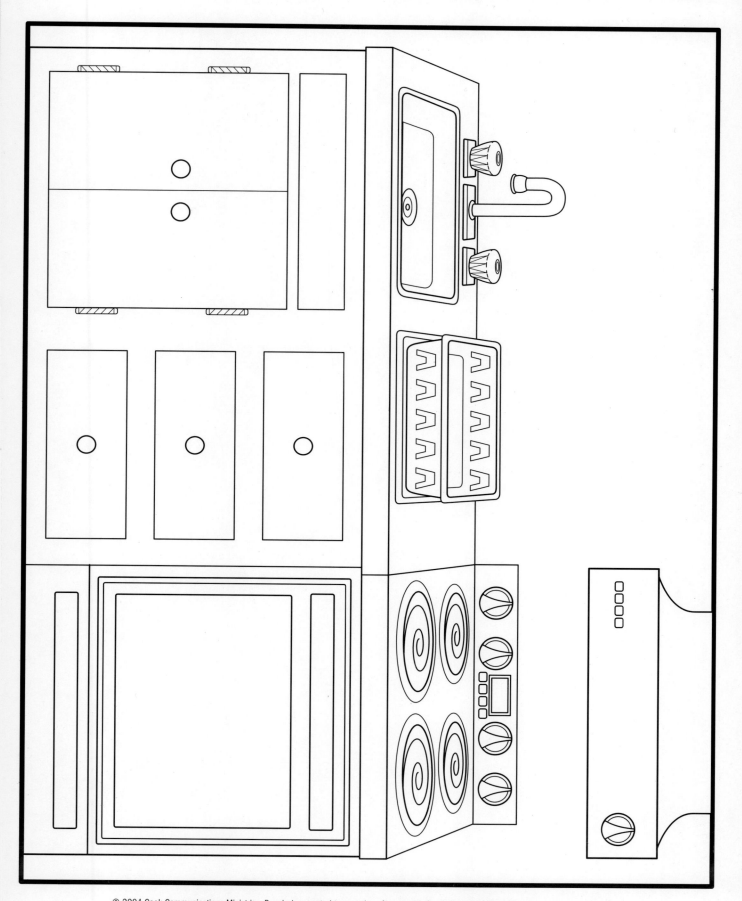

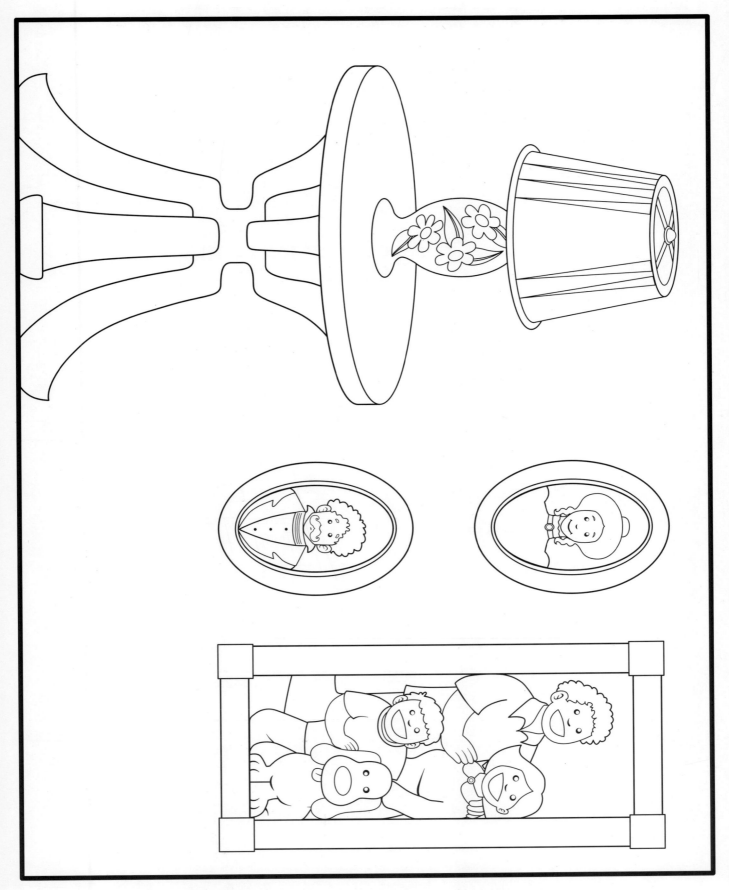

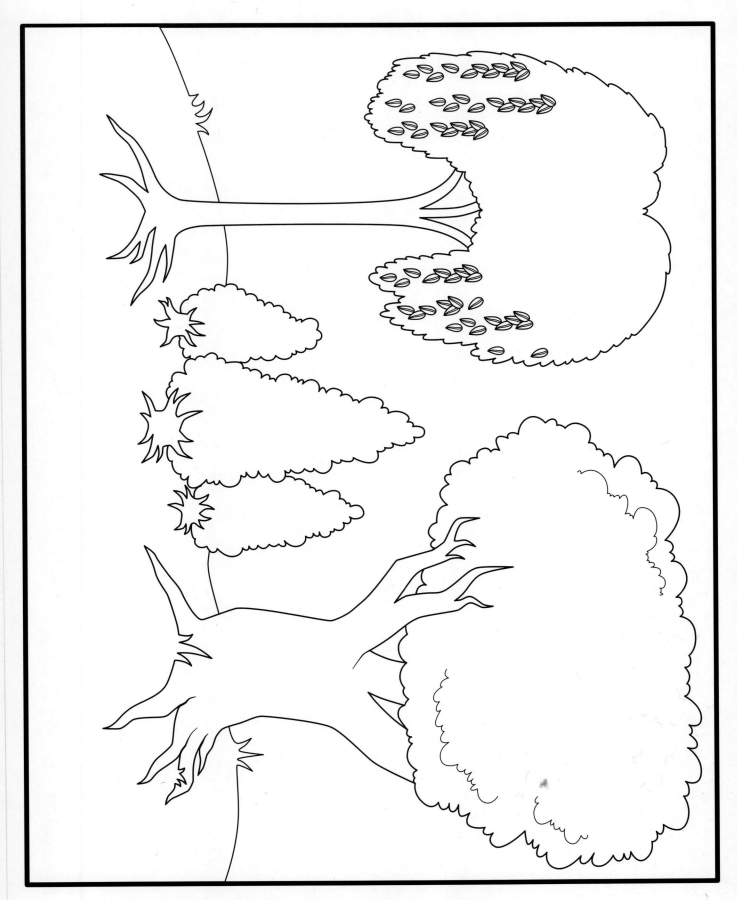

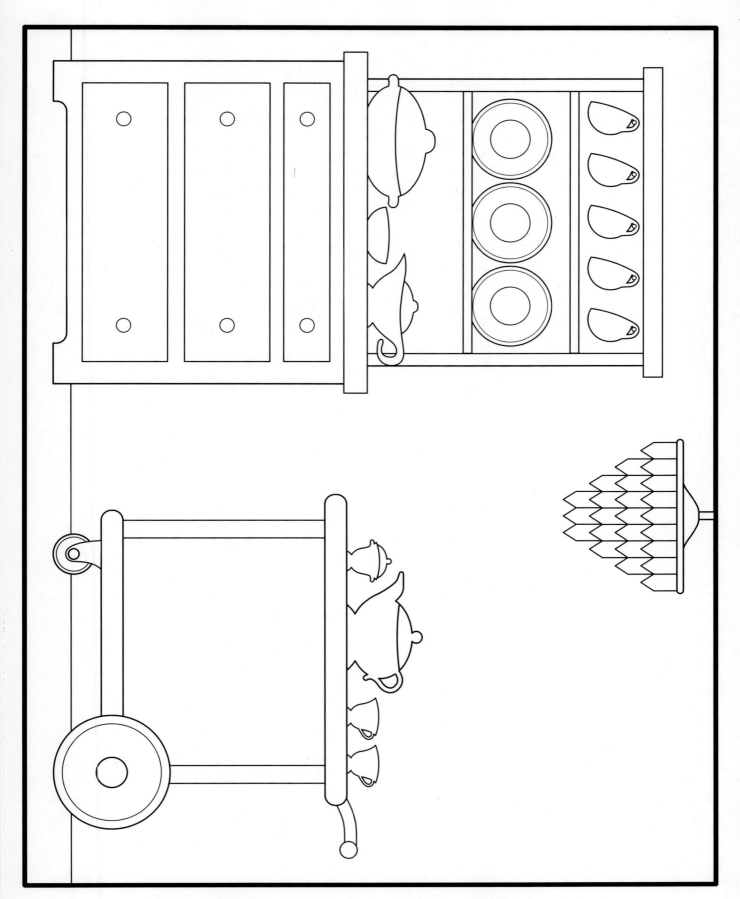

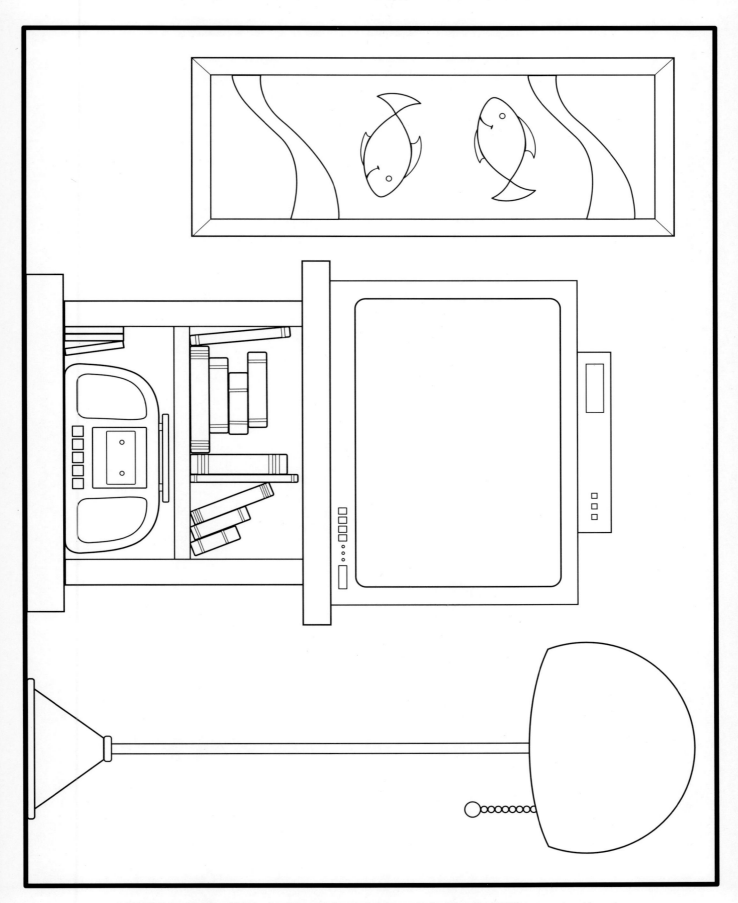

Discovering Jesus as Your Savior

God loves us, but He does not like our sin. The Bible teaches that all people have sinned or disobeyed God (Romans 3:23).

Have you sinned by disobeying God?

Jesus has made the way for us to be forgiven by God. Jesus is God's perfect Son. Jesus died on a cross to take the consequences for our sins (John 3:16). Because Jesus died for us, our sins can be forgiven.

Do you believe that Jesus died on the cross to forgive you of your sins?

The Bible says that our sin separates us from God (Romans 6:23). There is only one way that we can be connected to God and live with Him forever. We must be forgiven by God.

Do you want to know how to be forgiven by God?

Jesus didn't stay dead. The Bible tells us that He rose from the dead and is alive today. So we can talk to Him right now. If we believe that Jesus died on the cross to take the consequences for our sins (Romans 10:9-10), we can ask Him to forgive us of our sins. The Bible promises that if we ask Jesus to forgive us, He will (1 John 1:9).

Would you like to ask Jesus to forgive you of your sins?

Once we have asked Jesus to forgive us, our sins are forgiven. Jesus saves us from the result of our sins. When we trust Jesus as our Savior, we are part of God's family forever (1 John 5:11-12).

Because we are part of His family, we are to live in ways that please God and do things that help us learn more about Him (Colossians 1:10).

What are some ways you can learn more about Jesus?

Now that you are forgiven and part of God's family (John 1:12), you will want to share your decision with others.

With whom will you share your decision to trust Jesus as your Savior!

"Discovering Jesus as Your Savior."

Use the other side of this page to talk with kids who express interest in discovering Jesus as Savior. See Page D-10 for more about this resource.

Step 1 This is the necessary first step. Sorrow for our sin is appropriate (2 Corinthians 7:10). God loves us even though we sin (Romans 5:8). We must recognize that we deserve God's punishment, and His love is a free gift (Romans 6:23).

Step 2 We must truly believe in God and want to be forgiven by Him (Hebrews 11:6). Without sincere desire, we will not find God.

Step 3 We must declare our belief in Jesus and God's gift of salvation (Romans 10:9-10). Without belief there is no forgiveness.

Step 4 Asking in words that are meaningful to us is required. Once we ask in faith, we can celebrate new life in Christ and trust in God's faithfulness (1 John 1:9).

Step 5 Reading the Bible, praying, and coming to church to learn about God are ways to learn more. God wants us to "grow in grace, and in the knowledge of our Lord and Saviour Jesus Christ" (2 Peter 3:18).

Step 6 It is important to let children express their decision in their own words. It will ensure that they understand what has happened and prepare them to share the Good News with others. Jesus teaches us to tell others about Him (Matthew 10:32; 28:19).

DEAR PARENTS,

Today at VBS your child expressed his or her desire to accept Jesus Christ as Lord and Savior. After hearing the Bible truths and explanations printed on the other side of this paper, your child responded to the questions presented and prayed for salvation.

Please give your child the opportunity to tell you about his or her decision in his or her own words. The following questions may help guide your conversation.

- *Why did you decide to ask Jesus to be your Savior?*

- *What does this decision mean to you?*

- *How will you learn more about Jesus and what He wants you to do?*

- *Do you have any questions right now about God, or what it means to believe in Jesus as your Savior?*

If you'd like help answering your child's questions, talk with the leaders of the church where your child is attending VBS.

If you are seeking God's free gift of salvation for yourself, the leaders and members of the church where your child attends VBS would be happy to talk with you about how to receive forgiveness and become part of God's family.

Creative Bible Activities
for Children Series

100's of Songs, Games and More!

Bring the Bible to life and help your kids stay interested in learning with these fun activities, songs and crafts! Over 1200 action-packed ideas at your fingertips.

100's of Songs, Games and More! For Preschoolers

$16.99 (Can. $24.99), ISBN: 0-78143-968-X ITEM #: 102859 8.5 x 11, 157p

100's of Songs, Games and More! For School Kids

$16.99 (Can. $24.99), ISBN: 0-78143-965-5 ITEM #: 102858 8.5 x 11, 143p

Bible Memory Games

There's no better way to help children put God's word to memory! Includes circle games, movement games, craft games, use of puppets, puzzles, and many more fun, easy-to-teach activities.
$16.99 (Can. $24.99) ISBN 0-78144-119-6 ITEM #: 103617 8.5 x 11, 143p

One Rehearsal Christmas Play

The easiest Christmas plays ever! Everything you need for a one-hour or group practice that includes preschool through middle school children. Choose from 12 productions with a scriptural message and minimal preparation!
$12.99 ISBN 0-78144-120-X ITEM #: 103618 8.5 x 11, 96p

Spur-of-the-Moment Games

Instant games to fit your class needs! Keeps first though 6th graders interested and actively involved in learning. Loaded with music games, icebreakers, creative ways to review your lessons, team games, indoor games, and outdoor fun at a moment's notice. A must for every teacher's classroom!
$12.99 ISBN 0-78144-188-8 ITEM #: 103616 8.5 x 11, 96p

Spur-of-the-Moment Crafts

Instant crafts to fit your class needs! Keeps first though 6th graders interested and actively involved in learning. With over 200 crafts, it's loaded with the flexibility and creativity to help teachers make their classroom fun and the learning memorable.
$12.99 ISBN 0-78144-121-8 ITEM #: 103619 8.5 x 11, 96p

Life and Lessons of Jesus Series
(4-Volume Series)

Make Jesus real for kids with reproducible, easy-to-do and fun activities! Each volume is packed with dozens of projects that you won't find anywhere else!
$24.99 each (Can. $37.99), 8 1/2 x 11, Paperback

Volume 1—Jesus' Early Years   ISBN: 0-78143-847-0   ITEM #: 101841
Volume 2—Jesus' Ministry   ISBN: 0-78143-848-9   ITEM #: 101842
Volume 3—Following Jesus   ISBN: 0-78143-849-7   ITEM #: 101843
Volume 4—The Love of Jesus   ISBN: 0-78143-850-0   ITEM #: 101844

Prices subject to change.

Great NexGen Resources!

Bible FUNStuff Series

Excellent resources for children and teachers!

Children's ministry can be fun and meaningful when you use these incredible creative resources from Godprints. Every activity comes with a Godprint, Bible Truth and Bible Verse to help kids learn what God is like and how to become more like Him! Build your own lesson from these creative options, or use them as a supplement!

8.5 x 11, $16.99 each (Canada $24.99)

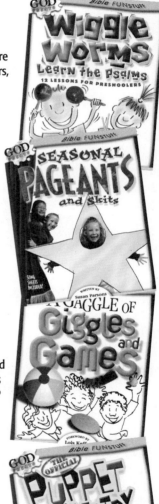

NEW! Down in Front Children's Sermons
Take kids on exciting adventures through Bible times where they'll discover that Bible places were real towns full of real people. ISBN: 0-78144-083-1 ITEM #: 103452 112P

NEW! Fun Science That Teaches God's Word
60 activities that reflect God's incredible creation in science with a craft or reproducible project.
ISBN: 0-78144-081-5 ITEM #: 103450 112P

NEW! Toddlerific
Faith building activities for Toddlers and twos. Includes reproducibles for creating Bible story "books" children can safely handle and take-home papers to help parents understand their developing children.
ISBN: 0-78144-082-3 ITEM #: 103451 112P

Children's Sermons In a Bag
A variety of bags are used as creative, out-of-the-ordinary object lessons in this terrific collection of 48 interactive children's sermons! ISBN: 0-78143-958-2 ITEM #: 102361 112P

Every Season Kid Pleasin' Children's Sermons
Great INTERACTIVE children's sermons that help kids understand what God is like—and how they can be more like Him! Sermons focus on the four seasons with holiday and special occasion sermons. ISBN: 0-78143-839-X
ITEM #: 101780 112P

FUNtastic Kid Crafts
Simply the most creative craft book ever! Contains 48 fun crafts in all, including: gifts, wearable crafts, hardware, food crafts, and toys. ISBN: 0-78143-838-1 ITEM #: 101777 112P

Paper Capers
The "funnest" paper craft book ever made, complete with pop-ups and 3-D crafts. Each reproducible craft is built on a Bible Verse and the verses go all the way through the Bible!
ISBN: 0-78143-836-5 ITEM #: 101778 112P

Prices subject to change.

A Gaggle of Giggles and Games
80 new games created for kids "K" and up! Games are organized into four sections: Cooperative, Ice Breakers, Rowdy, and Bible Memory games. There are "indoor/outdoor" options. ISBN: 0-78143-840-3
ITEM #: 101781 112P

Folder Games for Children's Ministry
Wander through a 3-D wilderness, explore Bible friendships, and learn from the experiences of Jonah, Moses, Joseph and more! Each game can be laminated, and easily stored in file folders for future use. ISBN: 0-78143-961-2 ITEM #: 102364 140P

The Official Puppet Ministry Survival Guide
Includes puppetry lessons, puppet patterns, stage building directions, and two fun scripts to get you going! ISBN: 0-78143-841-1 ITEM #: 101782 112P

Seasonal Pageants and Skits
Everything you need to put together a seasonal program or full-blown pageant! Easy-to-prepare skits and program outlines will boost and edify your children's ministry! ISBN: 0-78143-959-0 ITEM #: 102362 112P

Teaching Off the Wall: Interactive Bulletin Boards
Five types of bulletin boards include: 3-D; ceiling and floor; tagalong (portable); seasonal; and Church/HomeLink. ISBN: 0-78143-837-3
ITEM #: 101779 112P

Wiggle Worms Learn the Psalms
Preschoolers will have hours of Bible fun at church or at home with these crafts, music and games! Music sheets are provided for each lesson and the pages are reproducible for use over and over.
ISBN: 0-78143-960-4 ITEM #: 102363 112P